To Carey Stanton

(1923–1987)

*Who so generously shared his knowledge and appreciation of islands,
and made it possible for others to do so as well.*

And also to fellow islanders from whom I learned:

Justy Caire (1906–1987)
Marcia Caire (1905–1987)
Bill Connally (1929–1986)
Red Craine (1900–1989)
Henry Duffield (1921–1986)
Pier Gherini (1912–1989)
Ben Hughey (1906–1997)
Buster Hyder (1905–1994)
Steve Leatherwood (1943–1997)
Phil Orr (1903–1991)
Tom Thornton (1909–1996)

Proceedings of the Symposium on the Biology of the California Islands. 1967

CALIFORNIA'S CHANNEL ISLANDS

California's Channel Islands

1001 QUESTIONS ANSWERED

MARLA DAILY

SHORELINE PRESS
SANTA BARBARA • 1997

THIRD EDITION
ISBN 1-885375-01-8

Published by Shoreline Press
Santa Barbara, California

Cover photo by Franz Lanting
Title page photo of Anacapa Lighthouse by Steve Junak
Design and typography by Jim Cook/Santa Barbara

CONTENTS

PREFACE TO THE THIRD EDITION

Since the first edition of *California's Channel Islands: 1001 Questions Answered* was published a decade ago, numerous island changes have taken place. In particular, the two largest of the eight islands, Santa Cruz Island and Santa Rosa Island, have never before in history seen so many changes in such a short period of time. These changes have come about with those who own them, those who control them, and those who make decisions on their behalf. The faces of Santa Rosa and Santa Cruz islands have been altered forever, as the last of private ownership has become island history.

Santa Rosa Island was purchased at the end of 1986 by the National Park Service from Vail & Vickers whose interests date back to 1901. Although Vail & Vickers retained the rights to continue their cattle operations until A.D. 2011, increasing interactions with the National Park Service make this more difficult each year. The time of public visitation has arrived with multi-day camping or day trips by boat or plane.

On Santa Cruz Island, in the past decade three of the four Gherini family members who owned the island's east end sold their interests to the National Park Service. The last holdout, Francis Gherini, had his 25 percent ownership interest removed from him by Legislative Taking passed by Congress in November 1996, thus completing the government's acquisition of Channel Islands National Park.

Santa Cruz Island's western nine-tenths passed to The Nature Conservancy on December 8, 1987, upon the death of Carey Stanton, president of the Santa Cruz Island Company. Cattle ranching was discontinued, and the century old cattle chute was removed from the pier. The Santa Cruz Island Foundation, which was created by Stanton in 1985, became more active upon his death. Its purpose is to protect and preserve the cultural history of California's Channel Islands, to promote island research and education, and to collect, maintain and catalog items of real and personal property or interests regarding the California Channel Islands. To these ends, Santa Cruz Island Foundation activities have included: installation of a small archaeology museum in Pete's House at the Main Ranch on Santa Cruz Island in 1989; restoration and seismic upgrading of the chapel on Santa Cruz Island for its centennial celebration in 1991; installation of a visitors' center on Santa Barbara Island in 1993; and restoration of Campo del Norte on Santa Cruz Island in 1996. In addition, the Foundation publishes a series of Occasional Papers, eight to date, which deal with cultural aspects of California's Channel Islands.

As the adjacent mainland population has increased, so too has man's desire to visit the offshore islands. When it was created in 1980, Channel Islands National Park was the only national park in Southern California. Now it is one of three. Within the park, visitation to Anacapa Island remains the heaviest. Island Packers continues to be the park's boat concessionaire as it has been since 1968. Camping is now available on all five islands within the park. In 1995, Channel Islands Aviation became the first air concessionaire for visitation within the park. On the east end of Santa Cruz Island, Island Adventures, which operated under a private agreement with Francis Gherini for 14 years, closed its operations to make way for Channel Islands National Park.

Advances in cellular phone technology have bridged the former communication isolation, and now island visitors can phone home from isolated beaches and mountaintops. The world has indeed become smaller.

Finally, since the publication of the first edition of *California's Channel Islands, 1001 Questions Answered,* many island old-timers have died: Carey Stanton, Pier Gherini, Red Craine, Buster Hyder, Ben Hughey, Steve Leatherwood, Phil Orr, and Tom Thornton. With each death, a library of island information is lost. This third edition updates the many changes on California's Channel Islands.

—Marla Daily
Santa Cruz Island Foundation
1997

PREFACE TO THE FIRST EDITION

There seems to be an intrinsic quality of mystery shared by islands throughout the world. As one approaches a "new" island for the first time one wonders: What will be different? What will be the same? What will be entirely new? These and other questions naturally come to mind with each new island experience.

Millions of people inhabit Southern California, most of whom are aware of the existence of some islands offshore. Ronald Reagan has a bird's eye view of four of them from his west coast ranch. Some people know that there are eight islands, and fewer people can name them. Thousands of people have visited at least one Channel Island, but few have visited more than one. As an island naturalist, I am one of the fortunate few who has visited all eight California Channel Islands.

My first formal introduction to a California Channel Island came about in 1973 when, as a recent graduate of the University of California at Santa Barbara, I was included in a project conducting an archaeological survey on Santa Cruz Island. I was soon inescapably and happily involved with researching the California Channel Islands, collecting island books and references, conducting oral interviews, and learning more about their botany, biology, and history. My own curiosity soon led me to realize that many of the things I was curious about were not public information. Two of the islands are privately owned, and a third just passed from private to Government ownership in 1986. Active military maneuvers are conducted on two others. How was I to share this knowledge without being inappropriate, inaccurate or offensive?

It is with great care, an extreme respect for privacy, and the help and guidance of many generous people that this book has been made possible.

—Marla Daily
1987

ACKNOWLEDGMENTS

I am deeply indebted to a multitude of people, businesses and institutions for their generous support and assistance. Islanders have shared knowledge, in some cases, gained over a lifetime. Experts in various fields have not only contributed expertise and comments, but also photographs. Singularly important is the the safe island transportation provided both by air and by sea. In some cases my indebtedness spans more than twenty-five years. I thank you all.

Aspen Helicopters, Inc.
Brooks Institute of Photography
Channel Islands Adventures
Channel Islands Aviation
Channel Islands National Park
Island Adventures
Island Packers, Inc.
Naval Air Station, North Island, San Diego
Pacific Missile Range, Point Mugu
Petroleum Helicopters, Inc.
Santa Barbara Botanic Garden
Santa Barbara Historical Society
Santa Barbara Museum of Natural History, Channel Islands Archive
Santa Catalina Island Conservancy
Santa Catalina Island Museum
Santa Cruz Island Company
The Nature Conservancy
United States Navy, Port Hueneme
University of California Santa Barbara, Santa Cruz Island Reserve
University of California Santa Barbara, Library Map and Imagery Lab
Vail & Vickers

General Editorial Assistance: the late Carey Stanton, Natalie Daily, Clifton Smith, Steve Junak, Lyndal Laughrin, Alice Edwards, Dave Riedell

Botany: Steve Junak, Santa Barbara Botanic Garden; Clifton Smith, Santa Barbara Botanic Garden; Lichens: Charis Bratt, Santa Barbara Museum of Natural History

Vertebrate Zoology: Paul Collins, Santa Barbara Museum of Natural History; Lyndal Laughrin, Santa Cruz Island Reserve; the late Stephen Leatherwood, Hubbs Marine Research Institute; Pam Yochem, Hubbs Marine Research Institute

Invertebrate Zoology: F.G. Hochberg, Santa Barbara Museum of Natural History; Adrian Wenner, University of California Santa Barbara

Anthropology: John Johnson, Santa Barbara Museum of Natural History; Larry Wilcoxon, Robert Peterson, Archaeological Consultants; Clement Meighan, University of California, Los Angeles

Paleontology: John Cushing, Elmer Noble, Professors Emeriti, University of California Santa Barbara

Photographic Reproductions: William B. Dewey

Santa Cruz Island: the late Carey Stanton, the late Henry Duffield Jr., the late Justinian and Marcia Caire; the late Pier Gherini, Francis Gherini, Helene Caire, Lyndal Laughrin, Shirley Clarke

Santa Rosa Island: A.L. Vail, N.R. Vail Jr., the late Tom Thornton, the late Phil Orr

San Clemente Island: Kenneth Mitchell, Jan Larson, Andy Yatsko, Naval Air Station, North Island, San Diego; William Everett, Jennifer Stone

San Nicolas Island: Ron Dow, Grace Smith, Steve J. Schwartz, Pacific Missile Range, Point Mugu

Santa Catalina Island: Terry Martin, Santa Catalina Island Conservancy

Channel Islands National Park Service Islands: Kirk Connally and the entire Island Packers family; William Ehorn, former Channel Islands National Park Superintendant; Tim Setnicka, Channel Islands National Park Superintendent; Don Morris, Nick Whelan, Charles Drost, Dan Guthrie, Lois Roberts, Betsy Lester

Photographers: William B. Dewey, Steve Junak, Terry Martin, F.G. Hochberg, Ralph Clevenger, Lyndal Laughrin, Paul Collins and Steve L. Schwartz, each of whom generously contributed access to their island photographs to help illustrate this book.

A particular expression of gratitude goes to the late Denton O. "Buster" Hyder, octogenarian extraordinaire, whose accurate memories of his life on and around all eight Channel Islands were a source of much inspiration.

The four Northern Channel Islands as viewed from Landsat I, 560 miles high. From west to east (left to right) they are San Miguel, Santa Rosa, Santa Cruz and Anacapa islands.

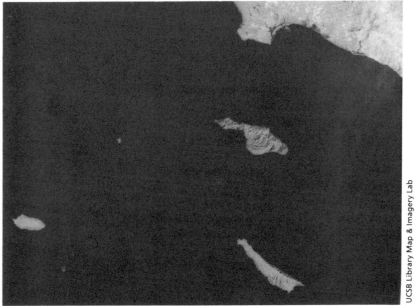

The four Southern Channel Islands as viewed from Landsat I, 560 miles high. From west to east (left to right) they are San Nicolas, Santa Barbara (small dot), Santa Catalina (above) and San Clemente (below).

CALIFORNIA'S CHANNEL ISLANDS

1. What are California's Channel Islands?

There are eight islands located off the coast of southern California which comprise California's Channel Islands. They are divided into two separate groups: the Northern Channel Islands (San Miguel, Santa Rosa, Santa Cruz and Anacapa islands), and the Southern Channel Islands (Santa Catalina, Santa Barbara, San Nicolas and San Clemente islands).

2. Where are the California Channel Islands?

The California Channel Islands extend in a northwest to southeast direction for about 160 miles from Point Conception to San Diego, and lie from eleven to sixty miles offshore.

3. Are there any other islands in California?

Yes. California's islands are divided into two groups: the Northern California Islands off San Francisco (Año Nuevo and the Farallon group); and the Southern California Islands (the Northern Channel Islands and the Southern Channel Islands). For research purposes scientists sometimes include the Baja California Islands in Mexico as a third group of California Islands, since they have close biological affinities to the Southern California Islands.

4. How are the California Channel Islands arranged according to size?

From largest to smallest they are:
1. Santa Cruz Island (96 square miles)
2. Santa Rosa Island (84 square miles)
3. Santa Catalina Island (75 square miles)
4. San Clemente Island (56 square miles)
5. San Nicolas Island (22 square miles)
6. San Miguel Island (14 square miles)
7. Anacapa Island (1.1 square miles)
8. Santa Barbara Island (1 square mile)

5. What is special about the California Channel Islands?

Among many things, there are plants and animals found on the California Channel Islands which are found nowhere else on earth. In addition, hundreds of miles of unspoiled coastline surrounding these islands offer undisturbed habitats to breeding colonies of sea birds, seals and sea lions.

6. Where can one obtain information about the California Channel Islands?

Information about the California Channel Islands can be obtained at a number of facilities: the Channel Islands National Park Visitor Center; The Nature Conservancy Santa Cruz Island Project office; the Santa Catalina Island Museum; the Channel Islands Archives at the Santa Barbara Museum of Natural History; and the Santa Cruz Island Foundation. (See directory).

7. What is the Santa Cruz Island Foundation?

The Santa Cruz Island Foundation is a private non-profit organization established in 1985 by the late Carey Stanton to protect and preserve the cultural history of California's Channel Islands, to promote island research and education, and to collect, maintain and catalog items of real and personal property or interests regarding the California Channel Islands. To these ends, Santa Cruz Island Foundation activities have included: installation of a small archaeology museum in Pete's House at the Main Ranch on Santa Cruz Island in 1989; restoration and seismic upgrading of the chapel on Santa Cruz Island for its centennial celebration in 1991; installation of a visitor's center on Santa Barbara Island in 1993; and restoration of Campo del Norte on Santa Cruz Island in 1996. In addition, the Foundation publishes a series of Occasional Papers, eight to date, which deal with cultural aspects of California's Channel Islands. The Foundation's office is located in Santa Barbara.

8. What is the Channel Islands Archives?

The Channel Islands Archives, housed in the Santa Barbara Museum of Natural History, was founded in 1977 as a research collection of materials relating to the natural and cultural histories of all eight California Channel Islands. A compendium of over 2,500 photographs, maps, theses, newspaper and magazine articles, books, paintings, deeds, personal diaries, letters, manuscripts, home movies and various island memorabilia comprises the archival holdings.

9. Which islands are a part of Channel Islands National Park?

Five of the eight islands fall within the boundaries of Channel Islands National Park: San Miguel, Santa Rosa, Santa Cruz, Anacapa and Santa Barbara islands. Of these, the western nine-tenths of Santa Cruz Island is privately owned by The Nature Conservancy as an inholding within the boundaries of Channel Islands National Park. Only the eastern portion of Santa Cruz Island is a part of Channel Islands National Park. Acquisition of this portion was completed on February 10, 1997, when Congress, through a Legislative Taking, acquired the last privately held interest.

10. Are there any other national parks in southern California?

Channel Islands National Park was the only park in southern California from 1980 until 1994 when both Death Valley National Park and Joshua Tree National Park were created.

11. Which islands are owned by the United States Government for military purposes?

San Clemente, San Nicolas and San Miguel are owned by the U.S. Government, although San Miguel is managed by Channel Islands National Park. Currently, military activity occurs on the islands of San Clemente and San Nicolas.

12.   Who owns the waters around Channel Islands National Park?

The State of California owns all submerged lands within three nautical miles of Channel Islands National Park. All submerged lands within one nautical mile of the park are inside the park boundary.

13.   What is the Channel Islands National Marine Sanctuary?

In 1980, in recognition of the significant marine life and resources around the Channel Islands, the waters within six nautical miles of the four Northern Channel Islands and Santa Barbara Island were declared Channel Islands National Marine Sanctuary. This includes about 1,252 square nautical miles of habitat. It is administered by the National Oceanic and Atmospheric Administration (NOAA).

14.   To which of the Channel Islands is there regularly scheduled public transportation?

All of the islands with the exceptions of San Clemente Island and San Nicolas Island have available public transportation by boat and/or by air. Transportation within Channel Islands National Park is provided by boat concessionaire, Island Packers, Inc. and air concessionaire, Channel Islands Aviation. (See directory).

15.   How should one dress to visit any of the Channel Islands?

Clothing depends in part upon the weather and the time of year. In general, it is best to dress in layers which can be added or removed throughout the day. Cold winds blow across the ocean's surface, so a warm jacket, sweater and windbreaker, along with long pants are recommended for channel crossings by boat. Wearing a hat or scarf will keep the wind from blowing hair in one's face. Sturdy shoes or hiking boots are a must for island exploration. While exploring tidepools, people often wear old tennis shoes which can get wet. Thongs are not recommended at any time. While hiking on an island, one can get very hot, so wearing a light shirt or t-shirt is often adequate during the summer months.

16.   What should one bring on a day trip to the Channel Islands?

It is a good idea to carry a small day pack with such items as sunscreen, chapstick, canteen of water, and your lunch. There are no stores available on any island with the exception of Santa Catalina. Outhouses are available on the Park Service islands at the campgrounds.

17. On which islands can one camp?

With a permit and/or reservations, camping is allowed on Santa Catalina, Anacapa, the east end of Santa Cruz, Santa Rosa, Santa Barbara, and San Miguel islands. Channel Islands National Park issues camping permits. Island Packers transports campers by boats to all Park islands. The Catalina Travel Connection, Hermit's Gulch and Doug Bombard Enterprises, and the Cove and Camp Agency issue camping permits for Santa Catalina Island. (See directory).

18. What should one bring for camping in primitive campgrounds such as those within Channel Islands National Park?
food
water
warm sleeping bag
tent (optional)
daypack
flashlight
messkit (plate, cup, utensils)
personal gear

19. What should one include in personal gear?

warm jacket	sturdy shoes
wind breaker	socks
sweater/sweatshirt	bathing suit
shirts: long and short-sleeved	towel
soap/brush/comb	sun glasses
toothbrush/toothpaste	sunscreen
long pants	hat/visor
shorts	journal/pen/pencil
underwear	camera/film
binoculars	

20. Is fishing allowed from the Channel Islands?

With some exceptions and with a valid California fishing license, yes. Anacapa, Santa Barbara and San Miguel islands have areas exempt from fishing as established by the California

Department of Fish and Game. Ecological Reserves extend one mile from the shore of these islands. Within each island reserve area, fishing is permitted in designated areas only.

21. What is the best time of year for tide-pooling on the Channel Islands?

The winter and summer months bring lower than average tides, and therefore they are the best times for tide-pooling.

22. Do any of the Channel Islands have good areas for surfing?

Yes. Good conditions for surfing exist around some of the Channel Islands. The surf depends upon a combination of conditions, including the time of year, currents, swell, wind, bottom conditions and depth of water.

23. Which currents surround the California Channel Islands?

The California Current brings cold, low-salinity water from the north to southern California. As the current flows toward Point Conception, it mixes gradually with warmer and saltier water from the western central Pacific Ocean. Off the Northern Channel Islands, the upper 300 feet of water circulates in a counter-clockwise gyre call the California Countercurrent. Here, surface water mixes with water than has welled up from depths below 300 feet, creating a region known as a "transitional zone."

24. What are the features of the Channel Islands "transitional zone"?

The transitional zone created by the meeting of warmer and colder waters around the Northern Channel Islands brings together northern and southern ranging organisms. A diverse array of fishes, plants, birds and marine mammals joins together to make this area one of the richest in biological productivity.

25. Are there different kinds of islands?

Yes. Islands can be categorized into one of two general types, continental islands and oceanic islands. Continental islands are assumed to have been connected to a mainland landmass or continental shelf, while oceanic islands have not. The California Channel Islands lie on the continental shelf of the North American continent. They have been called "fringing islands" by scientists.

26. How were the California Islands formed?

Current evidence suggests a very complex mixture of volcanic activity, the raising and lowering of sea levels, and plate tectonics as the creators of the California Channel Islands.

27. When were the California Channel Islands formed?

This is a question still asked by geologists. Fourteen million years ago the region now encompassing southern California was very active volcanically, creating basins and ranges. During this period, the forerunners of today's California Channel Islands were in the process of being formed, their sizes and shapes changing with each new period of volcanism and with each new ice age.

28. Were the California Channel Islands ever connected to the mainland?

The California Channel Islands probably have not been connected to the mainland by a landbridge at least since the Pleistocene Ice Age which began about one and a half million years ago.

The four Northern Channel Islands visually represent a seaward extension to the west of the Santa Monica mountains .

29. What evidence supports the fact that these islands were probably not connected to the mainland?

Geological evidence for such a connection is lacking. Some of the best evidence comes from the plants and animals present, or more importantly in this case, absent, on the islands. The depauperate aggregation of the fauna of the California Channel Islands is striking when compared to southern California's mainland. The absence of terrestrial mammals such as coyotes, bears, racoons, rabbits, gophers, moles, and other rodents would be highly unlikely if the islands had ever been connected to the mainland.

30. Without a landbridge, how can organisms get to an island?

There are a variety of means by which organisms can get to an island, including sea water flotation, rafting, air flotation or flying, and transport by birds or man.

31. What is dispersed by sea water flotation?

Sea water flotation is the primary means of dispersion for plants.

32. What is dispersed by rafting?

Rafting—accidental transport on debris or flotsam—is the most probable mechanism by which small land animals such as frogs, lizards, salamanders, snakes and mice can get to an island.

33. What is dispersed by flying or air flotation?

Flying or air flotation are the primary means for dispersal of birds and bats, as well as butterflies, moths, and a number of other insects, spiders, seeds and spores.

34. How do men or birds transport organisms to islands?

Transport by man may be either intentional or accidental. Sheep, pigs, cats and other domestic animals are often intentionally introduced, while seeds, undesirable insects or animals may accidentally result from man's activities on an island. Birds can act as carriers by depositing undigested seeds in their guano or by transporting seeds stuck to their feet or feathers.

35. What happens once an organism gets to an island?

Getting there is only half the problem. Once an organism reaches an island, it must successfully survive and reproduce in an environment that is conducive to its continued survival. Some things make it, while others do not. This hit and miss sort of colonization has been called the "sweepstakes theory of dispersal."

36. What features occur on the sea floor between the California Channel Islands and the mainland?

The area between the California Channel Islands and the adjacent mainland is called the Continental borderland. It is one of the few sea floors in the world which has seamounts, sea basins, escarpments and submarine canyons. Deep channels between and among some of these islands give them the name Channel Islands.

37. What is a seamount?

A seamount is a submarine mountain which was once an

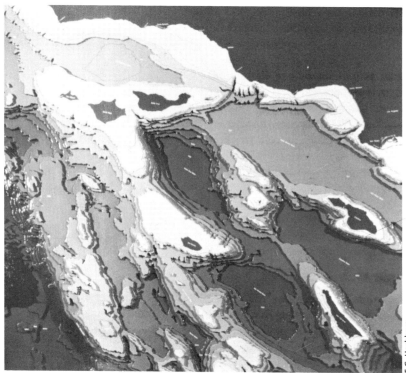

F.G. Hochberg

Deep sea basins surround the outer waters of the Channel Islands. When the sea level was much lower, the four northern islands were connected as one landmass known as "Santarosae."

active volcano. Several seamounts are submerged around the Channel Islands.

38. What is a sea basin?

Sea basins are related in form and origin to dry land basins, such as that of Los Angeles. The Santa Barbara basin lies between the four Northern Channel Islands and the adjacent mainland. The Santa Monica and San Pedro basins separate the Southern Channel Islands from the mainland. The Santa Cruz, San Nicolas and Santa Catalina basins lie to the southwest of the California Channel Islands.

39. How deep are these sea basins?

Depth varies with each basin, although the coastal basins are much shallower than the deep-water basins to the southwest of the Channel Islands. The Santa Barbara basin is about 1500 feet deep, while the Santa Monica and San Pedro basins are about 2250 feet deep. The Catalina basin is about 3750 feet deep. The deep-water basins of Santa Cruz and San Nicolas reach depths of over a mile.

40. What is an escarpment?

Escarpments are distinct steep slopes or cliffs that are formed by faults or folding of underlying rock.

41. What are submarine canyons?

Submarine canyons are steep, V-shaped canyons formed by cutting action of thick sediment-filled currents that flow down slope. Their upper sections are formed by river cutting during times of lower sea levels. The Hueneme Canyon, which lies off-shore between the east end of Anacapa Island and Port Hueneme, is an example of a submarine canyon.

42. What were the shapes of the Southern California Islands when the sea level was much lower?

Bathymetric measurements indicate that when the sea level was about 150 feet lower, the four Northern Channel Islands of San Miguel, Santa Rosa, Santa Cruz and Anacapa were joined together as one large island which scientists call "Santarosae." A submarine canyon between Port Hueneme and the east end of

"Santarosae" separated this land mass from a mainland connection, although the gap was probably only a few miles across.

43. How long ago did "Santarosae" exist?

About 18,000 years ago, the super-island of "Santarosae" covered about 724 square miles. Since then, the sea level has risen about 150 feet, separating "Santarosae" into the individual Northern Channel Islands of San Miguel, Santa Rosa, Santa Cruz and Anacapa.

44. When did the California Channel Islands attain their present size?

The California Channel Islands reached their present size about 2,000 years ago.

45. What Pleistocene mammals lived on "Santarosae"?

Mammoths, which evolved into a dwarf form, are the most notable mammals known from the fossil record. Pleistocene fossils also include sea otter remains, giant deer mice, and flightless geese.

46. On which islands have mammoth remains been found?

Mammoth remains have been found on the islands of San Miguel, Santa Rosa, Santa Cruz and San Nicolas.

47. Without a landbridge, how did mammoths get to some of the California Channel Islands?

Mammoths probably arrived on "Santarosae" by swimming. The fact that mammoths formerly existed on various Southern California Islands cannot be used to support a land bridge theory. It is a well documented fact that modern day elephants not only can, but do, swim. Presumably, their ancestors had the same capabilities. At a time when the sea level was much lower during the last ice age, the distance a mammoth would have to swim to reach the Channel Islands would have been much shorter—perhaps only as far as a few miles. As sea levels rose and increased the distance to the mainland, mammoths could have become stranded.

48. Do all of the Channel Islands mammoth finds represent a dwarf form of mammoths?

No. Mammoth remains from the Channel Islands cover a broad spectrum in size, ranging from the Imperial to the dwarf species.

49. Why were some of the mammoths on the Channel Islands dwarfs?

A dwarf mammoth seems a contradiction of terms. It is a well-documented phenomenon, however, that on an island, large mammals tend to evolve to a smaller size over a period of time. If the Imperial mammoths became stranded on "Santarosae", it is possible that given enough time, this large species would evolve into a smaller form.

50. How small were dwarf mammoths on the Channel Islands?

The smallest of these when fully grown was only about four feet high at shoulder. Examples are on display at the Santa Barbara Museum of Natural History.

51. Are there any other examples of island dwarfism among the California Channel Islands?

Yes. Both the island fox and the island skunk are smaller than their mainland counterparts and serve as examples of island dwarfism.

52. If large animals evolve to smaller sizes in island environments, do smaller animals evolve to larger sizes in island environments?

Yes. Given enough time, small animals may evolve to a larger size. The endemic Santa Cruz Island jays are a third again as large as mainland jays, and are a good example of island gigantism. Giant mice are known from the San Miguel Island and Santa Rosa Island fossil record, and today's island deer mice are slightly larger than their mainland counterparts.

53. What is an endemic animal or plant?

An endemic animal or plant is one which has evolved into a distinct form and which is restricted in its distribution to a particular locality.

54. Why are there so many endemic animals and plants on the California Channel Islands?

Isolation is one of the key factors responsible for endemism. Once organisms become stranded on an island, the gene pool from which they reproduce is limited to those organisms. Adaptations which are valuable for survival in a more competitive mainland environment, can become less important in an island environment. On the other hand, adaptations may develop which are beneficial for survival in an island environment.

55.   Did man coexist with mammoths on "Santarosae"?

This is a question which needs further study. To date, no direct evidence has been found to conclusively link mammoths and man as contemporaries on "Santarosae."

56.   When did the mammoths become extinct?

Current evidence suggests the mammoths lived on the Channel Islands until about 12,000 years ago.

57.   What is the earliest radiocarbon date for Indian occupation on the Southern California Islands?

Several confirmed radiocarbon dates in the range of 8000 years before present exist among the California Channel Islands. A few isolated incidents of older dates from Santa Rosa Island (12,600 years before present) and San Miguel Island (10,700 years before present) have been reported.

58.   What is a midden?

A midden, or kitchen midden as it is sometimes called, is an

Mammoth bones have been found on three of the Northern Channel Islands.

Middens, characterized by shell debris, represent habitation sites of former Indian populations.

area covered with the debris of everyday living, representing locations people once occupied over some length of time. On the California Channel Islands, middens characteristically contain pieces of many types of shells and fish bones scattered about in an area of very dark or black soil. Less noticeable may be pieces of other bone, burned stone from fire pits, and pieces of discarded tools or weapons.

59. What are marine terraces?

Marine terraces, also called wave cut terraces, are an erosional feature of emergent coastlines created by changing sea levels. Marine terraces become abandoned shorelines as islands rapidly rise or as sea levels rapidly fall. Terraces which are seen on some of the California Channel Islands today were formed over a period of perhaps two million years or more.

60. On which islands are there well-developed marine terraces?

San Clemente, San Nicolas, Santa Cruz and Santa Rosa islands have well-developed marine terraces. The southwest side of San

Clemente Island has the greatest display of marine terraces found on any of the California Channel Islands. As many as 19 terraces are exposed above water, with at least two more below sea level. On the west end of Santa Cruz Island, at least five terraces, exposed as "giant steps," are evident.

61. What is a blowhole?

A blowhole is a hole in a sea cliff from which columns of spray are forced upward, often accompanied by noise. Blowholes are formed by wave erosion which extends sea caves along joints or cracks to the surface. The expansion and compression of air in the hole, forced out as waves enter, creates the driving force which ejects water. There are many blowholes located around the California Channel Islands.

62. What is a fumarole?

A fumarole is a hole or vent from which fumes or vapors issue. They are usually found in volcanic areas. Fumaroles active in the recent past are known from Santa Cruz Island.

63. What are badlands?

Badlands are regions nearly devoid of vegetation where erosion has cut the land into an intricate maze of narrow ravines and

Badlands, an erosional feature, can be found on most of the California Channel Islands.

Marla Daily

15

sharp crests and pinnacles. Badlands occur on most of the California Channel Islands.

64. What is caliche?

Caliche is derived from the Latin "calix" meaning lime. Composed largely of calcium carbonate, gravel, sand, silt and clay, caliche forms weird shapes and sizes which have been referred to as "fossil forests" or "rhizoconcretions." Former trees and root systems turned to caliche form bizarre landscapes on some of the California Channel Islands.

65. Which islands have caliche?

The outermost islands of San Miguel, Santa Rosa, San Nicolas and San Clemente have extensive deposits of caliche. Little or no caliche landscapes occur on the other four Channel Islands.

66. What are native animals on an island?

Native animals are those animals which occur naturally on an island without having been introduced by man. The island fox, spotted skunk, California ground squirrel, ornate shrew, several species of mice, and bats are the native Channel Islands mammals.

67. On which islands are foxes found?

Foxes are found on six of the eight Channel Islands. They do not occur on the two smallest islands of Anacapa and Santa Barbara. Each island on which the fox occurs has its own distinct subspecies of island fox.

68. How does the Channel Islands fox differ from the mainland gray fox?

The Channel Islands fox is essentially a dwarf form of the mainland gray fox. Body proportions and coloring are similar, but the overall size of the island fox is much smaller.

69. How do the island fox subspecies differ from each other?

To the untrained eye, island foxes all look very similar. Differences are subtle ones of body and skeletal measurements.

70. Where do foxes live on the Channel Islands?

Foxes can be found in every island environment and plant community, but chaparral or woodlands seem to be the preferred fox habitats. Foxes are territorial, so frequently the same fox will be seen repeatedly in the same area.

71. What do foxes eat on the Channel Islands?

Foxes are omnivorous, opportunistic feeders. Their diet consists mainly of insects, berries and fruits, supplemented by birds, eggs, carrion, mice and occasional amphibians or reptiles. Plant foods vary with the season as does the availability of fruits and berries.

72. What are examples of plant materials eaten by foxes?

Island cherries, manzanita berries, toyon fruits, prickly pear cacti fruits, and gooseberries are among the items foxes will eat if they are available. Foxes will even climb trees in search of food.

73. When is the best time of year to see foxes on the Channel Islands?

Foxes can be seen during any time of the year, although during fall and early winter late afternoons and early evenings they are more commonly seen. In January and February they begin forming pairs and mating. Around May pups are born, with up to five

Marla Daily

Island foxes are found on six of the eight California Channel Islands.

17

Lyndal Laughrin

Spotted skunks occur on Santa Cruz and Santa Rosa islands.

in a litter. In September the pups start separating from their parents, and by the beginning of the year the pups are ready to begin their cycle of pair formation.

74. How long do island foxes live?

Island foxes live about six or seven years. Adult foxes have no natural enemies on the Channel Islands, so mortality is usually a result of old age and tooth deterioration. On some of the Channel Islands, fox mortality is increased by competition with introduced animals such as cats, and by the presence of automobiles which accidentally run over them.

75. What is the status of the island fox?

In 1971 the Channel Islands fox was placed on the California Rare and Endangered species list as a rare species.

76. On which islands are there spotted skunks?

Both Santa Rosa and Santa Cruz islands have populations of the island spotted skunk, which is a distinct Channel Islands subspecies. Skunks are known historically from San Miguel Island as well.

77. What is different about the island form of spotted skunk?

Island spotted skunks have a larger head and body but a

18

shorter tail than mainland spotted skunks. They also have less white on their bodies than do mainland spotted skunks.

78. What do the skunks eat on Santa Cruz and Santa Rosa islands?

Island skunks are known to eat insects, eggs, birds and mice.

79. Where do spotted skunks live?

Not much is known about the habitat or habits of the Channel Islands spotted skunk. They are primarily nocturnal, and are seldom seen.

80. Which islands have California ground squirrels?

Only Santa Catalina Island has the California ground squirrel. Skeletal remains of this species have been found in archaeological sites, indicating the population is not a recent introduction.

81. Which islands have ornate shrews?

Only Santa Catalina Island has native ornate shrews, where they are extremely rare.

82. Are there gophers, rabbits, or chipmunks on any of the California Channel Islands?

No. Rabbits introduced historically to Santa Barbara and Anacapa islands have been removed.

Marla Daily

The deer mouse is the only native terrestrial mammal common to all eight Channel Islands. Each island has its own distinctive subspecies.

83. **Are there any native terrestrial mammals common to all eight California Channel Islands?**

The deer mouse is the only one. Each island has its own distinctive subspecies of the deer mouse.

84. **How do island deer mice differ from mainland deer mice?**

Island deer mice are larger than mainland deer mice.

85. **Why are bats found on most of the Channel Islands?**

The power of flight has preadapted bats for island colonization. Twelve of the nineteen native mammalian species known for the California Channel Islands are bat species. They have yet to be collected on San Miguel and Anacapa islands, but attempts to catch them have been few.

86. **What is a pinniped?**

Pinniped means "fin footed" and refers to both true seals (harbor seals and elephant seals) and eared seals (sea lions and fur seals).

87. **How can one tell the difference between a true seal and an eared seal?**

True seals lack external ears, and they drag their bodies along on land. Eared seals have external ears, and they articulate their hind flippers forward to aid them while walking on land.

88. **Which pinnipeds are found around the California Channel Islands?**

California sea lions, Northern sea lions, Northern fur seals, Guadalupe fur seals, Northern elephant seals, and harbor seals are all found around the California Channel Islands. San Miguel Island is the only island on which all six occur.

89. **Which are the more commonly seen pinnipeds?**

California sea lions and harbor seals are found around most of the islands much of the time.

90. **Can you describe the California sea lion?**

The California sea lion is the best known of all the seals, since it is the one seen most commonly in zoos and circuses. Adult males can be up to nine feet long and weigh over 700 pounds.

Females may be six feet long and weigh 300 pounds. They are various shades of chocolate brown. Pupping and breeding take place between May and August, peaking in June and July. California sea lions feed mainly on squid and octopus, although they will also eat a variety of fish.

91. On which California Channel Islands do California sea lions breed?

California sea lions are known to breed on San Miguel, Santa Barbara, San Nicolas and San Clemente islands. They haul out—lie about or rest—on all eight islands.

92. Can you describe the Northern sea lion?

Northern sea lions, also called Stellar sea lions, are larger than California sea lions. Adult males can be up to eleven feet long and weigh nearly a ton. Males have a heavy muscular neck with a mane of longer coarse hair. Females are smaller. The coat, a dark chocolate brown at birth, changes to a lighter color approaching yellowish buff as the animal ages.

93. Can you describe the Northern fur seal?

Adult male Northern fur seals are just over six feet in length and weigh over 500 pounds. Females are much smaller. Adult males are dark brown with white hairs which give them a grayish tinge. Females are dark gray on their backs and lighter gray with tinges of brown on their undersides. Pups are born with black hair which is shed when they are about eight weeks old. Peak mating and pupping occur in June and July. Northern fur seals have a very short snout.

94. On which California Channel Islands do Northern fur seals breed?

They breed only on San Miguel Island.

95. Can you describe the Guadalupe fur seal?

Little is known about Guadalupe fur seals. Adult males are about five feet in length and weigh up to 300 pounds. Females are smaller. They have long pointed noses and are dusky black in color with some lighter tipped hairs. They breed only on Guadalupe Island off the coast of Mexico, although individuals are sometimes seen at San Miguel and San Nicolas islands.

96. Can you describe the northern elephant seal?

Northern elephant seals are the most spectacular in appearance of all the Channel Islands seals. Adult males may be up to eighteen feet in length and weigh up to two and a half tons. The inflatable trunk-like nose is the most outstanding feature of the adult male elephant seal. Fighting between adult bulls leads to heavy scarring and cracking of the neck region. Female elephant seals are smaller, usually under twelve feet in length, and both males and females are dark gray to gray brown in color. These seals pup and breed in December and January. Pups are born with a black coat which moults by the time they are seven weeks old.

97. How large are elephant seal pups when they are born?

At birth pups are about five feet long and usually weigh less than one hundred pounds. Within the first month of life, a pup's bodyweight will increase from three to seven times from its mother's milk alone. This added body weight will nourish the pup during a several month fasting period which occurs after the mother weans the pup and returns to sea.

98. For what purpose does the adult male elephant seal use his trunk-like nose?

Adult male elephant seals use their trunk-like noses for vocal-

Marla Daily

Adult male elephant seals use their large noses for vocalization.

ization. When the nose is inflated it acts as a resonating chamber, amplifying the roar of the male.

99. On which California Channel Islands do Northern elephant seals breed?

Northern elephant seals breed on the islands of San Miguel, Santa Rosa, San Nicolas and San Clemente. They also breed on the Northern California Islands and some of the Baja California islands.

100. Are Northern elephant seals very commonly seen around the Channel Islands?

Only during the pupping and breeding seasons are adults generally seen on land. The rest of the year they are pelagic, living in open waters, during which time very little is known about their activities. Pups, called weaners, and sub-adult animals remain on the beach after the adults have returned to the sea.

101. How many Northern elephant seals are there?

Today it is thought there are an estimated 80,000 animals on the eight California Channel Islands. The Northern elephant seal has made a remarkable recovery from near extinction a century ago. In 1890, less than 100 elephant seals were known to exist. From about 1818 to 1860 they were commercially hunted for their blubber as a source of oil. As the animals disappeared, so too did the industry.

102. How do scientists study Northern elephant seal populations?

Marine mammal scientists study elephant seal populations and movements by tagging their hind flippers with colored, numbered tags. The animals are tagged as pups, and each island upon which pups are born has a designated color tag. As tagged animals are re-encountered, detailed records can be kept of the individual animal.

103. Can you describe harbor seals?

Harbor seals, also known as spotted seals, principally live along the shorelines of the Channel Islands, feeding upon commercially unimportant fish. Adult harbor seals are about five feet long and weigh in the neighborhood of 130-170 pounds. They are easily recognizable by their spotted coats and lack of external ears. They pup and breed in March and April.

104. On which California Channel Islands do harbor seals breed?

Harbor seals are thought to breed and pup around all the California Channel Islands, with the possible exception of Santa Barbara Island. Unlike other species of seals and sea lions, harbor seals do not form large breeding colonies, and their pups are usually born in the water's spash zone.

105. How are pinnipeds counted?

The various species of seals are monitored both by aerial photography surveys and ground censuses conducted during peak pupping and breeding times.

106. Are there any sea otters on the California Channel Islands?

Sea otters are uncommon visitors around the California Channel Islands. Their remains have been found in archaeological sites on the six largest islands. Historically, they were present by the thousands all along the California coast. During the latter part of the 18th and early 19th centuries, they were the most sought-after marine fur-bearer during which time Channel Islands resident populations were hunted to extermination.

107. Why were sea otters considered so valuable?

Sea otters have reddish brown skin covered with a soft undercoat of hair frosted with longer, silver-tipped hair. Their hides were in great demand for use in fur coat manufacture. Otter pelts brought as much as $2500 each. In 1911 an international treaty was adopted to protect this greatly diminished animal.

108. What is a feral animal?

A feral animal is one which has reverted from domestication to a wild state.

109. Which feral animals are currently on which Channel Islands?

Sheep:	Santa Cruz
Goats:	Santa Catalina
Cats:	Santa Catalina, San Nicolas, San Clemente
Pigs:	Santa Cruz, Santa Catalina

110. Which feral animals have been successfully removed from which Channel Islands?

Sheep:	sheep have been removed from all but Santa Cruz

Goats: San Clemente
Cats: Anacapa, Santa Barbara
Rabbits: Anacapa, Santa Barbara
Burros: San Miguel
Dogs: San Nicolas
Pigs: Santa Rosa

111. Why are feral sheep and goats undesirable?

Sheep and goats have a direct impact on island vegetation, sometimes causing irreparable damage or even extinction to a species. Feral populations of these animals also compete with native fauna for some food resources, while destroying cover and essential breeding habitat for bird species. Insects and land snails are also adversely affected by habitat destruction. Mature sheep and goats are prey only to man.

112. Why are feral pigs undesirable?

Pigs are omnivorous. They will eat almost anything that has food value, including vegetation (foliage, fruits and seeds), invertebrates, reptiles, amphibians, mice, ground-nesting birds and eggs, and carrion. They also root up the soil and facilitate erosion. Pigs affect native populations of both the flora and the fauna. Mature pigs are prey only to man.

113. Why are feral cats undesirable?

Cats are opportunistic and feed on the most readily available and easily caught items, including the large insects, rodents, birds, lizards, and refuse. Cats are found most frequently about areas of human habitation and dump areas of the island they inhabit. They either directly impact native life forms by eating them (mice, lizards, birds), or they indirectly compete with them for food (foxes). Ground-nesting sea birds are particularly susceptible as prey for feral cats.

114. What are introduced or non-native animals?

Introduced animals include those which are intentionally placed on an island (e.g. bison, cattle, deer, and elk), and those which are accidentally introduced (e.g. rats). Technically speaking, introduced "wild" animals do not form feral populations by definition.

115. Which intentionally introduced animals live on which islands?
In addition to various domestic pets kept on some of the islands, the following animals are all introduced:

Cattle: Santa Rosa, Santa Cruz, Santa Catalina
Horses: Santa Rosa, Santa Cruz, Santa Catalina
Deer: Santa Rosa, Santa Catalina
Bison: Santa Catalina
Elk: Santa Rosa

116. Which islands have rats?
Rats have been accidentally introduced, probably via shipwrecks, to San Miguel, Anacapa, Santa Catalina and San Clemente islands. It is an amazing fact that rats have not made it to the two largest islands, Santa Cruz and Santa Rosa.

117. Are there snakes on all the California Channel Islands?
No. Snakes occur on Santa Rosa, Santa Cruz, and Santa Catalina islands. The islands of San Miguel, Anacapa, Santa Barbara, San Nicolas and San Clemente are all snake-free.

118. Are there rattlesnakes on any of the California Channel Islands?
Yes. There are rattlesnakes on Santa Catalina Island.

Gopher snakes are found on Santa Rosa, Santa Cruz, and Santa Catalina islands.

Maria Daily

Alligator lizards occur on all but Santa Barbara and San Clemente islands.

119. Are there lizards on all of the islands?

Yes. Five species of lizards are found on the Channel Islands The alligator lizard is the most widespread species, occurring on all but Santa Barbara and San Clemente islands.

120. Which islands have island night lizards?

The island night lizard is found only on Santa Barbara, San Nicolas and San Clemente islands.

121. Which islands have Pacific tree frogs?

Pacific tree frogs can be found on Santa Rosa, Santa Cruz and Santa Catalina islands.

122. Are there land snails on every California Channel Island?

Yes. Land snails occur on every California Channel Island.

123. What types of birds live on the California Channel Islands?

As a group, the Channel Islands off California support a wide variety of seabirds and land birds. Bird observations have been recorded around the Channel Islands for over a century. In some cases, these islands offer the last remaining nesting habitat for a species in an undisturbed natural environment.

124. How many different breeding land birds occupy the California Channel Islands?

About sixty species of land birds nest on the various islands.

125. Why do the Channel Islands have fewer types of birds than the adjacent mainland?

Islands have fewer types of habitats than the mainland, and small islands have fewer types of habitats than large islands. Also, not all birds will disperse over water. Therefore, the larger the island, and the closer it is to the mainland, generally the more birds there will be.

126. Are there any birds endemic to the Channel Islands at the species level?

Yes. There are thirteen types of birds which have evolved into one or more endemic races, the most distinctive of which is the Santa Cruz Island jay, classified as unique at the species level.

Marla Daily

Pacific tree frogs are found on Santa Rosa, Santa Cruz and Santa Catalina islands.

Ralph Clevenger

The Santa Cruz Island jay is a third again larger than its mainland counterpart, and it is a much brighter blue.

127. Which birds are recognized as having distinct island subspecies?

California quail	orange-crowned warbler
Allen's hummingbird	house finch
western flycatcher	rufous-sided towhee
horned lark	rufous-crowned sparrow
scrub jay (species)	sage sparrow
Bewick's wren (3)	song sparrow (3)
loggerhead shrike (2)	

128. Which endemic bird subspecies breed on a single island and do not disperse to other islands?

The Santa Cruz Island jay is found only on Santa Cruz Island, and the Santa Catalina Island variety of California quail is found only on Santa Catalina Island as a native. The quail on Santa Cruz and Santa Rosa islands were introduced from Santa Catalina Island and are therefore the Santa Catalina variety.

129. Do ospreys breed on any of the California Channel Islands?

No. Ospreys, once known to breed on San Nicolas, Santa Catalina and San Clemente islands, no longer nest on any California Channel Island. The last nesting record was in 1927 on San Clemente Island.

130. Do bald eagles nest on any of the California Channel Islands?

Bald eagles formerly nested on every Channel Island. The last nesting record on both Anacapa and Santa Rosa islands was in 1949, and on Santa Catalina Island they nested into the early 1950s. In 1980, a program to reintroduce the bald eagle to the Channel Islands began on Santa Catalina Island.

131. Why did bald eagles stop nesting on the California Channel Islands?

Several factors led to the bald eagle population decline. Large birds of prey were often shot as sport by early ranchers and visitors to the Channel Islands. Museums took birds as specimens, and egg collectors robbed the nests of their prized rare eggs. At least 125 bald eagle eggs in collections around the country can be traced to nests on the Channel Islands. Secondary agents such as poisoning and environmental pollutants also had significant effects on the population.

132. When did bald eagles become protected?

In 1940 under the Bald Eagle Act, and again in 1973 under the Endangered Species Act, bald eagles were afforded legal protection.

133. Have any other raptors (birds of prey) been reintroduced to the California Channel Islands?

Yes. Peregrine falcons, which are known to have nested on all but San Nicolas Island, were reintroduced in the 1980s to San Miguel Island in the hopes of establishing breeding status once again. Peregrine falcons continue to be seen as visitors to the Channel Islands.

134. How do plants get "introduced" to the Channel Islands?

Human use of the Channel Islands results in disturbances through cultivation, construction, and ranching activities such as grazing. These activities, especially during the dry years, open habitats to opportunistic annual grasses and undesirable weeds, which thrive in disturbed places. Seeds arrive, for example, on peoples' clothing and in supplies and cargo brought from the mainland. As human activity increases, so does the likelihood of new plant introduction. Awareness is the key to preventing unintentional introductions.

135. Are there any programs to prevent the introduction of plants to the Channel Islands?

Yes. On some islands, building materials (e.g. gravel) must be sterilized before they can be sent to an island. Some animals such as cattle or horses may be sprayed or quarantined before they enter the island environment.

136. What percentage of plants found on the Channel Islands are introduced as opposed to native plants?

About 20 percent of the total number of plant species found on the Channel Islands are introduced.

137. How many plants are Channel Islands endemics?

About 100 plants are found only on one or more California Channel Island. They are endemic at several levels: genus, species, subspecies and variety.

138. How many plants are endemic to the California Channel Islands at the genus level?

Two. *Lyonothamnus*, the island ironwood, and *Munzothamnus*, a shrub in the sunflower family found only on San Clemente Island, are the only endemic genera.

139. Which islands have island ironwood (*Lyonothamnus*)?

Island ironwood is found on the four islands of Santa Rosa, Santa Cruz, Santa Catalina and San Clemente. The ironwood on Santa Catalina Island is a different subspecies from that found on the other three islands.

140. Where are ironwood trees found on these islands?

Natural populations of island ironwood are commonly found on north-facing slopes where they form small groves. Present day populations are remnants of the once widespread mainland populations which occured from about 19 million to about six million years ago when they became extinct on the mainland.

141. In what plant family is the ironwood?

The ironwood tree is a member of the rose family.

▲ Ironwood trees, found on four of the Channel Islands, are known only from the fossil record on the mainland.

◄ Leaves of the Santa Catalina subspecies of ironwood (right) differ from leaves (left) of ironwood found on San Clemente, Santa Cruz and Santa Rosa islands.

142. How does the ironwood on Santa Catalina Island differ from that found on Santa Rosa, Santa Cruz, and San Clemente islands?

Santa Catalina Island ironwood has simple lobed leaves, while leaves on the other subspecies are fern-like lobed leaves with 5–7 leaflets each.

143. Which plant groups have a high degree of endemism among their species on the California Channel Islands?

Manzanita *(Arctostaphylos)*, buckwheat *(Eriogonum)*, bedstraw *(Galium)*, live-forever *(Dudleya)*, island-chicory *(Malacothrix)*, tarweed *(Hemizonia)* and tree-foil *(Lotus)* are among those which have a high degree of endemism on the Channel Islands.

144. What is *Coreopsis*?

Coreopsis is a bizarre-looking plant in the sunflower family. Its dry, brown, seemingly lifeless stalks come into full bloom with clusters of yellow daisy-like flowers in late winter and early spring. Once seen, this plant is not soon forgotten.

Coreopsis *grows on all of the eight Channel Islands. Its bright yellow daisy-like flowers bloom in the spring.*

Marla Daily

33

145. Does *Coreopsis* grow on every Channel Island?

Yes, *Coreopsis* is found on all eight California Channel Islands.

146. Are there native pine forests on any of the California Channel Islands?

Yes. There are native pine forests on both Santa Rosa and Santa Cruz islands. In addition to the Bishop pines found on both islands, Santa Rosa Island has a relict stand of Torrey pines. The only other native Torrey pines are found along a small area of coastline in San Diego County.

147. Which islands have endemic island cherry trees?

Santa Rosa, Santa Cruz, Anacapa, Santa Catalina and San Clemente islands have island cherry trees. They were once an important food source for the Canaliño Indians.

148. Which islands have endemic island oak trees?

Santa Rosa, Santa Cruz, Anacapa, Santa Catalina and San Clemente islands have island oak trees.

149. Are sycamore trees native to any of the Channel Islands?

They are native only to Santa Catalina Island. The few sycamore trees found on Santa Cruz Island have been planted since 1937.

150. On which island is there no poison oak?

Santa Barbara Island is the only California Channel Island without poison oak.

151. What is jimson weed?

Jimson weed (*Datura* sp.) is a member of the potato family. It has toxic properties which can induce hallucination, blindness, and even death. It was used by island Indians, and is found on the islands of Santa Rosa, Santa Cruz, and Santa Catalina.

152. Did the same tribe of Indians live on all the Channel Islands?

At the time of Spanish contact, no. The Indians of Southern California were divided by their linguistic affiliations. Chumash Indians occupied the Northern Channel Islands of Santa Cruz, Santa Rosa and San Miguel, and the adjacent channel mainland. Gabrieliño Indians occupied the Southern Channel Islands of San

Jimson weed, found on the three largest islands, is toxic and has hallucinogenic properties.

Clemente, Santa Catalina and San Nicolas, and parts of the adjacent mainland. Anacapa and Santa Barbara islands were probably only seasonally occupied.

153. What was the linguistic difference between Chumash Indians and Gabrieliño Indians?

Chumash Indians spoke a Chumashan dialect, shared among the Northern Channel Islands and the adjacent mainland coast. Gabrieliño Indians spoke a Shoshonian dialect, shared among the Southern Channel Islands and the adjacent mainland. There were some minor linguistic differences from island to island.

154. Is there a common term used to refer to all the California Channel Islands Indians collectively?

The term Canaliño refers to the entire group of island peoples in terms of their shared similar material cultures. It means channel people.

155. What is the first account of the Channel Islands Indians?

Accounts from Cabrillo's 1542 voyage described the Northern Channel Islands people: "The Indians of these islands are very poor. They are fishermen; they eat nothing but fish; they sleep on the ground; their sole business and employment is to fish. They say that in each house there are fifty souls. They live very swinishly and go about naked."

156. What were some of the differences between island and mainland Indians?

The primary difference was in their style of life and available resources. Island peoples depended heavily upon the sea for their resources, since the plant and animal life available to them was limited on each island. There were no large game animals to hunt. As a result, the maritime economy was very well developed to include utilization of over 125 species of kelp and pelagic fish; in addition to abalone, mussels, and other intertidal organisms.

157. Did the Channel Islands Indians hunt marine mammals?

Yes. Seals and sea lions were available on various islands. Sea otters lived among the Southern California Islands, and occasionally whales would become stranded ashore. Meat, pelts, bones, and oil were used either directly or as trade items for needed mainland commodities.

158. What items were traded by island Indians?

Shell beads, dried fish, sea otter pelts, shells and steatite (a soapstone found on Santa Catalina Island) vessels were among the items traded by islanders for mainland items such as seeds, acorns, various roots, obsidian, dried meat and mainland animal products.

159. Did the island Indians trade only with the mainland Indians?

No. The trade network included inter-island trading as well. It is perhaps by this method that foxes were distributed among the Channel Islands. Shell bead money was an important part of the economy for Santa Cruz Island, while steatite was a valued trade item from Santa Catalina Island. Today, archaeologists can trace some items to their place of origin by the materials of which they are made.

160. Did the island Indians trade with non-Indians?

Yes. After the Spanish contact period, island Indians readily traded with the Europeans for glass beads and iron items such as fishhooks and metal cutting tools. Archaeological sites are determined to be post European contact by the presence of such introduced items.

161. How did the island Indians make fishhooks?

Circular fishhooks of irridescent shell or bone were used as lures for kelp bed fish. Commonly, abalone shells were drilled and filed into the desired shape. These hooks had both a point and a shank for attachment. Composite fishhooks were also made, consisting of "V" shaped pieces of bone, shell or wood which were bound together to form an acute angle. Indians on the Southern Channel Islands also used twisted cactus spines as fishhooks.

162. In addition to using fishhooks, how else did the island Indians catch fish?

Harpoons and several models of spears were used in catching fish, as well as porpoise, seals, sea lions and otters.

163. Why was Santa Catalina steatite such a prized commodity?

Valued items such as game stones, small bowls, shaman's paraphernalia, pipes, flutes, weights, fish net sinkers, club heads, ornaments, effigies and cooking utensils could be made from steatite. Due to the soft nature of this soapstone, it could be worked more easily than other types of stone. It is a stable rock under exposure to heat, and it retains heat for a long time.

164. Does obsidian occur naturally on any of the California Channel Islands?

No. Obsidian artifacts found on various islands were made from mainland sources of this glass-like volcanic rock. Some of it has been matched with obsidian deposits found as far away as the Owens Valley and the eastern Mojave Desert.

165. What materials were used to make arrowheads and spear heads?

Fine projectile points and tools were fashioned from chert, which is found on several of the Channel Islands.

166. What is chert?

Chert is a compact rock type composed of microcrystalline quartz. It can be worked to produce a sharp cutting edge. Island chert is found geologically in the Monterey Formation, and its colors vary from light blonde to very dark brown.

167. How was shell bead money made?

Bead money was cut from pieces of *Olivella* shells. Each section was placed on a pitted stone slab and drilled by hand with a thin chert flake called a bladelet. The rough pieces were then strung on a rod or thong and rolled on a stone slab to smooth the bead edges to a uniform size.

168. Was there a division of labor among island Indians?

Yes. The basic division of labor was between men and women. The men were responsible for hunting and fishing while the women and children would collect plants, seeds, and shellfish. Women dominated basketmaking, and men did most of the woodworking, bead making, and arrowhead manufacturing. There were both part-time and full-time specialists.

169. What did the Canaliño use for shelter?

At the time of Spanish contact, some island Indians lived in thatched houses made of a framework of poles or whale ribs and covered with interwoven sea grass, rushes, bracken fern or other materials available on the islands. The floor was usually dirt and contained a firepit. A smokehole was left in the thatching. These houses were often occupied by one or more families.

Some Indian village sites left house-pit depressions.

38

Marla Daily

Indian petroglyphs, carved in rock, are scarce on the California Channel Islands.

170. How were these houses arranged?

When the Spanish arrived in California, they described Indian villages and rancherías on the islands which contained clusters or rows of Indian houses.

171. How did island Indians make fire?

A device called a fire drill was used for starting fires by means of friction. A straight, hardwood rod placed in a small depression of a softer wooden anvil was twirled between the hands until the resultant fine dust ignited. After Spanish contact and the introduction of steel, flint strikers using flint struck on steel in tinder were used.

172. What is the difference between a pictograph and petroglyph?

Pictographs refer to Indian paintings on rocks, while petroglyphs refer to Indian carvings on rock. Most of these were done in caves or shallow rock shelters.

173. On which islands are there pictographs?

Pictographs are generally simpler in color and design on the

Channel Islands as compared to those on the adjacent mainland. Pictographs have been found on Santa Rosa, Santa Cruz, Santa Catalina and San Nicolas islands.

174. On which islands are there petroglyphs?

San Nicolas, Santa Cruz and Santa Rosa islands have examples of petroglyphs. The "Killer Whale Cave" on San Nicolas Island is the most elaborate example of a petroglyph cave on the Channel Islands.

175. How did the island Indians get from island to island and to the mainland?

Island Indians traveled in plank canoes called tomols. These were constructed of wooden planks, held together with leather thongs and caulked with asphaltum.

176. How many of the California Channel Islands are named for saints?

The five islands of Santa Rosa, Santa Barbara, Santa Catalina, San Nicolas and San Clemente are named for saints.

177. Is San Miguel Island named for a saint?

No. Miguel, or Michael, was an archangel. In the case of San Miguel Island, it is thought the name Miguel was applied by Miguel Costansó, who mapped the Channel Islands in 1770. He originally mapped Santa Rosa Island as "Miguel", and the name was later transferred to the island to the west of Santa Rosa.

178. What are the habitation or ownership phases of the California Channel Islands?

There are four main phases of ownership and occupation for the California Channel Islands: the Indian occupation period, the Spanish era, the Mexican era, and the American era.

179. When was the Indian phase?

There are no records of the beginning of human occupation on the California Channel Islands. Dates vary from island to island, although about 8000 years before present is the generally accepted beginning of the occupation period. The Indian period lasted through the Spanish era into the Mexican era of the early 19th century, when the last of the Indians were removed to the mainland for "missionization." The last individual Indian known to live on one of the islands was "the lone woman of San Nicolas," who was brought to Santa Barbara in 1853.

180. When was the Spanish era?

Spanish occupation of California began in 1769 with the Portolá expedition, when title to all California land was vested in the King of Spain under the Law of the Indies.

181. When was the Mexican era?

The Mexican era was from 1821 until the Treaty of Guadalupe Hidalgo in 1848. In 1821 Mexico's long revolt against Spain ended. News of the success and end of the revolt reached Alta California in 1822. During the Mexican era, the three islands of Santa Cruz, Santa Rosa and Santa Catalina were granted to private individuals. At the close of the Mexican era, although the islands were not specifically mentioned in the Treaty of Guadalupe Hidalgo, they passed, along with the rest of California, to the United States.

182. When did the American era begin?

California was ceded to the United States by the Treaty of Guadalupe Hidalgo in 1848, and in 1850 California became a state. Of the eight California Channel Islands, five were ungranted. Titles to the three privately owned islands were confirmed by the United States, and the remaining five islands became the property of the U.S. Government.

183. Which of the California Channel Islands were granted to private individuals by the Mexican government in the 19th century?

Santa Catalina, Santa Rosa and Santa Cruz islands were granted to private individuals. Today, non-profit organizations own most of Santa Catalina Island (Santa Catalina Island Conservancy) and Santa Cruz Island (The Nature Conservancy). Santa Rosa Island was purchased by the U.S. Government in 1986 for inclusion within Channel Islands National Park. Purchase of all private interests in the east end of Santa Cruz Island was completed in 1997 by the National Park Service.

184. Who was the first non-native to discover the California Channel Islands?

Juan Rodríguez Cabrillo. In 1542, his expedition, consisting of the two ships *San Salvador* and *La Victoria,* traveled among the California Channel Islands. Reports from that expedition, recorded many years later, contain the first written mention of any of the Southern California Islands. Collectively the Northern Channel Islands were called "Islas San Lucas." This voyage marks the beginning of recorded Spanish contact with the island Indians.

185. Did any other 16th-century expeditions visit the California Channel Islands?

Yes. Although the 1579 voyage of Sir Francis Drake aboard the *Golden Hind* visited several California ports, no mention is made of the Southern California Islands. However, in 1595 Sebastián Rodríguez Cermeño visited some of the California Channel Islands aboard the ship *San Agustín.* Specifically which islands he visited is unclear, although they were probably the islands of Santa Rosa, San Miguel, and perhaps Santa Catalina. In 1598 the Manila galleon *San Pedro* wrecked at Santa Catalina Island, after which her crew and passengers spent several months on the island.

186. Which expeditions visited the California Channel Islands in the 17th century?

In 1602 Sebastián Vizcaíno traveled to the West Coast of North America under the orders of King Philip III of Spain. His expedition published extensive notes, plans and sketches of this voyage, which visited several California Channel Islands. After the Vizcaíno expedition, a lapse of 167 years occured until the next well-documented evidence of European contact with the Channel Islands.

187. Which expeditions visited the California Channel Islands in the 18th century?

In 1769 the Gaspar de Portolá expedition explored Alta California for the King of Spain by both land and sea. The sea-going part of the expedition, with the vessels *San Carlos* and *San Antonio,* examined several of the Channel Islands, including San Clemente and Santa Cruz. In 1793 the English expedition of George Vancouver standardized and finalized the names of the eight Southern California Islands.

188. When did the sea otter industry develop around the California Channel Islands?

Sea otter hunting around the California Channel Islands began in the late 1700s and continued until the mid-1800s, when the animals were no longer available in sufficient quantity to warrant hunting. Several nationalities participated in the hunting, including the Russian, Aleut, Spanish, English, French and Portuguese.

189. How did the sea otter industry develop?

During the Spanish era, Spaniards in upper and lower California began to collect otter skins traded from natives. Otter furs found their way aboard Manila galleons to the Orient, where the furs were prized more highly than fox or sable. Otter became the royal fur of China, where otter skin products symbolized high social standing. Russians, stimulated by this demand, came to the Channel Islands along with native Aleut Indians, who, joined by others, significantly overharvested the animals to near-extinction.

190. What ended the sea otter industry around the California Channel Islands?

By the end of the 19th century, the lack of animals was the primary factor responsible for the decline in the sea otter industry. In 1911 Russia, Japan, England and the United States signed a fur treaty giving the sea otter protection under law. A period of poaching and a black market continued, but eventually the fur became less fashionable and these illegal activities ceased.

191. When was the Chinese abalone fishing industry developed on the California Channel Islands?

The Chinese abalone fishing industry developed during the mid-19th century. Chinese who were brought to this country as cheap labor to help build railroads and work the mines began to develop the abalone industry in the early 1860s.

192. How did the Chinese operate the abalone industry?

Chinese abalone fishermen, as squatters, established abalone camps on several of the California Channel Islands. Here they would pry the abundant supplies of abalone off the rocks in great quantity. After removing the meat from the shell, the abalone meat was pounded and then boiled in a large kettle for a short time, after which it was placed in the sun to dry. When the meat was thoroughly dry, it was packed in sacks and shipped to the mainland.

193. Who ate this dried abalone product?

Most of the meat was shipped to San Francisco, where it was sold to both China and to the large Chinese community who lived in San Francisco. The meat was considered a great luxury and was consumed primarily by the more affluent Chinese.

194. What happened to the abalone shells collected by the Chinese?

The abalone shells were sent to markets in the United States, France and Germany for use in the manufacture of jewelry and buttons.

195. How long did the Chinese dominate the abalone industry?

For over two decades, the abalone industry was dominated by the Chinese. By the mid-1880s however, Americans, Portuguese, Italians, and Swedes moved on to the California Channel Islands to take advantage of the fishing industry which was rapidly developing. By the 1890s Chinese were effectively eliminated from the industry with the 1892 passage of the Chinese Exclusion Act, which forced Chinese to seek employment elsewhere.

196. What evidence remains of the Chinese abalone industry?

Archeological excavations have revealed opium tins and Chinese porcelain pieces from former camp areas. Seven of the islands have place names such as Chinese Harbor, China Camp, Chinese Point, and China Canyon.

197. What happened around the Channel Islands as the fishing industry developed?

In the late 1800s and early 1900s, an extensive fishing industry developed around the California Channel Islands. As the demand for fish increased, so too did the industry. Fishermen rented space on island shorelines or squatted as trespassers, living in makeshift shacks while conducting various fishing enterprises. Fishermen were often subsidized by businesses such as the Larco Fish Company or the Castagnola Brothers, who made frequent pickups of lobsters, crabs and fish from the island fishermen. World War II brought with it the end of the island fishermen, and the U.S. Government used all of the islands for Coastal Surveillance

Stations. Although the fishing industry resumed after the war, the system of fishermen living on the islands did not.

198. What happened on the Channel Islands during the Prohibition Era?

With the enactment of the Volstead Act of 1920, illegal liquor smuggling became a big business around the California Channel Islands. Secluded coves provided hiding places for caches of liquor awaiting smuggling onto the mainland. Over a half dozen law enforcement agencies cooperated in trying to outwit or outrun the crafty rumrunners. Enterprising moonshiners made alcoholic products in stills hidden in caves on some of the islands. With the repeal of Prohibition in 1933, rumrunning and bootlegging on the Channel Islands waned.

199. What happened on the Channel Islands during World War II?

The Coastal Lookout Organization was established to provide surveillance from Point Arguello to the Mexican border. Ten stations were established, three on San Clemente Island and one on each of the other Channel Islands, whose purpose was to report enemy vessels. Station personnel were trained in night surveillance and vessel recognition, and each station was supplied with binoculars and arms. On July 1, 1945, the Coastal Lookout Organization was abolished.

200. What happened in the waters surrounding the Channel Islands during World War II?

As a part of the Coastal Lookout Organization, both offshore and inshore patrol vessels cruised the local waters. The Inshore Patrol had twelve vessels and the Offshore Patrol had three. One of these, the *Hermes,* is credited with discovering a foreign submarine outside San Pedro Harbor.

N

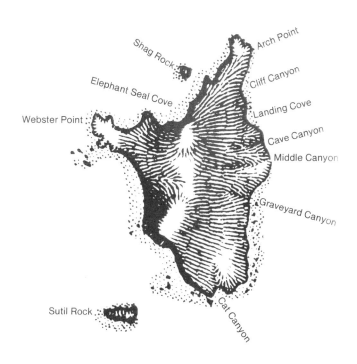

Shag Rock

Arch Point

Cliff Canyon

Elephant Seal Cove

Landing Cove

Webster Point

Cave Canyon

Middle Canyon

Graveyard Canyon

Cat Canyon

Sutil Rock

SANTA BARBARA ISLAND

SANTA BARBARA ISLAND

201. How large is Santa Barbara Island?
Santa Barbara Island is the smallest of the eight California Channel Islands. Its area is one square mile in size or 638.72 acres.

Aerial view of Santa Barbara Island, 1 square mile in size.

47

202. In what county is Santa Barbara Island?

Surprisingly, Santa Barbara Island is in Santa Barbara County, even though geographically it is closer to Los Angeles and Ventura counties.

203. How far is Santa Barbara Island from the mainland?

Santa Barbara Island is 38 miles from the mainland coast of California. Twenty-eight miles out to sea from Santa Barbara Island lies San Nicolas Island. It is 24 miles to Santa Catalina Island.

204. What is the highest point on Santa Barbara Island?

Signal Peak, at 635 feet in elevation, is the highest point.

205. Who owns Santa Barbara Island?

The U.S. Government owns Santa Barbara Island. Today, the National Park Service manages and preserves this island as part of the Channel Islands National Park, created in 1980. Santa Barbara Island has never been privately owned. In 1848 it became a part of the United States, and in 1938 it was made a part of Channel Islands National Monument.

206. What are the physiographic features of Santa Barbara Island?

Santa Barbara Island is roughly triangular in outline and emerges from the ocean as a giant twin-peaked mesa with steep cliffs. Marine terraces slope away from the two rounded hills, Signal Peak and North Peak. Offshore, there are two named rocks, Shag Rock off the northerly shore, and Sutil Rock off the southwest end. Santa Barbara Island has no well-developed sandy beaches. A few narrow rocky beaches surround the island at various points, and most of these are submerged at high tide. Along the eastern side of the island are a few named canyons. Precipitous cliffs drop to the sea around most of the island.

207. How many canyons are there on Santa Barbara Island?

There are six major canyons along the east side of Santa Barbara Island. From north to south they are: Cliff Canyon, Landing Cove, Cave Canyon, Middle Canyon, Graveyard Canyon and Cat Canyon. These canyons contain some of the denser vegetation found on the island, and they are good areas for birdwatching. Some of the canyons are off-limits to visitors to help ensure protection of the fragile habitat.

208. Are there any badlands on Santa Barbara Island?

Yes. On the southeast portion of the island there is a small area of badlands. The trail crosses this area.

209. How was Santa Barbara Island formed?

Geologists think this island was formed by underwater volcanic activity. Pressures beneath the earth's surface uplifted this island, which has never had a landbridge to the mainland or to other islands. During different periods of the uplifting process, wave erosion caused several marine terraces, which are evident today. The island was submerged during the Pliocene or early Pleistocene eras, and therefore the colonization by plants and animals began only within the last several hundred thousand years.

210. What are Santa Barbara Island's rock types?

The island is made of up tuffs and breccias. The soils of the terraces consist mostly of silt and clay.

211. What type of weather is there on Santa Barbara Island?

The overall climate on Santa Barbara Island is generally very temperate. During hot summer days, the temperature may reach into the 90s. Prevailing northwest winds average seven to sixteen miles per hour, depending upon the exposure of the area. Heavy fogs may set in, which bring with them associated moisture.

212. What is the average rainfall on Santa Barbara Island?

Annual rainfall averages 12 inches a year, and is supplemented by wet fogs and high relative humidity. Most of the rain falls between October and April.

213. Is there any fresh water on Santa Barbara Island?

There is no reliable supply of fresh water on Santa Barbara Island. Small temporary seeps occur during wet years; however no permanent fresh water source is known. The island surface area is small and relatively impermeable, so that no aquifers exist.

214. How can one visit Santa Barbara Island?

One can visit Santa Barbara Island either by private boat or via the Channel Islands National Park concessionaire, Island Packers. Regular trips are run to this island from Memorial Day throughout the summer months.

Gear brought to Santa Barbara Island must be carried up a short, steep zig-zagged trail to the island's mesa from Landing Cove. Today, a new ranger's residence and visitor center are at the top of the trail.

215. Does one need a permit to land on Santa Barbara Island?

To land on Santa Barbara Island for day use, a permit is not necessary. However, for overnight camping, one must obtain a free permit from Channel Islands National Park headquarters.

216. What is the best time to visit Santa Barbara Island?

Each season varies. Most people visit this island in the spring, when the wildflowers bloom, or during the summer months, when regular boat transportation is available. Visitation is allowed year-round, as is camping with the proper permit.

217. What are the landing conditions on Santa Barbara Island?

The only way to get onto this island is by skiff at Landing Cove on the island's east side. There is no dock, although there is a landing platform built by the Park Service. The ascent to the top of the island is quite steep, and resting places are provided along the way. Approximately 160 steps lead to the top of the mesa where the visitors' center, ranger's residence and campgrounds are located.

218. How long may one camp on Santa Barbara Island?

With a permit from the Channel Islands National Park, campers are allowed on the island for up to one week. Most camping activities are dictated by the available boat transportation provided by Island Packers, Park concessionaire.

219. What are the camping facilities?

A primitive camping area with nine sites and outhouses is provided on Santa Barbara Island, where up to 30 campers are allowed at any one time. One must bring all the necessities of life, including water. Camp sites are bordered by railroad ties and contain a picnic table. There are no trees or vegetative cover. Gear must be carried from the landing cove to the top of the hill, a distance of about one-quarter mile.

220. Does the Park Service have any facilities on Santa Barbara Island?

Yes. The former Quonset hut which served as a ranger's residence for many decades was replaced in 1991 with a modern facility. A modest visitors' center attached to the residence was installed in 1993 by the Santa Cruz Island Foundation in conjunction with the National Park Service. Displays interpret the island's cultural and natural history, and a large hand-painted mural illustrates offshore life underwater. A small helipad is within walking distance from the facility.

The campground on Santa Barbara Island is located next to the ranger's residence and visitor center. Campers must bring their own water.

221. Is there electricity on Santa Barbara Island?

Solar power is used to provide electricty to the ranger residence on the island. No electricity or water is provided to the campgrounds.

222. Are there any motor vehicles on Santa Barbara Island?

No.

223. What are the hiking conditions on Santa Barbara Island?

There are several trails looping around and over the top of Santa Barbara Island. Periodically one or more of these may be closed due to bird nesting activity. All of the trails are easy walking, with elevation changes of less than 200 feet. "Silent policemen" (railroad ties) mark parts of the trail.

224. Are there any dangers to look out for on Santa Barbara Island?

Yes. One must be aware of dangerous cliff edges and crumbling slopes, and stay only on the open trails.

225. What happens in the event of an emergency on Santa Barbara Island?

The island's National Park Service ranger has radio communication to the mainland. In the event of an emergency, a helicopter pad facility atop Santa Barbara Island is used, if weather and fog permit.

226. Is there a view of anything but water from Santa Barbara Island?

Yes. Since Santa Barbara Island is located centrally among the eight California Channel Islands, on a clear day, every island in the chain with the exception of San Miguel Island, which is hidden from view by Santa Rosa Island, is visible.

227. What is the intertidal zone on Santa Barbara Island?

A total of five miles of shoreline surrounds Santa Barbara Island. The intertidal zone on the east coast typically consists of a narrow, steeply sloping shore which is covered by high tides backed by steep cliffs. The northern, western, and southern portions are composed of isolated, exposed boulder-strewn beaches against precipitous cliffs. Small sandy beaches are present in Elephant Seal Cove and south of Webster Point.

228. Are there any accessible sandy beaches along Santa Barbara Island?

No. Only at Landing Cove is the ocean accessible. It comes up to the island along a rock-faced shoal where diving and snorkeling can be very good. The few inaccessible cove areas on Santa Barbara Island serve as breeding and haul-out grounds for marine mammals.

229. How is the fishing around Santa Barbara Island?

This island is less impacted by commerical fishing than some of the other more easily accessible islands. Sea urchins, abalone, sea bass, rock cod, anchovy, shark, lobster and mackerel are among the principal resources of the area.

230. What are the diving conditions around Santa Barbara Island?

Along the calmer eastern side of the island, diving can be incredibly clear and excellent. Encounters with playful sea lions are common. Snorkeling areas are accessible from Landing Cove.

231. Are there any native terrestrial mammals on Santa Barbara Island?

Yes. The endemic subspecies of deer mouse *(Peromyscus maniculatus elusus)* is the only native terrestrial mammal on Santa Barbara Island.

232. Where do the mice live?

On Santa Barbara Island, mice can be found in every habitat. They are in grasslands, iceplant, coastal bluff communities and in the maritime cactus scrub.

233. Do the mice harm anything?

The mice can be pests, especially for campers who leave food in bags which can be chewed through. It is a good idea to store edibles on a table and in mouse-proof containers such as coolers. If a mouse is picked up, it may bite.

234. How are the mice controlled?

Various species of owls and hawks prey upon the mice in great quantity. With the removal of feral cats, the mice have no mammalian predators. Santa Barbara Island supports a higher density of deer mice in comparison with the other islands.

235. Are there bats on Santa Barbara Island?

Yes, although bats are probably migrant visitors to Santa Barbara Island and not permanent residents. One species of bat, the hoary bat *(Lasiurus cinereus)* has been collected. Bats can be seen flying about at night.

236. Are there any non-native animals on Santa Barbara Island?

No. In the past, various domestic animals including horses, mules, cats, sheep, rabbits, chickens and turkeys have lived on Santa Barbara Island. The Park Service will not allow pets to be taken to the island.

237. What is the earliest evidence of a non-native animal on Santa Barbara Island?

In *Life, Adventures and Travel in California* by T.J. Farnham, written in 1849, he states: "Farther offshore and southward are the islands of Santa Barbara, San Nicolas and San Clemente . . . They are densely populated with goats." In 1897 J.R. Britton wrote that the island was "scattered . . . skulls and hoofs of sheep put on the island as a business venture some years ago."

238. How did rabbits get to Santa Barbara Island?

Rabbits were introduced to this island twice. The first time

During the early ranching era on Santa Barbara Island, goats were free to roam the island. Circa 1918

Buster Hyder Collection

was around 1918, when the lessees of the island, the Hyders, brought up to 2000 Belgian hares *(Dryctolagus cuniculus)* to be set free as a source of food. Occasionally they would bring people to the island and allow them to hunt a rabbit or two. According to Buster Hyder (1986 interview) the rabbits had a hard time competing with the feral cats, and within a short time the rabbit population had been drastically reduced. This population is thought to have been eliminated sometime prior to World War II.

239. When was the second introduction of rabbits to Santa Barbara Island?

The New Zealand red rabbit was introduced to the island sometime during the early 1940s, when the island was being used by military personnel as an aircrft early warning outpost. Several years passed before this population began to have a substantial impact on the island's vegetation. A rapid and destructive rabbit population surge occured in the early 1950s.

240. How were rabbits eliminated from Santa Barbara Island?

In 1954 a rabbit extermination program was instituted by the National Park Service and U.S. Fish and Wildlife Service. Control efforts included hunting, trapping, contact poison and the use of strychnine-coated bait. These methods were only partially successful due to the inaccessibility of many of the rabbit burrows. After each attempt to remove the rabbits, the population recovered. With an intensive effort by the National Park Service, rabbits were finally eliminated in 1984 by hunting. Vegetation has slowly begun to recover from the grazing pressures placed upon it by the rabbits, adding habitat for nesting birds, land snails, and night lizards.

241. How did cats get to Santa Barbara Island?

It is not known when or how cats were first introduced. Presumably fishermen brought them to keep the native mouse population down. These cats multiplied, lost their domesticity, and eventually flourished as a feral population. They were on the island prior to 1896. When the Hyders arrived to live on Santa Barbara Island in 1915, cats were prolific enough to be considered pests. They caused a decline in nesting populations of Xantus' murrelets and Cassin's auklets. They also preyed upon the rabbits introduced by the Hyder family. According to Buster

Hyder, the cats eventually died off years later due to a cat fever. A lone cat was trapped in 1978 by Park Service personnel.

242. What marine mammals can be seen at Santa Barbara Island?

California sea lions, harbor seals and Northern elephant seals are commonly sighted about the rocky coves and ledges of this island. Sea lions and elephant seals breed here. Santa Barbara Island ranks third of the eight Southern California Islands in pinniped importance, after San Miguel and San Nicolas islands.

243. Are there any sea otters on Santa Barbara Island?

No. As early as 1810, Santa Barbara Island was used by hunters to take otters, seals and sea lions. The otters and elephant seals were hunted to extermination here, and thus far, only the elephant seal population has made a recovery.

244. Can whales be seen from Santa Barbara Island?

During migration, gray whales can sometimes be seen on their southward or northward trek. Historic accounts recount killer whales beaching themselves temporarily to catch and eat seals or sea lions on some of the rocky haul out and breeding areas of this island. Boaters often see other species of whales while traveling to or from Santa Barbara Island.

245. Are there any snakes on Santa Barbara Island?

No.

246. What reptiles are found on Santa Barbara Island?

Only one reptile, the island night lizard *(Xantusia riversiana)* is found on this island. It is an endemic lizard, also found on San Nicolas and San Clemente islands. It also occurs on Sutil Rock off the west side of Santa Barbara Island. The 1973 Endangered Species Act lists this lizard as threatened.

247. Why is the night lizard threatened?

The reduction of the lizards' habitat, which has occurred historically as a result of fires, farm and ranch activities, threatened the existence of this species. Vegetative cover is important in providing shelter, refuge and food sources. It is unlawful to disturb rocks on Santa Barbara Island since they often provide habitat for the island night lizard.

Gray whales annually migrate past the California Channel Islands on their way to their breeding grounds in Baja California.

248. What is known about the island night lizard population?

The population density is very low, and it is thought there are between 550 and 700 lizards. Females do not mature sexually until their third or fourth year, and they reproduce only every other year.

249. What amphibians are found on Santa Barbara Island?

None.

250. Is there an interesting insect fauna on Santa Barbara Island?

Little is known about the insects on the Channel Islands. The California Department of Food and Agriculture conducted an insect survey of Santa Barbara Island in 1974, and the Santa Barbara Museum of Natural History has conducted several surveys. The Los Angeles County Museum of Natural History has an important collection from this island as well. The beetles and grasshoppers are the best studied groups. Many of the collected insects lack identification, a common problem in entomology.

251. What are some of the insects found on Santa Barbara Island?

Familiar insects include at least six species of grasshoppers, silverfish, praying mantids, thrips, stink bugs, leafhoppers, aphids, mealybugs, ground beetles, carrion beetles, scarab beetles, soft-winged flower beetles, lady beetles, scavenger beetles, darkling beetles, long-horned beetles, and many species of weevils, flies, ants and bees.

252. Are there any butterflies or moths on Santa Barbara Island?

Yes. Pyralid moths, leaf-roller moths, geometrid moths, Tussock moths, Sphinx moths, and an endemic tortricid moth which feeds on giant coreopsis have been collected on Santa Barbara Island. Butterflies include white sulphur butterflies, milkweed butterflies, brush-footed butterflies, blues and hairstreaks.

253. Are there any scorpions, spiders or ticks on Santa Barbara Island?

Yes. One type of scorpion has been collected. Crab spiders, jumping spiders and an orb weaver are known for the arachnid fauna, and ticks have been found on mice.

254. Are there any land mollusks on Santa Barbara Island?

Yes. Santa Barbara Island supports the highest diversity of land mollusks on a National Park Service island. Seven living and three fossil snail species are known to occur on the island. Snails are found only where there is adequate shelter (vegetation, rocks and soil), moisture, and a source of calcium for shell building.

255. What animals prey on snails on Santa Barbara Island?

Deer mice, western gulls, and various beetles are known to eat snails. In addition, the Durant's snail *(Haplotrema duranti)* found on this island eats small or juvenile snails and snail eggs.

256. What birds are found on Santa Barbara Island?

At least seventy types of birds are reported. Among the more interesting are peregrine falcons, California brown pelicans, horned larks, three types of owls, Costa's and Allen's hummingbirds, Xantus' murrelets, Cassin's auklets, and both black and ashy storm petrels. The endemic Santa Barbara song sparrow is thought to be extinct.

257. Which land birds are known to nest on Santa Barbara Island?

American kestrel
mourning dove
barn owl
short-eared owl
burrowing owl
Costa's hummingbird
Allen's hummingbird
horned lark
northern raven
rock wren
common starling
orange-crowned warbler
western meadowlark
house finch

258. Did bald eagles nest here?

Yes. There are historical records of bald eagles nesting on Santa Barbara Island. In 1916, two bald eagle chicks were removed from a nest on Sutil Rock by early island residents Alvin Hyder and his brother. The birds later died in captivity.

259. What marine birds nest on Santa Barbara Island?

ashy storm petrel
black storm petrel
California brown pelican
double-crested cormorant
pelagic cormorant
Brandt's cormorant
black oystercatcher
western gull
pigeon guillemot
Xantus' murrelet
Cassin's auklet

260. Which birds on Santa Barbara Island are endemic Channel Islands subspecies or races?

The horned lark, orange-crowned warbler, and house finch are Channel Islands endemics on Santa Barbara Island, and the song sparrow was a Santa Barbara Island endemic.

261. What happened to the endemic Santa Barbara Island song sparrow?

This bird is thought to be extinct. Its sage brush *(Artemisia)* nesting habitat was severely reduced by a fire in 1959, after which the bird survived only another eight years. The last field sighting was in August 1967. With no suitable habitat in which to breed and nest, they would more likely fall prey to the barn owls and feral cats which were present on Santa Barbara Island. This sparrow *(Melospiza melodia graminea)* was one of the smallest forms of song sparrow, differentiated by its very grey back.

262. What is the vegetation on Santa Barbara Island?

There are no trees on Santa Barbara Island, and only a few shrubs. The vegetative aspect is that of herbaceous plants and grasses, verdant in the spring and appearing dry and brown during the hot summer. The island supports about 120 different species of plants, about 30 percent of which are introduced weeds.

Maria Daily

The endemic Santa Barbara Island live-forever, Dudleya traskiae.

263. How many plants endemic to the California Channel Islands are found on Santa Barbara Island?

There are fourteen endemic plant species or subspecies which occur on Santa Barbara Island and at least one other California Channel Island.

264. What are the three plants endemic to Santa Barbara Island?

The three plants restricted to Santa Barbara Island are a low shrubby buckwheat *(Eriogonum giganteum compactum)*, a small succulent *(Dudleya traskiae)*, and an annual poppy *(Platystemon californicus ciliatus)*.

265. What are the major plant communities on Santa Barbara Island?

There are five plant communities on Santa Barbara Island: grasslands, coastal bluffs, maritime cactus scrub, coastal sage scrub, and introduced ice plant and exotics.

266. Which plant families are best represented on Santa Barbara Island?

The sunflower *(Asteraceae)* and grass *(Poaceae)* families comprise the largest portion of the flora of this island. Of the known 120 different plant species, 30 are in the sunflower family and 22 are grasses.

267. Are there any ferns on Santa Barbara Island?

Only one species of fern, California polypody *(Polypodium californicum)* has been found. It is rare and known only from a few locations.

268. Why is there so much crystalline ice plant?

Crystalline ice plant *(Mesembryanthemum crystallinum)* is an introduced plant which is native to South Africa. It thrives in maritime areas with disturbed soils, and its fleshy "wet" leaves contain a high concentration of salt. When the plant dies back after turning reddish in age, the salts are deposited onto the soil, making it too saline for other plant seeds to germinate. It is "saving its place" for the next generation of ice plant. With the soil disturbance caused by early farming activities on Santa Barbara Island, the ice plant quickly spread.

269. Are there any plants to be wary of?

Yes. Coastal Cholla *(Opuntia prolifera)* occurs near the trail in a few places. Its spines can be very painful. Should a piece of cactus "jump" onto a person, it can be removed with a stick or a comb. During the hot summer months, "foxtails" from introduced annual grasses will get stuck in socks as one hikes the trails.

270. May one pick the flowers on Santa Barbara Island?

No. As a Park Service island, the vegetation is protected. All hiking activities are confined to the trails to protect the vegetation and habitat.

271. Why do lichens seem so abundant on Santa Barbara Island?

Lichens are actually a combination of an alga and a fungus growing together in a controlled parasitic relationship. Each relies upon the other for survival. The rocks of Santa Barbara Island provide good growing medium for lichens. Undisturbed, many of them will grow for over a century, obtaining the necessary moisture from fog and occasional rainfall.

272. Did Indians ever live on Santa Barbara Island?

Archaeological evidence shows that the island was inhabited, at least on a seasonal basis, by Indians, perhaps as a result of population growth on larger neighboring islands such as Santa Catalina. Due to the lack of firewood, water and basic subsistence materials, this island would be less desirable as a home when compared to some of the others. Given this island's central location, it may have served as an important stopover point for inter-island travel.

273. What archaeological investigations have been conducted on Santa Barbara Island?

The first archaeological reconnaissance was carried out in 1958 by archaeologists from UCLA, who recorded the location of one site. Later in 1958, the National Park Service sponsored a survey which located an additional four sites. In 1961 a sixth site was added. In 1964, Charles Rozaire of the Los Angeles County Museum of Natural History located a total of fifteen archaeological sites, only two of which had been previously recorded. Excavation of one site was conducted which yielded about fifty artifacts, including fishhook fragments, bone awl tips, and mortar and pestle fragments. The Park Service began further research in 1986.

274. Are the Santa Barbara Island sites still intact?

Due to the history of ranching and farming operations after the turn of the century, it is not known to what extent the archaeological sites have been altered. Wind and water erosion have affected some areas of archaeological interest. Grazing by sheep and goats, and burrowing by rabbits also has had an impact. A few sites located where activities have been minimal are less disturbed than others.

275. When was Santa Barbara Island named?

In 1602, explorer Sebastián Vizcaíno named Santa Barbara Island in honor of the saint whose day is December 4. Sutil Rock off the southwest shore was named by the Geographic Board after a ship of the Galiano expedition of 1792.

276. When was Santa Barbara Island surveyed by the U.S. Government?

In the early 1850s Santa Barbara Island was visited by U.S. Coast and Geodetic Survey employee W.E. Greenwell. In 1871, a survey station point was established on the island's highest hill, Signal Peak.

277. Who has lived on Santa Barbara Island in historic times?

Several people squatted on Santa Barbara Island before Government leasing took effect in 1901. A Coast Survey employee reported a fishermen's hut on the island as early as 1871. In 1897 a Chinese lobster fisherman was living in a small hut on the rocks above Landing Cove accessible by a wooden bridge. Also in the 1890s, H. Bay Webster (lessee of Anacapa Island) lived part-time on Santa Barbara Island as a fisherman and seal hunter. He built a cabin on the northwest portion of the island which now bears his name, Webster Point.

278. Who was the first to lease Santa Barbara Island?

J.G. Howland was the first to lease Santa Barbara Island. The first lease began July 1, 1909, for five years at a rate of $26 per year. Although Howland's lease forbade the subletting of Santa Barbara Island, in October 1909 he rented a portion of the island to C.B. Linton of Long Beach for $125 for the propagating of

Webster Point, Santa Barbara Island, was once the location of a shack built by H. Bay Webster. Today the bare area is used as a haul-out by California sea lions. Coreopsis stalks stand in the foreground.

pearls in abalone. Howland also issued fishing rights for a fee to Japanese and Chinese fishermen. When his lease expired, it was not renewed.

279. Who was the second lessee of Santa Barbara Island?

Alvin Hyder was the second lessee. After the Howland lease expired in 1914, public notices were issued advertising the five-year lease for bid. T.D. Webster of Carpinteria bid $225, and was outbid by Alvin Hyder of San Pedro, who bid $250. The lease ran from 1914 until 1919. It is with the Hyder lease that Santa Barbara Island saw its most active development.

280. What type of facilities did the Hyders build?

The Hyders built a two-room wooden ranch house on top of the island above Landing Cove. One room was occupied by Alvin Hyder and his family, and the other room was occupied by Alvin's brother Clarence and his family. A barn and chicken houses were constructed nearby.

281. How did the Hyders get their supplies to the top of the island?

In 1915, the Hyders constructed a wooden track with a sled on it which ran from the landing cove to the top of the hill by their house. A long rope was attached to the sled which they tied to their horse, Old Dan. Dan would pull the rope, which raised the sled, and stop at just the right place so the sled could be loaded or unloaded. The tracks for the sled were attached to the volcanic rock by spikes which were set in hand-drilled holes and fixed with cement. Today parts of the track and the hand-drilled holes still remain along the hillside.

282. How many people lived on the island during the Hyder years?

The number of people living on Santa Barbara Island varied, with up to as many as seventeen. Alvin Hyder had a wife and two children, and his brother Clarence had a wife and four children, all of whom lived together in the ranch house. Brother Cleve Hyder and his wife lived on the island in a separate house built partway up from Landing Cove.

During the Hyder ranching years, hay was raised on Santa Barbara Island. Circa 1918

Buster Hyder Collection

Cleve Hyder with his horses Dan and Charlie next to their haycrop on Santa Barbara Island. Circa 1918

283. How did the Hyders obtain fresh water?

The Hyders built three small reservoirs: one at the house, one on the west side of the island near Webster Point, and one near the south end of the island above Cat Canyon. Water was delivered from the mainland in their boat, *Nora II,* in fifty-gallon barrels, 25 at a time. From the boat, the water was pumped by engine to the house reservoir through a half-inch pipe which ran up the hillside from the landing cove to the reservoir. The other reservoirs held rain water.

284. What crops did the Hyders raise on Santa Barbara Island?

Several acres of potatoes were cultivated near the edge of the upper west slope. Barley hay was planted for three years in the area of the badlands on top of the island. One of the crops of hay was raised, baled, and sent to the mainland for sale only to have the buyers refuse to pay the bill. Because of this, the Hyders decided not send hay to the mainland again.

285. How did the Hyders clear the land?

Giant *Coreopsis* and crystalline ice plant were cut and cleared by hand, allowed to dry, and burned. This activity was practiced from about 1917 until 1921. Two horses and two mules were used to pull farm equipment such as plows and scrapers. No motorized vehicles of any kind were used.

286. What animals did the Hyder family raise on Santa Barbara Island?

In addition to the rabbits which were set loose, ducks, chickens, turkeys, geese, pigs, goats, and sheep were raised by the Hyders. The rabbits and sheep persisted after the Hyders left. During heavy winds, oftentimes some of the chickens would be blown out to sea and lost.

287. What was on the island when the Hyders arrived?

According to Buster Hyder in a 1986 interview, cats ran rampant on the island. No other animals except mice were present. A fisherman's shack existed in the landing cove when they first arrived. The Hyders built all the ranch buildings. They brought with them household goods, furniture and lumber for building purposes.

Buster Hyder Collection

Sheep were offloaded from a skiff to swim ashore on Santa Barbara Island by the Hyders. Circa 1918

67

Cleve Hyder shearing a sheep on Santa Barbara Island. Circa 1918

Buster Hyder Collection

288. Where did the Hyders get their sheep?

The Hyders purchased about three hundred sheep from the Caire ranch on Santa Cruz Island, and transported them to Santa Barbara Island by boat. The raising of sheep for wool and meat became the mainstay of their operation.

289. How were the sheep controlled?

The sheep were turned loose on Santa Barbara Island. No corrals or fences were needed. The animals were rounded up by horseback and by men on foot, and herded along a wooden wing-fence. They were tied and put upon the Hyder's wooden sled, which ran down the hill to the landing cove. Here they were loaded aboard the Hyder's boat for transportation to the mainland. Sheared wool was hand packed into large burlap sacks for transport.

290. Did the Hyder family utilize any of the island's natural resources?

Yes. In addition to marine resources of the island, gull eggs were systematically harvested, with one egg being taken from each nest. Due to the oily nature of gull eggs, they had to be boiled to be eaten. Cormorant eggs do not solidify with boiling, so the Hyders did not collect these.

291. What happened to the Hyder ranch?

When the Hyders left the island in 1922, they tore down the buildings for the lumber. They removed all their animals with the exception of the rabbits, probably a few sheep, and one mule, which later disappeared. The Hyders thought she was eaten by fishermen soon after they left the island. Leases required that all buildings be removed at the time of lease expiration. Even though the Hyder lease expired in 1919, they continued to live on the island for several more years.

292. Where did the Hyders go when they left Santa Barbara Island?

The Hyders moved to San Pedro where they started the 22nd

Octogenarian Buster Hyder returned to visit the island of his child-hood in 1986 after an absence of almost 60 years.

Street Landing, a sportfishing business. Alvin Hyder's son, Buster, ran the landing until 1966, when he retired to the family homestead in Cuyama Valley. The Hyders had the sportfishing business for almost fifty years.

293. Who had the lease after the Hyders?

In 1919, Santa Barbara Island was again advertised for lease. Two sealed bids, one for $25.50 a year, and the other for $1250 were received. The latter was accepted and was from the Venice Chamber of Commerce. A Mr. Abbot Kinney, board member, applied for the lease in his name. The Chamber wanted to develop the island for public uses such as camping, fishing, and a biological station and aquarium. They requested a twenty-five-year lease to justify expenditures the city would have to make, but the request was denied. In 1920, Mr. Kinney failed to pay the rent and the lease was revoked. By 1927, the island was still without a lease. The Hyders had moved off the island, and in 1929 again the lease was placed for bid. On November 1, 1929, the fourth lease was granted to Arthur McLelland and Harry Cupit for grazing land. They made only one $75 payment and never occupied the island for any length of time. In 1932 their lease was cancelled and no other leases were issued.

294. Have there been any fires on Santa Barbara Island?

Yes. In addition to some small agricultural burn-offs conducted by the Hyders between 1917–1921, a large fire of accidental origin burned most of the island's mesa in 1959. Winds from the west stopped the fire from continuing to the western edge of the island, although it did burn to the eastern edge. Approximately two thirds of the island was burned to the soil.

295. Is there a navigational light on Santa Barbara Island?

Yes. August 24, 1905, President Theodore Roosevelt issued the following proclamation: "It is hereby ordered that an unsurveyed island known as Santa Barbara Island . . . containing approximately 638.72 acres, is hereby reserved for lighthouse purposes." It was not until 1929 that the light began operation near the northwest corner of the island "to protect inter-island navigation in general and particularly for the protection of the Hawaiian Island and Trans-Pacific traffic, which follows a course passing six miles to the northward of the island."

Marla Daily

The navigational light on Santa Barbara Island is now solar powered.

296. What type of navigational light was designed?

The first light was an acetylene lantern equipped with a flasher adjusted to show a one-second light every six seconds. It cost $2286 to build and was set on top of a white wooden pyramid one hundred ninety feet above the water. It was an unmanned light. In 1986, a solar powered battery-operated light replaced the previously used system. Approximately 16 acres are set aside for navigational light purposes.

297. Have there been any other navigational lights on Santa Barbara Island?

Yes. A second light tower was constructed at the south end of the island in 1934. It was 486 feet above sea level. This light was burned in the 1959 fire and a "permanent discontinuance" was ordered by the Coast Guard, leaving just one functioning unmanned light on Santa Barbara Island.

298. What happened on Santa Barbara Island during World War II?

From 1942 through 1946 the island served as a military outpost. Motor vehicles and dirt roadways appeared during this occupation. Miscellaneous buildings, barracks and a boat-landing facility were constructed. At the outbreak of the war, both navigational lights were extinguished during the blackout. They were relighted in 1943 when the immediate threat to the Los Angeles area was thought to be over.

299. What happened to the Navy facilities?

After World War II, the Santa Barbara Island naval structures became the targets of extensive vandalism. By 1953, some of the buildings had been demolished, while others stood with doors blown off and windows broken. The 1959 fire burned some of the structures to the ground. Other materials had been dumped into the surrounding waters. In the early 1960s, a photo-tracking station was set on the island by the Navy. Two Quonset huts and three cement camera pads were installed. A jeep road ran between the photo pads and Quonset huts. When the Navy left the island, the camera pads, eight to ten generators, and one Quonset hut were left behind. The remaining Quonset hut served as a ranger residence for several decades until it was replaced with new facilities in 1991.

300. Are there any historic structures left on Santa Barbara Island?

No major structures of historic importance exist on this island. At the end of the early occupation of the island by fishermen, ranching and farming families, all the structures were removed. The ranger-visitor center Quonset hut was placed on the island in the early 1960s and was not of historic importance. Plow furrows from the early farming activities can still be seen on the west slope when viewed from North Peak. Occasional lumber and wire can be found from ranching days, as can the Navy's cement pads left from the 1960s. The trackbed leading from Landing Cove to the top of the mesa is still visible, but most of the track and the winch are gone.

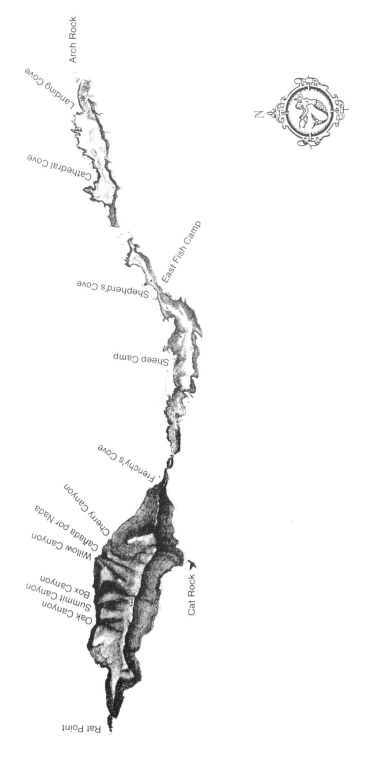

Arch Rock

Landing Cove

Cathedral Cove

East Fish Camp

Shepherd's Cove

Sheep Camp

Frenchy's Cove

Cherry Canyon

Cañada por Nada

Willow Canyon

Box Canyon

Summit Canyon

Oak Canyon

Cat Rock

Rat Point

N

ANACAPA ISLAND

ANACAPA ISLAND

301. How large is Anacapa Island?

Anacapa Island is almost five miles long, but only one-quarter to one-half mile wide. It is actually composed of three islets, East, Middle and West, bounded on most sides by sheer cliffs and connected only occasionally at extremely low tides. Together, the three islets are 1.1 square miles in size and contain approximately 700 acres. Anacapa Island is only slightly larger than Santa Barbara Island, making it the second smallest of the eight California Channel Islands.

Aerial view of East, Middle and West Anacapa Island.

302. What does Anacapa mean?

The name Anacapa is thought to be derived from the Chumash Indian word "Eneepah" meaning ever-changing or deception. Depending on the weather and approach to Anacapa, the three islets often appear as one large mesa or tableland. At other times, they are reflected in a mirage, making them appear much larger and closer. The name first appeared on British navigator George Vancouver's charts in the early 1790s.

303. How far from the mainland is Anacapa Island?

Anacapa Island is eleven miles from the mainland. The shortest distance is between the eastern end of East Anacapa and the Oxnard/Port Hueneme area.

304. In what county is Anacapa Island?

Ventura County. Originally Anacapa Island was placed within Santa Barbara County, but in 1873 that county was split into Santa Barbara and Ventura counties. With the projection of county lines seaward, Anacapa was placed in Ventura County.

305. What is the highest point on Anacapa Island?

Summit Peak on West Anacapa, at 930 feet in elevation, is the highest point. Elevations on Middle Anacapa reach 325 feet, and on East Anacapa reach 250 feet.

306. What is the physiography of East Anacapa Island?

East Anacapa is the smallest of the three islets, rising from the sea as a seemingly inaccessible mesa. The slightly terraced top of approximately 100 acres lies about 200 feet above sea level. Facilities on East Anacapa include the fog signal, lighthouse, Park Service buildings, and campground.

307. What is the physiography of Middle Anacapa Island?

Middle Anacapa Island is the second largest of the three islets. It is a little over three miles long, but seldom over one-eighth mile wide. Several small pocket beaches along the south side are only accessible by boat. East Fish Camp, the largest landing on the south side, was once the home of several fishermen. Landing is possible on the north side near the middle of the island at Sheep Camp. Due to the fragile ecology of Middle Anacapa, visitation is not permitted without permission from the Park Service.

308. What is the physiography of West Anacapa Island?

West Anacapa Island is the largest, highest, and most topographically diverse of the three islets. Visitation is strictly limited to the Frenchy's Cove and tide pool areas due to pelican and sea bird nesting activity.

309. What is the geology of Anacapa Island?

Anacapa Island is predominantly volcanic in orgin, composed mainly of highly weathered Miocene volcanic rock that has been eroded by wind and waves. It was probably uplifted not by volcanic activity, but by faulting. Many submarine lava flows can be seen on the island. In a few locations, sedimentary rocks can be found, including the blue-green San Onofre breccia on the south shore of West Anacapa near Cat Rock. Fissures forming sea caves and blow holes are common. Visually, Anacapa Island, along with the three other Northern Channel Islands, represents a seaward extension of the Santa Monica mountains.

310. Where are good examples of blow holes?

A good example of a blow hole can be found in the vicinity of Cat Rock on the south shore of West Anacapa. Adjacent to the blow hole is a large surge channel. A smaller blow hole is at Landing Cove on East Anacapa Island.

311. What and where is Cathedral Cave?

Cathedral Cave is located on the north side of East Anacapa Island to the west of Landing Cove. It is a large, multi-chambered sea cave which can be entered and explored by skiff on calm days. There may be a large surge running in the cave, so caution is advised.

312. What and where is Arch Rock?

Arch Rock, the easternmost extension of Anacapa Island, is a natural bridge formed by sea erosion. This forty-foot-high arch is considered by many to be the Anacapa Island trademark. It was first pictured on an engraving in 1854 by James Whistler.

313. What is the annual rainfall of Anacapa Island?

Though long-term meteorological data are unavailable, East and Middle islands are thought to receive an average of about eight inches of rain a year. West Anacapa may receive as much as thir-

Island Packers Collection

Arch Rock, East Anacapa Island with Island Packers' boat, Sunfish, *on a day trip.*

teen inches a year. Due to its height and location, West Anacapa Island forms a rainshadow effect over the other two islets.

314. Is there any fresh water on Anacapa Island?

No. There is not a dependable supply of fresh water available year around. A few caves seasonally have fresh water seepage. Water is shipped to East Anacapa Island and pumped into storage tanks for the use of Park Service personnel only. Visitors must provide their own water.

315. Who owns Anacapa Island?

Anacapa Island is owned by the U.S. Government. Unlike neighboring Santa Cruz and Santa Rosa islands, Anacapa Island has never had a private owner. In 1848 with the Treaty of Guadalupe Hidalgo, Anacapa Island became a part of California territory. Eighteen-fifty brought statehood to California, and in 1853 Anacapa Island was surveyed by the U.S. Coast and Geodetic Survey to determine the need for a lighthouse. In 1854, Anacapa Island was set aside for lighthouse purposes, and was administered by the Lighthouse Bureau until 1938, when President Franklin Roosevelt assigned National Monument status to both Anacapa and

Santa Barbara islands. In 1939 the Lighthouse Bureau went out of existence, and Anacapa Island was assigned to National Park Service management. Channel Islands National Monument fell under the supervision of Sequoia National Park until 1957 when it was transferred to San Diego and the Cabrillo Monument headquarters. In 1967, headquarters were established in Oxnard. In 1980, legislation creating Channel Islands National Park was passed by Congress and signed by President Carter. Anacapa Island's status then changed to that of a National Park. Certain areas on Anacapa Island are reserved by the U.S. Coast Guard.

316. How can one visit Anacapa Island?

Only East Anacapa Island is open to public visitation on a regular basis. Island Packers of Ventura, National Park Service concessionaire, runs scheduled boat trips to East Anacapa usually daily, if weather permits. Middle Anacapa has limited visitation. West Anacapa, with the exception of Frenchy's Cove and some tide pool areas, is closed to the public. East Anacapa Island is limited to 75 day visitors and 30 overnight campers at any one time.

317. Does one need a permit to land on Anacapa Island?

For day use on East Anacapa Island, a landing permit is not necessary. Overnight visitors are required to obtain a camping permit from the Park Service. Day use permits are required for Middle and West Anacapa (Frenchy's Cove), and are free from the Channel Islands National Park office in Ventura.

318. What is the best time of year to visit Anacapa Island?

Each season is very different. Spring offers the beauty of green grass and a multitude of wildflowers, though winds and seas may be a bit more choppy than during other times of the year. Summer brings sunny days and calm seas while offering a variety of plants in bloom. The lowest tides occur in summer and winter.

319. What types of trips are offered to Anacapa Island?

Island Packers offers half-day trips to Anacapa Island with no landing, or full-day trips with landing at either Landing Cove on East Anacapa or Frenchy's Cove on West Anacapa. Campers are accommodated by drop-off and pick-up service in coordination with regularly scheduled runs to the island. Sea cave explorations and floating classroom trips are also offered.

320. What can one see on a day trip to Anacapa Island?

In crossing the channel, whales or dolphins are often encountered. As one approaches the island, sea birds become more frequent. Around the island itself, harbor seals *(Phoca vitulina)* and California sea lions *(Zalophus californianus)* are seen regularly.

321. Does visitor use affect East Anacapa Island?

East Anacapa Island receives as many as 20,000 visitors a year. It is hoped that with camping on East Santa Cruz Island opened by the Park Service in 1997, this will alleviate some of the pressures now felt on East Anacapa. All public activity on East Anacapa Island is limited to the trail systems and campground areas to minimize impact.

Marla Daily

The landing at East Anacapa Island.

322. Can one swim or dive around Anacapa Island?

Yes. Although swimming and diving around Anacapa are somewhat difficult without a boat, the landing ladder area of East Anacapa offers access to the water for day and camp visitors during days of calm seas. Frenchy's Cove on West Anacapa is a good area for snorkeling from the beach.

323. How does one gain access to East Anacapa Island?

Access to East Anacapa is on the north side of this island in a small cove bounded by cliffs on all sides. On the west edge of the inlet is a dock and a series of concrete and metal steps which lead to the top of East Anacapa. Getting on to the island is a minor adventure in itself. A vertical ladder at Landing Cove leads from the bobbing skiff onto the landing where the 154 steel steps begin that zig-zag to the island's top. Visitors are advised to be agile and in good health.

324. What are the hiking conditions on East Anacapa Island?

A well-marked nature trail roughly the shape of a figure eight, and about one and a half miles long, is laid out on top of the mesa. One may take as much or as little time as desired in exploring the wonders of East Anacapa Island. The elevation gradient is approximately 40 feet.

325. Are there any dangers on East Anacapa Island?

Yes. The entire islet is surrounded by steep cliffs. One must stay on the well-established nature trails and their spurs. The cliff edges are vertical, crumbly, unstable and dangerous. One should not approach them for that slightly better view.

326. Are there any restricted areas on East Anacapa Island?

Yes. The trail to the lighthouse and foghorn is a restricted area. Approaching the foghorn can cause permanent hearing damage.

327. What should one bring to camp on East Anacapa Island?

Camping on East Anacapa Island is primitive. There is no water available, and all personal supplies, food and gear must be transported by the camper. If something is forgotten, one goes without. A two- or three-day stay is recommended. The Park will permit camping for up to two weeks, and permits are free from the Channel Island National Park Service office in Ventura. Since

Marla Daily

The campground on East Anacapa Island in 1987.

campers are restricted in number, one must call either Island Packers or the Channel Islands National Park office in advance to schedule overnight trips.

328. What are the campground conditions on East Anacapa Island?

There are seven camp sites, each with a fire pit for use in cooking meals. There is no water or fuel, and both must be brought by the visitor. Camping stoves are permitted. There are outhouses at the campground as well. Up to 30 campers are allowed at any one time.

329. What is the building that looks like a church on East Anacapa Island?

The building is a façade covering two redwood water tanks of 55,000 gallons each. In the past, vandals passing the island on boats shot at the tanks, releasing their precious supply of fresh water. In an attempt to stop the sniping, the churchlike structure was built to camouflage them. It has been relatively successful.

330. What is the large cement slab structure on East Anacapa Island?

Originally this slab served as a catchment basin for rain water. It was built in 1932 during the development of the current lighthouse. Gulls use this area for roosting and nesting. The cement slab now serves as a landing pad for helicopters.

Church façade surrounding water tanks on East Anacapa Island.

331. Have there ever been natural wild fires on Anacapa Island?
No. At least during historic times, no fires have been recorded.

332. What happens in the event of a fire on Anacapa Island?
No historical fires are known for Anacapa Island. In the event of a fire, the Channel Islands National Park would ask for assistance from Los Padres National Forest fire crews, who would respond with air tankers and hand crews. The island is classified as having a relatively light fuel load, in part due to previous grazing by introduced animals.

333. Are there any wharfs on Anacapa Island?
No.

334. Are there any roads or motor vehicles on Anacapa Island?
Although there are no cars on Anacapa Island, the Park Service keeps a small tractor on East Anacapa Island.

335. Are there any telephones on Anacapa Island?
Yes. Communication to the mainland is available for administrative and emergency use only. There is also a two-way radio communication from Anacapa Island to the mainland and to offshore boats. Most cellular phones work from Anacapa Island.

336. What type of emergency transportation exists for Anacapa Island?

In the event of an emergency, it is possible for a helicopter to land on East Anacapa Island, weather permitting. Customary transportation is by boat.

337. Are there any native animals on Anacapa Island?

Yes. The native deer mouse *(Peromyscus maniculatus anacapae)* is an endemic subspecies found on all three islets and in all habitats.

338. Are there any bats on Anacapa Island?

Although bats may occur on Anacapa Island, none has been collected thus far.

339. What introduced animals live on Anacapa Island?

Black rats *(Rattus rattus)* live on all three islets, and were probably introduced by shipwrecks. They are highly successful colonizers whose oppportunistic feeding habits are supplied by a variety of plants, intertidal invertebrates, mice, lizards, carrion, birds and eggs. In turn, rats are preyed upon by owls and hawks.

340. Do the introduced rats cause any harm?

Yes. They interfere with the native mice, lizards, plants and nesting land and marine birds. Their population is very hard to control or eliminate.

341. Are there any snakes on Anacapa Island?

No.

342. What lizards are found on Anacapa Island?

Two species, the side-blotched lizard *(Uta stansburiana)* and the alligator lizard *(Elegaria multicarinatus multicarinatus)* occur on Anacapa Island. The side-blotched lizard is the more abundant of the two, and is easily recognized by the dark blotches behind the fore limbs, and by its slender tail. The alligator lizard is recognized by the unmistakable undulating movement of its body as it runs. It is often mistaken for a snake.

343. Is either species of lizard harmful?

No. However, alligator lizards may bite if handled.

344. Are there any amphibians on Anacapa Island?

Yes. One species, the Pacific slender salamander *(Batrachoseps pacificus pacificus)* is found in the winter in moist areas of leaf litter and under boards and rocks, although it is not abundant. Its very small legs give it a wormlike appearance.

345. What is the insect fauna of Anacapa Island?

West Anacapa Island, with its greater plant diversity, has the most diverse insect fauna, followed by Middle and East islands. Several species of grasshoppers and crickets are found, along with ground beetles, carrion beetles, soft-winged flower beetles, sap beetles, lady beetles, darkling beetles, weevils, craneflies, mosquitoes, black flies, robber flies, bee flies, seaweed flies, house flies, flower flies, fruit flies, blow flies, flesh flies, ants and bees. The Los Angeles County Museum of Natural History and the Santa Barbara Museum of Natural History have major collections of Anacapa Island insects.

346. Are there any butterflies or moths on Anacapa Island?

Yes. Pyralid moths, leaf-roller moths, clear-winged moths, geometrid moths, tiger moths, owlet moths, milkweed butterflies, brush-footed butterflies, skippers, blues and hairstreaks have all been collected on Anacapa Island.

347. Does Anacapa Island have spiders?

There are about two dozen types of spiders known for Anacapa Island.

348. Are there any unique insects on Anacapa Island?

Yes. An endemic subspecies of shield-backed cricket has been described from Middle and West islands.

349. How did scale insects get to Anacapa Island?

The cochineal insect *(Dactylopius opuntiae)* spread to Anacapa Island from neighboring Santa Cruz Island, where it was intentionally introduced to reduce the prickly pear cacti population.

350. What land mollusks are found on Anacapa Island?

Four different types of snails and one slug have been collected on Anacapa Island: two subspecies of California blunt-top snail,

Shepard's snail, and a greenhouse slug. The slug was accidentally introduced and is not known to still occur here.

351. What are the breeding land bird species on Anacapa Island?

bald eagle (former resident)	barn swallow
peregrine falcon (former resident)	northern raven
red-tailed hawk	Bewick's wren
American kestrel	rock wren
black oystercatcher	northern mockingbird
mourning dove	loggerhead shrike
barn owl	European starling
white-throated swift	Hutton's vireo
Allen's hummingbird	orange-crowned warbler
black phoebe	western meadowlark
western flycatcher	house finch
horned lark	rufous-crowned sparrow

352. What marine birds nest on Anacapa Island?

California brown pelican
double-crested cormorant
Brandt's cormorant
pelagic cormorant
western gull
pigeon guillemot
Xantus' murrelet

353. Which birds on Anacapa Island have evolved into separate Channel Islands subspecies or races?

Allen's hummingbird
western flycatcher
horned lark
Bewick's wren
loggerhead shrike
orange-crowned warbler
house finch
rufous-crowned sparrow

354. Where do the California brown pelicans nest on Anacapa Island?

Pelicans *(Pelecanus occidentalis)* nest on the north-facing cliffs of restricted West Anacapa Island.

355. Why did the pelican become threatened?

The brown pelican is once again a fairly common sea bird of the west coast. In the late 1960s and early 1970s, a critical population "crash" occurred which endangered its future success. High levels of DDT concentrated in the birds' eggs which resulted in thin shells which were then crushed by the weight of the parent bird during nesting. With the ban of DDT, an immediate response was seen which enabled the pelicans to make a comeback. On West Anacapa, the birds nest without danger of harassment or disturbance.

356. What plant communities are on Anacapa Island?

Coastal bluff, island grassland and coastal sage scrub are found on all three islets. In addition, West Anacapa has chaparral and woodland communities. Anacapa Island lacks the extensive crystalline ice plant community so prevalent on Santa Barbara Island.

Brown pelicans nest undisturbed on Anacapa Island.

357. How many different plants are found on Anacapa Island?

The flora of Anacapa Island contains over two hundred different native and introduced plants. Some are rare and endangered. Unlike similarly sized Santa Barbara Island, Anacapa Island supports a number of trees and shrubs, particularly in the canyons on West Anacapa.

358. Are any plants endemic to just Anacapa Island?

No. All of the plants on Anacapa Island are also found on at least one other Channel Island, although some are Channel Islands endemic plants.

359. Of the Channel Islands endemic plants, how many are found just on Anacapa Island?

Seventeen Channel Islands endemic plants are found on Anacapa Island.

360. Are there any poisonous plants on Anacapa Island?

Poison oak *(Toxicodendron diversilobum)* grows on West Anacapa Island where it is part of the chaparral community.

361. Who planted the Eucalyptus trees on Middle Anacapa Island?

It is believed the trees were planted sometime around 1885 by a man named Elliott who raised sheep and built several houses here. These trees are now over a century old, and are native to Tasmania.

J.V. Elliott's Sheep Camp on Middle Anacapa Island circa 1885. Note the Eucalyptus trees.

362. Did Chumash Indians live on Anacapa Island?

It is not known if Chumash Indians lived year around on Anacapa Island in permanent settlements. They did occupy all three islets at least seasonally however. There is evidence of at least twenty-three kitchen midden areas. Perhaps a lack of a dependable supply of fresh water was a deterrent, although the intertidal areas were rich in their offerings for these maritime people. There are no Spanish accounts which reported people living on Anacapa Island.

363. What 19th-century archaeological work was conducted on Anacapa Island?

In 1877–1879, Leon de Cessac conducted field work on the Channel Islands for the French Ministère de l'Instruction Publique. He was looking for museum specimens, and did not cite the exact location where he conducted his work on Anacapa Island. In the 1880s, Lorenzo Yates explored archaeological sites on Anacapa Island and made a small collection of artifacts.

364. What 20th-century archaeology has been conducted on Anacapa Island?

David B. Rogers visited Anacapa Island for the Santa Barbara Museum of Natural History in the 1920s, followed by a Los Angeles Museum of Natural History survey around 1941. Phil Orr did field work in 1956 on East Anacapa for the Santa Barbara Museum of Natural History, and in 1958 UCLA conducted an archaeological survey during which time a site was excavated on the east island. In the early 1960s, Charles Rozaire visited Anacapa several times, conducting research and mapping site locations. UCLA sponsored limited field work in the 1970s which yielded a small collection of artifacts now housed in their anthropology department.

365. Who was the first explorer to find Anacapa Island?

Probably the first European explorer to discover Anacapa Island was Juan Rodríguez Cabrillo, navigator for the Spanish Empire. He passed Anacapa Island in 1542.

366. Who else saw Anacapa Island?

Most early explorers failed to specifically mention Anacapa Island in their charts or logs. In 1769, Portolá's sea expedition referred to it as "Las Mesitas" or little tables. Juan Perez, ship's captain for Portolá, called it "Vela Falsa," false sail.

367. What is the first mention of a structure on Anacapa Island?

In an unsigned logbook of the U.S. Coast and Geodetic Survey dated September, 1853 the following appears: "There are two landings on the middle island, one in the north, and the other on the south side at either of which it is practicable to get to the signal. At present there is the remains of an old house just at this landing and a trail from here will lead you up the slope of the hill."

368. How was the artist James Whistler involved with Anacapa Island?

Whistler, known for the portrait of his mother, never visited Anacapa Island. In 1854 however, he was employed by the U.S. Coast and Geodetic Survey as an engraver at the salary of $1.50 per day. As such, he was assigned the task of preparing an engraving of East Anacapa Island. In completing the assignment, he took artistic license and added a number of seagulls to his work. Previously, he had received a warning for adding such touches, and shortly after the Anacapa Island assignment he was discharged. The 1854 version of the map shows the seagulls. When the map was reprinted two years later, the birds were omitted. An original of Whistler's Anacapa Island engraving with the gulls is valuable as a collector's item today.

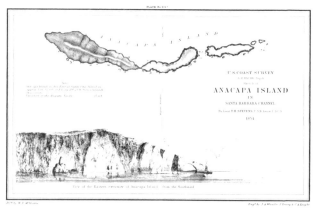

Marla Daily Collection

Anacapa Island as sketched by artist James Whistler in 1854. The 1856 version deleted the controversial seagulls from above Arch Rock.

369. What happened on Anacapa Island during the 19th century?

Although since 1848 Anacapa Island has been U.S. Government property, until 1902 Uncle Sam appears to have taken little interest in what went on on the island. Several different persons used the islets for fishing and ranching purposes, selling what interests they could to others as they left. In 1902, these possessory interests stopped when the Government instituted a formal lease agreement policy.

370. Who was the first person to live on Anacapa Island during historic times?

During the 19th century, seasonal fishermen used Anacapa Island as a base. Captain George Nidever was one of the first persons to have interests on Anacapa Island where he raised sheep, even though it was Government property. A July 1869 deed records the sale of the Islands of Anacapa from William Dover to Louis Burgert and W.H. Mills for $1500. In 1872, Anacapa Island and the property contained thereon was transferred to the Pacific Wool Growing Company, which also bought interest in several other Channel Islands that year. In 1882, Anacapa Island was quit-claimed to Ezekiel and J.V. Elliott.

371. Who were the official lessees of Anacapa Island?

According to Government records, the island was leased as follows:

1902–1907	Le Mesnager
1907–1917	H. Bay Webster
1917–1927	Ira Eaton
1927–1932	(no lease recorded)
1932–1937	C. F. Chaffe

372. What is known about the Le Mesnager lease of 1902–1907?

In 1897, Frenchman Louis Le Mesnager bought the Elliott interests on Anacapa Island for $8000. April 1, 1902, the U.S. Government officially leased Anacapa Island to Le Mesnager for five years at $25 a year. Under the terms of the lease, it was formally acknowledged that Anacapa Island was U.S. Government property. Le Mesnager was not to "erect any permanent buildings upon any part of said island." It was to be used for grazing and farming only.

373. What is known about the H. Bay Webster lease of 1907–1917?

Heaman Bayfield Webster, Ventura businessman, contracted with the Government to run sheep and have a fishing concession on Anacapa Island. During these ten years, Webster, his wife Martha, and two sons Morris and Harvey, lived on Anacapa much of the time.

374. How did H. Bay Webster become interested in Anacapa Island?

In 1884, Webster paid his first visit to Anacapa Island. At that time, he said there was a shack on West Anacapa Island occupied by a Chinese fisherman. From 1890 to 1895, Webster hunted seals for their pelts and oil, but quit the business because prices were too low. Webster sold his last skins for 75 cents per 100 pounds, and sold the seal oil for only 20 cents a gallon. By the end of the 19th century, the animals were no longer found in sufficient numbers to make the business profitable.

375. What did H. Bay Webster do once he acquired the lease in 1907?

Webster's main interest was in sheep raising. Upon taking over the lease, he purchased from previous lessee Le Mesnager, the 40-50 sheep already on the island. In addition, Webster purchased another 250 sheep from neighboring Santa Cruz Island.

376. How did Webster manage all the sheep?

Webster raised sheep for wool and not for meat. He used his boat, *Ana Capa,* to transport the sheep from islet to islet as needed. Sheep to be moved to Middle or West Anacapa Island were hog-tied while aboard the boat, and then untied and thrown overboard to swim ashore to their new islet. Shearers were imported from the mainland to do the shearing. By the time Webster sold his sheep interests, there were about 500 head total. Flocks suffered repeated poaching by fishermen, and their numbers declined heavily in years of drought due to lack of water and feed.

377. Where did H. Bay Webster and his family live?

The Websters lived on Middle Anacapa Island at Sheep Camp, the location of the main headquarters for the sheep operation.

378. Did H. Bay Webster's children go to school?

Yes. In 1911, Webster brought out a governess/tutor for his sons, and erected Anacapa Island's first and only school in a tent.

379. What happened to the Webster lease in 1917?

H. Bay Webster tried to renew his lease when it expired in 1917 for 25 years instead of the usual five-year period outlined. He found that an Act of Congress would be required to change the terms of the lease, and since World War I had begun, Congress had little time to devote to such small matters. He lost his bid to Captain Ira Eaton, who bid $607.50 per year for this 1917–1922 Anacapa Island lease. In 1912, East Anacapa Island was excluded from the lease so that the Lighthouse Bureau could erect and maintain lighthouse facilities there.

380. What happened with East Anacapa Island after 1912 when it was excluded from the lease agreement?

East Anacapa, set aside for lighthouse purposes and personnel, remained off-limits to all others. In 1926, Superintendent Rhodes of the Lighthouse Bureau issued a public notice for the "sale of rock at Anacapa Island Lighthouse Reservation" in which 160 tons of rock could be taken. The points from which the rocks could be quarried were to be subject to Governmental approval. Presumably, this offer was to attract builders of mainland harbors, jetties and breakwaters such as those being constructed at Santa Barbara and San Pedro. Ten dollars was the highest bid received, and it was not accepted.

381. How long did Ira Eaton have the lease for Middle and West Anacapa Islands?

Ira Eaton had the lease for ten years, from 1917–1927. Eaton was able to secure two consecutive five-year leases, during which time he ran a resort operation on neighboring Santa Cruz Island. Eaton used Anacapa Island as a storage place for bootlegged liquor during prohibition. His lease fees were in part paid by the Santa Barbara fish company owned by the Larco Brothers, who placed fishermen on Anacapa Island.

382. What happened when Ira Eaton's lease ran out?

No lease is recorded for 1927–1932, although it is known that during this period Frenchman Raymond "Frenchy" LaDreau moved to West Anacapa Island. Frenchy made good money during Prohibition by helping rumrunners. Several times he stored liquor in caves or in his chicken coop on the island. A heavy drinker himself, oftentimes Frency took partial payment in liquor or a percentage of the cache.

383. Who was the last lessee on Middle and West Anacapa Islands?

C. Fay Chaffe was awarded the lease from April 1, 1932 for five years at $760 a year. Although his lease had the usual limitations allowing farming and grazing and preventing subletting, Chaffe, like Eaton before him, pursued subletting. His sole interest was in developing a sport-fishing camp on the island, for which he planned a sea wall and pier. Chaffe took in three partners, Al Derby, Merl Allyn and a Mr. Philbrick for this venture, but his elaborate plans never came to fruition.

384. Did Chaffe sublet to anyone else?

Yes. He entered into an agreement with the Redlands Investment Company, run by J.M. Johnson, who wanted to stock Anacapa Island with game birds and to conduct reforestation programs. Chaffe was anxious to diversify his interests, but the Lighthouse Bureau rejected this proposal.

385. Why was the leasing of Anacapa Island terminated in 1937?

In 1932, the Bureau of Lighthouses brought Anacapa and Santa Barbara islands to the attention of the National Park Service, proposing that they be turned over for park purposes. By 1935, Congress had created a statute dealing with unused Government property, under which Anacapa Island was placed. In 1937, the Commissioner of Lighthouses advised against any further lease agreements on Anacapa Island, and hence leasing was terminated.

Channel Islands National Park Service facilities on East Anacapa Island.

386. Did all of Anacapa Island transfer to National Monument status in 1938 and then National Park status in 1980?

No. The Lighthouse Bureau retained four parcels of land: all of Cat Rock on the south side of West Anacapa; 46.72 acres of West Anacapa; 7.68 acres of Middle Anacapa; and 106.88 acres of East Anacapa. In 1939, the Lighthouse Bureau went out of existence, and these parcels were transferred to the Coast Guard. In 1970, the Coast Guard and the National Park Service signed an agreement whereby the Park Service would assume the responsibility of these islands except of the lighthouse itself.

387. What did the Park Service do with the Coast Guard buildings?

The buildings erected by the Lighthouse Bureau and transferred to the Coast Guard were in a bad state of disrepair by 1970 when the Park Service assumed responsibility for them. The complex was refurbished and repaired, keeping a Spanish-style architecture. Buildings include a three-bedroom ranger residence, a generator building combined with living quarters, a fuel storage

Channel Islands National Park Service

A rare photograph with long-time island resident Raymond "Frenchy" LaDreau (left) and former island lessee H. Bay Webster (right). Circa 1940.

Frenchy's cabins, West Anacapa Island circa 1940. None is left today.

building, and a combination maintenance-storage building with a portion of it converted into a visitor center.

388. For whom is Frenchy's Cove named?

Frenchy's Cove is named for Raymond "Frenchy" LaDreau, long-time resident fisherman on West Anacapa Island. He arrived sometime around 1928, prior to the island's establishment as a National Monument. For about twenty-eight years he lived a hermit-like existence on Anacapa Island, serving as the unofficial Park Service representative, reporting acts of vandalism and island activities. He was well-known among fishermen from Monterey to Ensenada. Described as "a hermit who enjoyed company," Frenchy lived alone with his cats in one of several cabins built at the cove which now bears his name. He left Anacapa Island in 1956 at age eighty after incurring injuries in a fall. What became of him is a mystery.

389. What were Frenchy's living accomodations?

Four shacks lined the bluffs at Frenchy's Cove. They were built in 1925 by promoters from Ventura who had hoped to develop a sport fishing camp. Frenchy lived in the largest of these shacks, which had board and bat walls lined with magazine pictures to help keep out the wind. From a tiny window, Frenchy had a million dollar view across the channel from which he could see steamers and potential visitors passing by. A narrow path led from his shack to the beach where he kept his skiff and mooring device.

390. What was Frenchy's mooring device for his skiff?

To pull the skiff high above high water, Frenchy built a pulley system using an old anchor chain, steel cable, pulleys and rollers anchored to the island by steel rods driven into the rocks and hard earth. His lobster traps and other fishing gear were stored in a small cave above his mooring spot on the island.

391. Since Frenchy seldom visited the mainland, how did he obtain fresh water?

Water was always a problem for Frenchy. He begged it from

Frenchy's Cave, West Anacapa Island with a source of brackish water.

all the vessels that anchored off his beach, but even so he would often run out, particularly during bad weather months when few boats visited the island. In a sea cave located about a quarter of a mile west of his home was a brackish water seep where water dripped from the ceiling. When necessary, Frenchy would prop a bucket under the drip, and within 24 hours he could collect two to three quarts of brackish water.

392. What happened to Frenchy's home site?

After Frenchy left Anacapa Island, the Park Service decided to set up headquarters at Frenchy's Cove. In 1959, one of the four shacks was torn down, and the other three were temporarily repaired. An outhouse was constructed, and more than a ton of trash and debris was either burned or shipped off of West Anacapa Island.

393. What is it like at Frenchy's Cove today?

This cove offers the best landing spot on West Anacapa Island.

Frenchy's Cove today. Day trips to West Anacapa Island land on this beach.

It is a small, narrow two-hundred-foot-long cobblestone beach backed by cliffs on the northeastern part of the island. A narrow sea channel separates it from Middle Anacapa Island. At low tide, one can walk through to the south side to visit an expanse of tide pools. All of the shacks have been removed.

394. When was the first navigational light placed on Anacapa Island?

Shortly after the 1853 wreck of the *Winfield Scott*, the Coast Survey pointed out the need for a permanent lighthouse facility on Anacapa Island. It was not until 1911, however, that funds became available for the erection of an unmanned light. Powered by acetylene, this light could be seen for twenty miles. The signal consisted of a one-second light on a ten-second cycle. It was located atop a fifty-foot metal skeleton tower on the extreme eastern end of Anacapa Island.

395. When was the first fog signal device installed?

In 1911, with the erection of the first navigational light, a whistling buoy was anchored five-eighths of a mile off the east end of East Anacapa Island. By 1921, however, it was found to be inoperative. In 1928, the Lighthouse Bureau began allotting funds for a fog signal and radio apparatus on East Anacapa Island, which was completed in 1932.

396. When was the current lighthouse built?

The lighthouse light on Anacapa Island was turned on for manned operation on March 25, 1932. After dealing with several different construction firms, the Lighthouse Bureau finally had construction completed which included a 30,000 square foot concrete rain collecting pad, a water tank, light tower, powerhouse for the generator, an oilhouse, a fog signal building and several lighthouse keepers' dwellings. This is the only true lighthouse found on a California Channel Island.

397. When was the light automated?

The light was automated in 1968. Until that time (1932–1968) the light was tended around the clock by a rotating crew of Coast Guard personnel. During World War II, from 1942–1945 the light was turned off during the Pacific Coast blackout.

398. Are there any shipwrecks on Anacapa Island?

Yes. Anacapa is the site of over a dozen major shipwrecks, the most famous of which was the *Winfield Scott*. Ships traveling between San Francisco and Los Angeles have historically followed the Santa Barbara Channel shipping lanes, where many have made their last voyage.

399. What happened to the steamer *Winfield Scott*?

This 225-foot steam paddlewheeler owned by the Pacific Mail Steamship Company was built in 1851 to make the run from Panama to San Francisco with passengers, mail, and supplies. On December 2, 1853, in a dense fog she went aground on the north side of Middle Anacapa Island due to pilot error. It was about midnight, after most of the passengers had gone to sleep, when she landed on Middle Anacapa to await rescue, which for some was not to be for a week. On December 4, the Pacific Mail's steamer *California* picked up the women and children while enroute to San Francisco, returning a week later for the rest of the passengers and crew, who had to ride to Panama. Today, divers can swim around parts of the wreck, which includes the paddle-wheel.

400. Have any deaths occured on Anacapa Island?

Several people have died on Anacapa Island. In 1928, a Swede named "Slim" Melander was drowned while caring for his lobster traps. In 1931, Iver Steen was found in Frenchy's Cove with his throat slit. Frenchy had gone to town for a month, and Steen was watching his place. Frenchy found the body upon his return. It is thought that Steen, an alcoholic, was experiencing alcohol withdrawal and took his own life with one of Frenchy's knives. In 1938, Charles Johnson, erstwhile "mayor" of Anacapa Island, was found dead in one of the cabins at Frenchy's Cove, apparently of old age. In 1973, National Monument employee Bob Timmons died of a heart attack on East Anacapa Island. In 1991, East Anacapa Island camper Kent Sayre fell from the island to his death. In 1992, two brothers, Bryan and Monte Bolton, were killed in their inflatable dinghy while exploring caves.

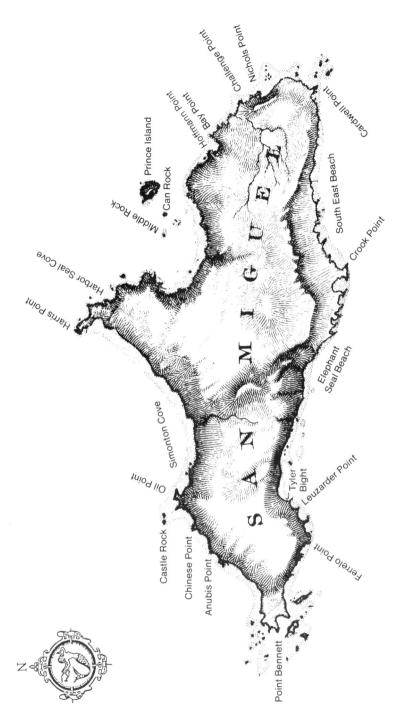

SAN MIGUEL ISLAND

SAN MIGUEL ISLAND

401. How large is San Miguel Island?

San Miguel Island is 14 square miles, and ranks sixth in size of the eight California Channel Islands. Including Prince Island, which lies in the entrance to Cuyler's Harbor, San Miguel Island contains 9325 acres. It is approximately eight miles long and four miles wide, and is the westernmost of the Northern Channel Islands.

402. How large is Prince Island?

Prince Island, located in Cuyler's Harbor, contains 39.4 acres and has an elevation of 296 feet.

403. Where is Richardson Rock?

Richardson Rock is an islet five and a half miles from San Miguel's western point. It is almost fifty feet high and five hundred feet wide.

404. In what county is San Miguel Island?

San Miguel Island is in Santa Barbara County.

405. How far is San Miguel Island from the mainland?

The closest mainland is Point Conception, which is approximately 26 miles away. The closest neighboring island, Santa Rosa, is 3 miles to the east.

406. What is the highest point on San Miguel Island?

Green Mountain, at 831 feet in elevation, is the highest point.

407. What is the physiography of San Miguel Island?

The topography of San Miguel Island is quite low in contrast to the high rugged peaks, ridges and canyons found on some of the larger islands. Waters surrounding the island are often rough and hazardous due to submerged rocks and shoals. Prevailing northwesterly winds are almost constant, blowing sand quite readily. Dense fog often shrouds the island from view. It is the least accessible of the four Northern Channel Islands, and has been called the "graveyard of the Pacific" due to the large number of shipwrecks.

408. What is the geology of San Miguel Island?

San Miguel Island is composed of Tertiary rocks and Pleistocene terrace deposits. In addition, Eocene marine sediments are present on the western part of the island, and Miocene volcanic rocks are confined to the eastern part.

Steve Swartz

Prevailing northwesterly winds oftentimes make the Point Bennett area of San Miguel Island unnavigable.

The caliche forest found on San Miguel Island is the most spectacular example to be found on any Channel Island.

409. Is there caliche on San Miguel Island?

Yes. There is an extensive, very well-developed caliche forest on San Miguel Island. It offers good evidence that the island once supported large trees and shrubs, unlike today. This is the most spectacular caliche to be found on any of the California Channel Islands.

410. Has anyone ever filed a mining claim for San Miguel Island?

On July 28, 1891, José Guadalupe Espinosa recorded with the County of Santa Barbara a gypsum lode discovery on San Miguel Island. He described it "on the southeast end of said island, running northerly there from 1500 feet and from the center of said lode 300 feet on each side thereof. Discovered January 8, 1891." The mine was never worked.

411. Have any earthquakes been reported on San Miguel Island?

Yes. In 1895, William Waters, possessory owner of San Miguel Island, wrote to the Director of the State Weather Service in Sacramento: "There has been quite a commotion on San Miguel Island. The land which formed a high bluff on the west side of the harbor [Cuyler's Harbor] has sunk more than sixty feet and forced itself under the beach, not only raising it, but stones which had lain at water's edge for years are now fifteen feet above it . . . So sudden was the change that fish and crabs were left high and dry and thirty feet above the harbor."

412. What is the average rainfall on San Miguel Island?

There are no long term rainfall records for San Miguel Island. The records known are marked by wet and dry trends. Temperatures are mild year around and marked by a lack of extremes. It is known that severe droughts occurred in 1863–64, 1870–71, and again in 1876–77. Another dry trend existed from 1897–98 and again in 1923–24.

413. Is there any fresh water on San Miguel Island?

Yes. Unlike smaller Santa Barbara and Anacapa islands, San Miguel Island has several springs which provide water year around in modest quantity. Of the 28 known springs, only a few produce water of potable quality. The spring in Nidever Canyon off Cuyler's Harbor is contaminated with the intestinal bacterium *Escherichia coli.*

414. Who owns San Miguel Island?

San Miguel Island is owned by the U.S. Government. Cooperative agreements exist between the Navy and the Department of the Interior (May 7, 1963, as amended October 20, 1976) in which the Navy allows employees of the Interior Department (National Park Service) to manage and preserve the scientific and cultural values of the island.

415. When did the Navy get control of San Miguel Island?

In 1934 the Secretary of Commerce transferred the control of San Miguel Island and its offshore Prince Island to the Navy.

416. How can one visit San Miguel Island?

Currently, San Miguel Island has limited visitation by boat for either day trips or for overnight camping. There is an undeveloped campground with an outhouse and seven sites where up to 30 people are permitted to camp at one time. Persons are also allowed to visit the island via private boat. Hiking is restricted to established trails. Visitation permits are available through Channel Islands National Park.

417. Does anyone live on San Miguel at present?

San Miguel Island is occupied by Park Service personnel and scientists. There are no permanent residents.

418. What park service facilities are on San Miguel Island?

The original ranger station and composting toilet are above Cuyler's Harbor in Nidever Canyon. A new complex was constructed in 1996 adjacent to the airstrip above Cuyler's Harbor.

419. Are there any other facilities on San Miguel Island?

Yes. The National Oceanic and Atmospheric Administration (NOAA) has a facility located above Point Bennett. Scientists studying the marine mammal populations stay here.

Landing is permitted only at Cuyler's Harbor on San Miguel Island.

Park Service personnel and researchers often travel to San Miguel Island by plane, landing on a dirt runway.

420. Are there any motor vehicles on San Miguel Island?

There are no cars on San Miguel Island.

421. Are there any telephones on San Miguel Island?

No. The only communication available is by radio. Powerful cellular telephones, however, may work from the island.

422. Are there any airstrips on San Miguel Island?

There are two airstrips on San Miguel Island. Hammond Field, originally placed eastward of today's strip, is located in the vicinity of the old ranch complex on top of the island toward the east end. The plane of George Hammond first landed here July 22, 1934. Hammond Field appeared on aeronautical charts until 1965, when its poor condition prompted the Navy to have it deleted. The Dry Lake strip is located toward the west end near Green Mountain. Both strips are unimproved dirt runways. Landings are restricted to servicing Park Service personnel and researchers.

423. Have any planes ever been wrecked on San Miguel Island?

Yes. In 1942, a B-24 military aircraft crashed on the north side of Green Mountain, spreading wreckage over several acres. Today the instrument panel, propellers, and pieces of the plane are still on the side of the mountain.

424. Are there any native terrestrial mammals on San Miguel Island?

Only the fox *(Urocyon littoralis littoralis)* and the deer mouse

(Peromyscus maniculatus streatori) are known to inhabit San Miguel Island. Archaeological evidence suggests that ornate shrews *(Sorex ornatus)* and the spotted skunk *(Spiloglae gracilis)* also occurred here.

425. Are there any bats on San Miguel Island?

Reports of bats flying about San Miguel Island are known, although none has been collected. It is thought the California myotis *(Myotis californicus caurinus)* probably occurs here. An extinct vampire bat *(Desmodus stocki)* is known from bones of at least eight individuals, indicating a population of this species on the island in the past.

426. Are there any other extinct animals known from San Miguel Island?

Yes. The giant mouse *(Peromyscus nesodytes)* is known from archaeological evidence. It may have been a contemporary of the extinct dwarf mammoth also once found here. An extinct flightless goose *(Chendytes)* is also known from the fossil record.

427. Are dwarf mammoths known from San Miguel Island?

Yes. Pleistocene fossil elephant remains were first reported by Herbert Lester in 1932 when he unearthed two large tusks. Since then, several other finds have been recorded.

428. Are there any feral animals on San Miguel Island?

No. For at least 127 years, introduced sheep grazed on the island. Burros were used as early as 1906 by island ranchers to haul supplies. Both of these animals formed feral populations which have since been eradicated.

429. When were the sheep removed from San Miguel Island?

The last remaining sheep on San Miguel Island were removed in 1966. Sheep had been grazing on the island for over a century, but when island lessee Robert Brooks was evicted from the island in 1948, he was unable to remove all his flock. From July 17–20, 1966, Navy personnel, a biologist and a Park Ranger hunted down the remaining 148 sheep.

430. What happened to the feral burros?

By the early 1970s, there were about two dozen burros roaming the island. Their hooves curled from living on sandy substrates, and they had been inbreeding for decades. In 1977, Park Service personnel eliminated the population to allow for better vegetative recovery and to help curb erosion on San Miguel Island.

431. Have there been any results from the removal of the feral sheep and burros on San Miguel Island?

Yes. Measurable recovery of the island has occurred for the past three decades. Plant communities are spreading and stabilizing the island's soil and sand. As a result, less sand is blowing about, and the once extensive sandspit at Cardwell Point on the island's east end has all but disappeared.

432. Are there any introduced mammals currently living on San Miguel Island?

Yes. Like Anacapa Island, San Miguel Island also is the home of the introduced black rat *(Rattus rattus)*. It is not known how long they have been on the island, but they appear to be confined to the northwest shore of the island and in the Cardwell Point area. They are thought to have been introduced by shipwrecks.

433. How many species of seals and sea lions are found here?

Six. San Miguel Island supports more species of pinnipeds than anywhere in the North Pacific. At certain times of the year, the Point Bennett area has in excess of 10,000 animals, which can be heard and smelled for miles. It is the most outstanding wildlife display found anywhere on the Southern California Islands.

434. What are the seals and sea lions that use Point Bennett?

California sea lion *(Zalophus californianus)*
Northern sea lion *(Eumetopias jubatus)*
Northern fur seal *(Callorhinus ursinus)*
Guadalupe fur seal *(Arctocephalus townsendi)*
Northern elephant seal *(Mirounga angustirostris)*
Harbor seal *(Phoca vitulina)*

435. Didn't all these pinnipeds attract hunters?

Yes. In the late 18th and early 19th centuries, sea-mammal hunters were drawn to San Miguel Island in search of the fur-bearing sea otter *(Enhydra lutris)*. Yankees, Russian-sponsored

Six species of pinnipeds use San Miguel Island for breeding and hauling out. As many as 10,000 animals may be on the beach at one time.

Aleuts, Kanakas (Hawaiians) and others were among those who came here to hunt.

436. Can one visit the Point Bennett area to see the pinnipeds?

Yes. Although Point Bennett itself has restrictions due to all of the breeding and pupping activity of the seals and sea lions, the point can be viewed from either offshore by boat or from an overlook position on the island. The Park Service permit system applies to the latter method of viewing.

437. How close may one get in a boat to Point Bennett?

No entry is allowed within 300 yards of shore, except during March 15–April 15 and October 1–December 15 when boats may approach to 100 yards.

438. Do airplanes bother the pinnipeds?

Since airplane noise is a potential threat to large pinniped breeding colonies on San Miguel Island, the California Fish and Game Code prohibits flights below 1000 feet above ground level over San Miguel Island. The only aircraft allowed to land on the island are those necessary for official administrative reasons.

439. Are there any amphibians on San Miguel Island?

The slender salamander *(Batrachoseps pacificus pacificus)* is the only amphibian recorded for San Miguel Island. They are found in association with springs and seeps and in dense vegetation cover.

440. What lizards are found on San Miguel Island?

Two species are known for this island: the alligator lizard *(Elegaria multicarinatus)*, and the western fence lizard *(Sceloporus occidentalis)*.

441. Are there any snakes on San Miguel Island?

No. Although there is prehistoric fossil evidence of the occurrence of the rattlesnakes and gopher snakes on San Miguel Island, there are no historic records of snakes of any kind.

442. Are there any land mollusks on San Miguel Island?

Yes. Both live and fossil specimens of the Ayres' snail can be found in abundance on San Miguel Island. In addition, a subspecies of California blunt-top snail occurs here.

443. What land birds nest on San Miguel Island?

bald eagle – former resident
peregrine falcon – former resident, reintroduced
red-tailed hawk
American kestrel
common barn owl
Allen's hummingbird
horned lark
barn swallow
northern raven – former resident
rock wren
European starling
orange-crowned warbler
song sparrow
western meadowlark
house finch

444. What marine and shore birds nest on San Miguel Island, including Prince Island and Castle Rock?

Leach's storm-petrel
ashy storm-petrel
California brown pelican – former resident
double-crested cormorant
Brandt's cormorant
pelagic cormorant
black oystercatcher
snowy plover
western gull
tufted puffin – former resident
common murre – former resident
pigeon guillemot
Xantus' murrelet
Cassin's auklet

445. Which birds on San Miguel Island are endemic Channel Islands subspecies or races?

The horned lark, orange-crowned warbler, house finch and song sparrow have evolved into distinct island races.

446. Have any birds been reintroduced to San Miguel Island?

Yes. Although peregrine falcons nested historically on San Miguel Island, they have not nested here for many years. In 1985, the Channel Islands National Park began a peregrine falcon rein-

Fossil specimens of land snails carpet some areas of San Miguel Island.

Coreopsis *and lupine bloom above Cuyler's Harbor in the spring.*

troduction program, which hopes to establish a breeding colony on San Miguel once again.

447. What is the vegetative aspect of San Miguel Island?

There are no large trees or shrubs on San Miguel Island. With the episodic cycles of droughts, overgrazing and soil stripping this island has experienced, along with wind and water erosion, the island's vegetation has been severely affected in the past. With the removal of feral animals in the 20th century, vegetative recovery is in process.

448. What plant communities are found on San Miguel Island?

Beach and coastal vegetation are well-developed on this island. The dunes are constantly being formed and moved in the areas of Cuyler's Harbor, Cardwell Point and Simonton Cove, among others. In addition, unlike smaller Anacapa and Santa Barbara islands, San Miguel Island has long stretches of sandy beaches. Coastal bluff, coastal sage scrub, grassland and coastal salt marsh communities occur here as well.

449. How many different plants are found on San Miguel Island?

About 220 different plants are found on San Miguel Island, including natives, island endemics and introduced plants.

450. Are there any plants endemic to only San Miguel Island?

Although there are no plants at the species level endemic to San Miguel Island, a subspecies of buckwheat *(Eriogonum grande dunklei)* is known only from this island.

451. Are there any ferns on San Miguel Island?

Interestingly, this is the only Channel Island on which ferns had not been found until 1987.

452. Did Chumash Indians live on San Miguel Island?

Yes. Archeological surveys have mapped 542 Indian sites on San Miguel Island, evidence that the occupation was more than casual or temporary.

453. How long ago was San Miguel Island occupied by Indians?

A radiocarbon date of 10,700 years before present indicates human occupation on San Miguel Island at least that long ago.

454. What did the Chumash call San Miguel Island?

San Miguel Island was called Tuqan.

Marla Daily

Beach and coastal dune vegetation helps to stabilize the wind-blown sand on San Miguel Island.

455. Have any archaeologists ever worked on San Miguel Island?

Yes, several. Early archaeologists visited the island looking for museum specimens, and excavation techniques were much different than those used by today's scientists. As early as 1873–74, surface collections were made. In 1875, the Smithsonian sponsored field work conducted by Paul Schumacher. He excavated hundreds of burials with their associated artifacts. In 1878, France sponsored Leon de Cessac to make collections. Continuing through the 20th century, various field work was conducted, including excavations for the Santa Barbara Museum of Natural History. Recently, the National Park Service has participated in further archaeological excavations.

456. In terms of disturbance, how have the archaeological sites survived?

The Indian sites on San Miguel Island have suffered major disturbances on the surface from continued sheep grazing and from the resulting erosion of the prevailing northwestly winds. In addition, relic or "pot hunters" have disturbed many of the sites. The sites are protected by Federal Law which is enforced by the National Park Service.

457. Who was the first person to discover and name San Miguel Island?

Juan Rodríguez Cabrillo. On October 18, 1542, the expedition of Cabrillo discovered and named the islands of San Miguel and Santa Rosa "Islas de San Lucas." He changed the name of San Miguel to "Posesión" for one of his ships. After Cabrillo's death, the name was changed to "Juan Rodríguez" or "La Capitana" in his honor. In 1748 it appeared on a map as "San Bernardo," the name which was adopted by Costansó on his 1770 map of the Channel Islands. The name "San Miguel" won acceptance from the charts of English explorer George Vancouver in 1793.

458. Is San Miguel the burial place of Juan Rodríguez Cabrillo?

Experts disagree on this subject. It is known that Cabrillo wintered at San Miguel Island in 1542 during which time he broke either an arm or a leg, which later became infected. Knowing he was a dying man, Cabrillo turned his expedition over to his chief pilot, Bartolome Ferrer. On January 3, 1543, Cabrillo died as a

A monument honoring explorer Juan Rodríguez Cabrillo was placed above Cuyler's Harbor in 1937.

result of his injury, and many say he was buried on the island. In 1937 to honor this great explorer, the Cabrillo Civic Clubs of California, a statewide Portuguese organization, placed a 40-inch-high monument to Cabrillo on a knoll overlooking Cuyler's Harbor.

459. Was San Miguel Island granted to anyone during the Mexican period?

No. In 1848 with the Treaty of Guadalupe Hidalgo, San Miguel passed to the U.S. Government.

460. Who first lived on San Miguel Island after the Chumash Indians?

As on various other Channel Islands, squatters, fishermen and otter-hunters lived on this island during historic times.

461. When did ranching begin on San Miguel Island?

Ranching probably began sometime around the 1850s on San

Miguel Island. The early "owners" of San Miguel Island were not legal owners, but owners by possession only. Until 1911, when the Government began issuing recognized leases, the various ranchers were squatters without rights. The first record of a long-term resident is that of frontierman and trapper Captain George Nidever.

462. How did George Nidever obtain an interest in San Miguel Island?

On June 30, 1863, the Santa Barbara County Sheriff held a sale of the property of Samuel C. Bruce to pay Bruce's debts which amounted to $1486.57. George Nidever was the highest bidder at $1800 for "all the right, title, interest and ownership . . . in and to all the sheep, cattle and horses upon the said Island of San Miguel, consisting of 6000 sheep, more or less, 125 head of cattle, more or less, and 25 horses. Also the right, title, interest, claim and ownership . . . consisting of a possessory claim to an undivided one-half of the said island." This is the first deed recorded for San Miguel Island. It is not known how Samuel Bruce obtained this interest.

463. Where did George Nidever live on San Miguel Island?

Nidever built an adobe house at an elevation of 400 feet above Cuyler's Harbor. Today only a few remnants can be found. A stream channel has cut through the structure, and sand has blown over much of it, adding to its decline.

464. What happened to George Nidever's interest in San Miguel Island?

On May 8, 1869, Nidever and his two sons Mark and George sold, for $5000 "one undivided half of all interest, right, title and possession" of San Miguel Island to Hiram W. Mills. Nidever's sons were tired of living on the island, and urged their father to sell. On April 26, 1870, for $10,000 Hiram W. Mills purchased their remaining interest in the island, including all their livestock.

465. What did Hiram Mills do with San Miguel Island?

The same day Mills bought out George Nidever and his sons, he entered into a sale of "all the undivided 3/4ths of San Miguel Island" with P.F. Mohrhardt, J.M. Leuzarder, and Warren H. Mills. The following year, 1871, Hiram Mills sold his remaining 1/4 interest to these three men for them to "share and share alike."

466. What did P.F. Mohrhardt, Warren H. Mills and J.M. Leuzarder do with San Miguel Island?

In 1872, these three men engaged in various transactions which resulted in Mohrhardt leaving the partnership and being replaced by Elmer Terry. In 1872, the three new partners formed the Pacific Wool Growing Company and took in investors. This company invested in not only San Miguel Island, but also in Anacapa and San Nicolas islands. In 1876 they were listed on the delinquent tax records in Ventura County, and in 1887 the company sold its interests.

467. Who bought the Pacific Wool Growing Company in 1887?

David Fitzgibbons bought the Company's assets on November 18, 1887, and sold them three days later back to Pacific Wool Growing Company president, Warren Mills.

468. What did Warren Mills do with San Miguel Island?

In 1887 he sold half interest in San Miguel Island to Captain William G. Waters for $10,000. At the time of the sale, there were 4000 sheep, 30 cows and horses, some pigs, turkeys, chickens, two cats and a dog on the island. Captain Waters and his wife and adopted daughter moved to the island in 1888, taking with them a maid and some ranch hands. The following years, Mills sold his other half interest to W.I. Nichols for $4000, who in turn sold it for $10,000 to William Schilling.

469. What is known about Waters' life on San Miguel Island?

Captain Waters maintained an interest in San Miguel Island for about thirty years (1887–1917). His wife, who spent only a part of one year on the island, kept a diary the first six months of 1888. She wrote: "I like the island, it has many advantages over town life as well as disadvantages, but for awhile will be good for us all. Had I a nice cozy house with a bathroom and other conveniences, heat for me, I would be content to stay half the year here." She wrote that the wind was always blowing, sometimes a gale, which blew the roof off their house one night. Her husband worked hard planting grain, gathering abalone and raising sheep and cattle. Mrs. Waters left the island in June, 1888 and died the following year.

470. Who sheared the sheep on San Miguel Island?

William Waters brought extra help to the island from Santa Barbara. The men were paid with brass San Miguel Island tokens made by Waters as a form of currency. Each coin had a hole in the center through which it could be strung. Tokens were redeemable for cash before the sheep shearers returned to town.

471. When was the San Miguel Island Company formed?

On March 4, 1897, William Waters and investor Jeremiah Conroy formed the San Miguel Island Company with a capital stock of $49,500. The company listed its assets: 3000 sheep, 1 otter boat, 3 skiffs, 2 small boats, 1 wagon, 1 cart, 3 plows, 1 harrow, 25 head of cattle, 18 horses and mules, 5 saddles and bridles, 1 set kitchen furniture and utensils, 1 mowing machine, picks, shovels, seeds and various other equipment. Also all the improvements, buildings, sheds, fences and materials on the island.

472. What happened to William Schilling's interest?

Schilling transferred his interest in the island to Elias Beckman in 1892. Waters continued to operate sheep and farming endeavors on the island, strengthening his possessory right. In 1908, Beckman and Waters were involved in a lawsuit over the island which resulted in the U.S. Government exercising its right of ownership.

473. When did the Government step in and exercise its right of ownership?

In 1909, President Taft issued an executive order reserving San Miguel Island for lighthouse purposes. In 1911, Captain Waters, who was still living on the island at the time, wrote to Taft to ask that the light be placed on Richardson Rock offshore instead. He explained that he had been living on the island, having bought his interest in 1887. To remove his stock and buildings would constitute an extreme hardship. On November 1, 1911, Waters was awarded a five-year lease for $5 a year. In signing the lease, Waters acknowledged the island was Government property.

474. Who were the official lessees of San Miguel Island?

1911–1916   William G. Waters
1916–1920   William G. Waters, Robert Brooks and J.R. Moore
1920–1925   Robert Brooks and J.R. Moore
1925–1948   Robert Brooks

475. What happened with the island lease when Waters' first five-year lease expired in 1916?

In 1916 the Government renewed Waters' lease. In 1917, Waters took in partners Robert Brooks and J.R. Moore since his lease had no clause to prevent doing so. Although the Lighthouse Bureau objected to the Waters-Brooks-Moore arrangement, the lease held. Waters died in 1917. By 1919, a six-room house, shearing pens, a wool house, barn, roads and four miles of fencing had been constructed. In 1920, Brooks and Moore renewed the lease for five years at $200 a year.

The 120-foot long ranch house which stood above Cuyler's Harbor was destroyed by a fire in 1967. (The Legendary King of San Miguel Island, McNally & Loftin 1979.)

476. What happened to the 1920–25 lease when it expired?

The Lighthouse Bureau placed the lease for bid. Bidding without a partner, Robert Brooks was the highest bidder at $3000 for five years. Second was Lewis Penwell, who bid $2550. Brooks tried to buy the island from the Government in 1927, but he was turned down. Instead, his lease was extended. He was evicted from the island by the Navy in 1948.

477. When did the Lesters live on San Miguel Island?

Robert Brooks hired Herbert Lester to manage the island for him in 1930. He had met Lester during World War I in the Army. Lester suffered from shell-shock and was in Walter Reed Hospital for a time recovering. Brooks thought the island life would be good for his friend, and he desperately needed some long-term help on the island. In 1930, Herbert Lester and his bride, Elizabeth Sherman Lester, moved to San Miguel Island.

478. Where did the Lesters live on San Miguel Island?

The Lesters occupied a large wooden ranch house originally built by Captain Waters in 1908. Most of the building materials were salvaged from lumber schooner wrecks on the island. Port holes served as some of the windows. The ranch was built around three sides of a court and was one story high. It had eight large rooms and a bath, with running water in several rooms. Lester called it "Rancho Rambouillet" after a breed of sheep.

479. What was life like for the Lesters on San Miguel Island in the 1930s?

The Lester family increased to include two daughters, Betsy and Marianne, all of whom lived in the large house on top of the island above Cuyler's Harbor. They lived a "Swiss Family Robinson" style of life which attracted attention nationwide. They seldom went to the mainland. A supply boat brought them the necessary food and goods, and their friend George Hammond flew mail and odds and ends to them. Herbert Lester developed his private collection of memorabilia in his "Killer Whale Bar," which included a whaler's bomb lance, a collection of guns, several cap and ball pistols, and the safe from the wreck of the ship *Cuba*. In the yard were such finds as lifeboats, ships' blocks, masts, booms, tackle gear, cleats, casks, and an old-time locomotive bell taken from a wrecked ship. Herbert Lester proclaimed himself "King of San Miguel."

480. How did the Lester girls go to school?

As the Lester daughters grew older, it became necessary to educate them. A schoolhouse, which was called the "tiniest schoolhouse in the world," was given to them by their neighbors on Santa Rosa Island. Mrs. Lester obtained teaching aids from the Santa Barbara County schools department, and instructed the girls herself. Occasionally they would have to pass proficiency exams.

481. When did the Lesters leave the island?

One June 18, 1942, Herbert Lester, despondent over his health, committed suicide. Later that same day, the children, then ages nine and eleven, were sent to the mainland. The Coast Guard picked up Mrs. Lester and the family's possessions July 4, 1942, and took her to Santa Barbara where she would begin her new mainland life.

482. Where is Herbert Lester buried?

Herbert Lester is buried above Harris Point on San Miguel Island. In 1981, his widow Elizabeth died in Santa Barbara. She is buried next to her husband on the island.

483. Who managed the island for Robert Brooks after the Lesters?

Ulmar Englund, an old sailor from Norway, and his wife Rae lived on the island for awhile, after which a couple named Al and Rosie Baglin came to live and work on the island. In 1948 when the Navy terminated the Brooks lease, everyone had to leave the island.

484. What happened on San Miguel Island during World War II?

As part of the Coastal Lookout Organization, the Department of the Navy established a lookout on San Miguel Island. A two-room shack with glass windows was placed with an observation tower near the ranch house. A road was bulldozed from the ranch to the wooden tower lookout and on to Point Bennett. Communication was via radio transmitter and receiver.

485. What happened to the island after World War II?

Robert Brooks, who held a revocable grazing lease on San Miguel Island for 33 years, was given a 72-hour eviction notice from the Navy in 1948. The Navy decided to use the island "for military purposes of a confidential nature." The Navy had been using San Clemente Island as a bombing range, and they decided a second range was needed on San Miguel Island. Coast Guard notice was issued December 17, 1948, declaring the San Miguel Island bombing range a danger area.

486. Did the U.S. Navy actually practice bombing on San Miguel Island?

Yes. Bombing of the island continued through the 1950s, scattering bomb casings and shrapnel all over the island. From June 16 to July 9, 1950, bombing operations were temporarily halted to allow former lessee Robert Brooks to go to the island to get the livestock he was unable to remove during his 72-hour eviction. In 1961 when draft plans were being formed for National Park operations, the Navy refused to give up San Miguel Island.

487. Why wouldn't the Navy release its interest in San Miguel Island?

San Miguel Island was considered by the Navy to be one of the most strategically located areas for the Pacific Missile Range. In 1963 the Navy transferred partial responsibility for the island to the commander of the Pacific Missile Range. The Navy and the Department of the Interior signed an agreement to jointly protect the "natural values and historic and scientific objects" on the island.

488. What happened on the island during the 1960s?

Both the Navy and the Pacific Missile Range continued active operations involving San Miguel Island. Radar guidance systems were tested, and major fleet exercises occurred around San Miguel Island. It continued to be used as a tactic target for both planes and ships. Small boaters interfering with operations continued to be a problem. Warning area notices would be issued to mariners and airmen before each operation, but by this time, protests from scientists, environmentalists, fishermen and pleasure boat owners began to increase.

489. What happened to the 120-foot long wooden ranch house?

In 1967 the ranch house burned to the ground. Though by this time it had been heavily vandalized, it contained the remnants of personal belongings of various ranch residents. The house was vacated in 1948 when the Navy terminated its lease, though occasionally Navy personnel or others would use it for shelter. The cause of the fire was a Navy aircraft dropping a warning flare which caused a grassfire blaze which in turn engulfed the house.

490. Are there any historic structures on the island?

The remains of the Nidever adobe can still be seen in an arroyo with a stream-cut channel going through it. The site of the extensive wooden ranch house is evidenced by the ruins of two chimneys and two cisterns. Miscellaneous associated debris is scattered about the area as well. This site remains a symbol of the previous hard-working ranch efforts by many people, and the futility of its success.

491. Have there been any accidental deaths on San Miguel Island?

Yes. In addition to Herbert Lester's suicide in 1942 and the fatalities in the 1942 plane wreck, Ralph Hoffmann, director of the Santa Barbara Museum of Natural History, fell to his death on San Miguel Island in 1932 while collecting plants.

492. Has any movie company used San Miguel Island?

Yes. In 1955 parts of *Mutiny on the Bounty,* which won Best Picture of the Year, were filmed around San Miguel Island.

493. Are there any lighthouses on San Miguel Island?

No. San Miguel Island was reserved by Executive Order for lighthouse purposes on April 23, 1909. Richardson Rock was reserved January 30, 1911, and Prince Island was reserved November 5, 1917. Of these three, only Richardson Rock was equipped with a lighted whistle buoy anchored northwest of the rock. It was rebuilt in 1948 and still serves to warn traffic of the obstacle nearby. An unwatched light was established on the south side of the island at Crook Point in 1943, but it was discontinued in 1953. A nun-buoy is anchored off the southwest tip of the island.

494. What major shipwrecks have occurred on San Miguel Island?

A Spanish galleon (1801) and the *J.F. West* (1898) are two shipwrecks known from the 19th century. In the 20th century, the *Kate and Annie* (1902), the *Coleman* (1905), the *Anubis* (1908), the *Comet* (1911), the *Watson A. West* (1923), and the steamer *Cuba* (1923) were some of the major disasters.

495. What happened to the *Coleman*?

The schooner *Coleman,* built in 1888, wrecked just inside Point Bennett on August 30, 1905. She carried 800,000 feet of lumber, 60,000 of which were salvaged. The rest of it, mostly redwood, washed ashore. John Russell, manager of the island for Mr. Waters, was able to salvage much of it using burros to haul it to the top of the island above Cuyler's Harbor, where he constructed the large 120-foot long ranch house. It was completed in 1908.

496. What happened to the *Anubis*?

On July 18, 1908, the German steamer *Anubis,* loaded with lumber, tallow, wheat and 67 people went aground a half mile east of Castle Rock on the west end of San Miguel Island. Captain Frank Nidever, grandson of former island resident George Nidever, was able to rescue some of the people. Two other steamers, the *Fulton* and *Dee Westport,* relieved the sinking ship of most of her cargo. On July 30th the crew pumped out holds, and using the tug *Goliath,* was able to pull her off the rocks. In Cuyler's Harbor she was repaired and then towed to San Francisco.

497. Where did the *Comet* wreck?

The *Comet,* carrying 620,000 feet of redwood lumber to San Pedro from Gray's Harbor, ran into Wilson Rock on the northwest side of San Miguel Island. With a badly damaged hull, she drifted ashore and came to rest. Island resident Captain Waters bought salvage rights for $1,000. As late as 1962, her hull could be seen on the beach buried in the sand with only her anchor exposed.

498. What happened to the *Watson A. West*?

In 1923, the schooner *Watson A. West* ran aground in a heavy fog at the west end of San Miguel Island. The lumber she carried allowed the wreck to remain afloat long enough for the crew to escape before she sank. Some of the lumber from this wreck was used in fencing and in the buildings on the island.

499. Where did the *Cuba* wreck?

On September 8, 1923, Pacific Mail luxury liner *Cuba* went aground on a reef 500 yards from Point Bennett. Her 115 passengers and 65 crew were rescued, along with the $2,500,000 in gold and bullion she carried. She was headed north to San Francisco when she became stranded in the fog. Captain Ira Eaton, who was running a resort on Santa Cruz Island at the time, was able to salvage much of the ship's furnishings, including tables, linens and silverware.

500. Are there any boat facilities on San Miguel Island?

No. Although some coves and harbors offer relatively safe anchorages from the strong prevailing northwest winds, San Miguel Island has no wharf or dock facility.

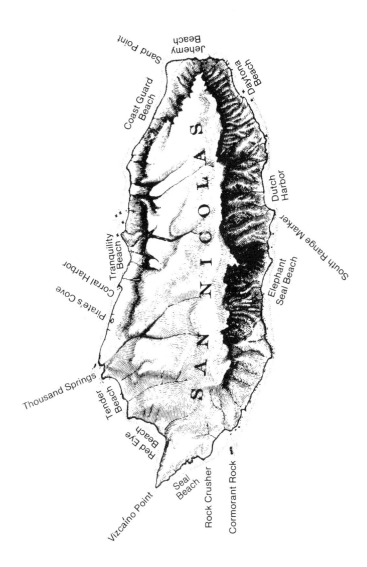

Jehemy Beach
Sand Point
Daytona Beach
Coast Guard Beach
Dutch Harbor
South Range Marker
Tranquility Beach
Elephant Seal Beach
Corral Harbor
Pirate's Cove
Thousand Springs
Tender Beach
Red Eye Beach
Vizcaíno Point
Seal Beach
Rock Crusher
Cormorant Rock

SAN NICOLAS

SAN NICOLAS ISLAND

501. How large is San Nicolas Island?

San Nicolas Island is 22 square miles and ranks fifth in size of the California Channel Islands. It is roughly oval in shape, with the axis just under ten miles long, and a maximum width of 3.6 miles.

502. In what county is San Nicolas Island?

San Nicolas Island is in Ventura County.

503. How far is San Nicolas Island from the mainland?

It is 61 miles to the nearest mainland, Laguna Point near Point Mugu. San Nicolas Island is the outermost island of the Channel Islands chain. Santa Barbara Island, its closest neighbor, is 28 miles to the east-northeast.

504. What is the highest point on San Nicolas Island?

Jackson Hill, at an elevation of 907 feet is the highest point. It is named after one of the Navy men once stationed on San Nicolas Island.

505. What is the physiography of San Nicolas Island?

The island is relatively flat-topped with a mesa-like profile. The western end contains large shifting sand dunes, while the eastern end is very precipitous with a small sand spit extending eastward. The southern or leeward side of the island is a giant escarpment which rises from the sea to 700 feet within a mile of shore. The northern side of the island has cliffs which rise as wave-cut terraces to the mesa at 300–400 feet above sea level.

Official photograph U.S. Navy by Steve Junak

The military base on San Nicolas Island is located on the island's flat-topped mesa.

506. What is the average rainfall on San Nicolas Island?

Rainfall records, which have been kept on San Nicolas Island since 1933, indicate an average annual rainfall of about 8 inches. A difference of over 18 inches occurs between the driest year recorded (3.3 inches in 1948) and the wettest year (21.59 inches in 1941). No thunderstorms, frosts or snowfall have been recorded.

507. Is there fresh water on San Nicolas Island?

Yes. San Nicolas Island contains a number of springs which have formed as a result of precipitation percolating into the ground. There are a few brackish seeps along fault lines, particularly on the island's south side. Fresh water needs for island personnel are met by harvesting water from wells.

508. What is the geology of San Nicolas Island?

The bedrock of San Nicolas Island is mainly composed of sandstone of Eocene age that has been carved into wave-cut terraces. Sediments of Pleistocene and Holocene age lie on top. The island is gently folded and intensely faulted. The marine sedimentary rocks forming marine terraces are composed of conglomerates, sandstone, siltstone and shale.

Official photograph U.S. Navy by Steve Junak

Constant wave action gradually alters the shape of coastal sandstone on San Nicolas Island.

509. Has anyone placed a mining claim on San Nicolas Island?

Yes. In 1900, Edmund Burke formed the San Nicolas Oil Company and filed a claim for oil exploration on San Nicolas Island in an attempt to sell stock in his oil company. No developments occurred on the island, however, and his claim was declared abandoned. In 1920, Burke wrote to the U.S. Government requesting preferential rights for oil exploration due to his previous claim. His request was denied and considered a "wild cat" scheme for promotion purposes.

510. Are there any badlands on San Nicolas Island?

There are extensive areas of badlands on the south side of San Nicolas Island which have been likened to those found in South Dakota.

511. Are there sand dunes on San Nicolas Island?

Yes. There are several types of sand dunes on San Nicolas Island, including cemented sand dunes, vegetated sand dunes, and active sand dunes. About three-fourths of the dunes on San Nicolas are active and in a constant state of movement.

512. Is there any caliche on San Nicolas Island?

Caliche is well-developed on the western third of San Nicolas Island, particularly among the sand dunes and Sea Lion Beach, Vizcaíno Point and 1000 Springs where these rhizoconcretions form unusual and bizarre landscapes.

513. Is it windy on San Nicolas Island?

Yes. Prevailing winds are from the northwest, and only a few days a year are wind-free. The average wind speed is about 14 knots. This almost constant wind action has created the large sand dunes on the western part of the island.

514. Is there a sandspit on San Nicolas Island?

Yes. There is a small sandspit located off the eastern end of San Nicolas Island which has been created by excessive sand deposition and prevailing northwesterly winds. A jetty built on the northern side of the sandspit has greatly reduced the size of this once much larger sandspit.

515. Are there marine terraces on San Nicolas Island?

Fourteen marine terraces are particularly well-developed on San Nicolas Island along the northeastern sector of the island. Pleistocene age marine shells can be found near the top of this island.

516. Who owns San Nicolas Island?

San Nicolas Island is owned by the U.S. Government. President Hoover's executive order of 1933 placed San Nicolas Island under the jurisdiction of the U.S. Navy. In 1947 it was placed under the control of the U.S. Naval Air Weapons Station, Point Mugu from where it continues to be administered today.

517. Can one visit San Nicolas Island?

No. San Nicolas Island is closed to the public. Limited scientific access is permitted. Clearance must be obtained in advance from the Point Mugu Naval Air Weapons Station.

518. What activities occur on San Nicolas Island?

Among other things, the Naval Air Warfare Center installations on San Nicolas Island study by radar, telemetry, photography, and other means, both internal and external missile data.

Official photograph U.S. Navy by Steve Junak

San Nicolas Island's "Housing and Business District"

The information gathered is entered into computers for scientists and engineers to study in great detail.

519. What facilities are on San Nicolas Island?

The U.S. Navy has spent millions of dollars making San Nicolas Island serviceable. Permanent structures include barracks, technical facilities, a large mess hall/cafeteria, medical and fire facilities, and a Navy exchange.

520. Are there any recreational facilities on San Nicolas Island?

Yes. Tennis courts, a racquet ball court, a hobby shop, a weight room, a jacuzzi, a movie theater, a bowling alley and a recreation center were built by the government on San Nicolas Island.

521. Is there a road system on San Nicolas Island?

The road system on San Nicolas Island consists of both paved and unpaved roads. Jackson Highway traverses most of the length of the island from Jackson Hill in the east to the far west end.

522. How many people are stationed on San Nicolas Island?

Currently, the island is home to about 200 military and civilian personnel. Most Navy personnel are assigned to the island for periods of two years. Duty here is considered equal to sea duty.

523. How does San Nicolas Island receive its supplies?

The bulk of the supplies are sent by barge or landing craft. Loading and unloading is done at Daytona Beach, the only suitable landing location on San Nicolas Island. Cargo planes also make two flights a week for small, non-restricted items.

524. Does the Navy import water to San Nicolas Island?

No. Adequate water is supplied by various wells and seeps on the west end of the island where the water percolates into the sand and flows underground along impervious strata toward the ocean to the north. A reverse-osmosis system augments wells.

525. How do military and civilian personnel travel to and from San Nicolas Island?

The Navy has a contract with a private airline company to provide regularly scheduled air transportation to San Nicolas Island. Flights are based out of Point Mugu.

An abandoned plane wreck lies northeast of the runway on San Nicolas Island.

526. What type of airstrip is on San Nicolas Island?

A paved 10,000 foot runway located on top of the east end of San Nicolas Island accommodates military air traffic to San Nicolas Island. The runway has a ground controlled approach facility, and can accommodate supersonic target aircraft and planes.

527. What are the flight restrictions for private aircraft around San Nicolas Island?

Aeronautical charts warn of extensive fleet and air operations conducted to approximately 100 miles seaward of San Nicolas Island. The California Fish and Game Code prohibits flights below 1000 feet above ground level over San Nicolas and Santa Barbara islands to minimize pinniped disturbance.

528. Is there a fire station on San Nicolas Island?

There are two fire stations on San Nicolas Island, one at the airport and one near the main military complex.

529. Have any fires occurred on San Nicolas Island?

No major fires have occurred on San Nicolas Island in recent time. There have been a few fires caused by electrical equipment or target launches, but all have been extinguished quickly.

530. Are there any telephones on San Nicolas Island?

Yes. A microwave system provides phone service to San Nicolas Island. It is a part of the 989 prefix area.

531. How does San Nicolas Island get its electricity?

Electricity is provided by a power plant of diesel generators which operates 24 hours a day.

532. What happens to sewage on San Nicolas Island?

Sewage is secondarily treated in a small plant near the main compound. Most of the effluent evaporates in the ponds, and the rest is spray irrigated after chlorination onto the adjacent hillside.

533. Is San Nicolas Island available for scientific study?

Yes. Limited access is accommodated through the facilities on San Nicolas Island. All research is screened through an independent review board. Approval, clearance, and arrangements must be obtained in advance from the Point Mugu Naval Air Weapons Station. Field station accommodations are available.

534. Are there any good boat anchorages or facilities on San Nicolas Island?

No. The majority of anchorages around San Nicolas Island are open roadsteads, offering little protection in inclement weather. No facilities are available except in the gravest emergency.

535. Are there any lighthouses on San Nicolas Island?

Although there are no lighthouses on San Nicolas Island, there are three navigational lights. They are located on the north side, south side and east end of the island. There is also an aerobeacon located on top of the middle of the island which flashes brightly.

536. Where is Begg Rock?

Eight nautical miles northwest of the west end of San Nicolas Island lies the volcanic protrusion known as Begg Rock. It is about fifteen feet high. Since it is a navigational hazard, it is marked by a whistling buoy and a flashing light. It was named for the *John Begg*, a schooner which ran against it in 1824.

537. What native terrestrial mammals are found on San Nicolas Island?

San Nicolas Island has both an endemic subspecies of island fox *(Urocyon littoralis dickeyi)*, and an endemic subspecies of deer mouse *(Peromyscus maniculatus exterus)*.

A curious fox under some Coreopsis *on San Nicolas Island.*

538. What species of bats occur on San Nicolas Island?

Two species of bats have been collected here, the California myotis *(Myotis californicus),* and the lump-nosed bat *(Plecotus townsendii).*

539. Are there any feral animals on San Nicolas Island?

Currently there are feral cats on San Nicolas Island. In the past, feral populations of sheep, goats, dogs and cats have been reported, but today only the cats remain as a feral population.

540. Do the feral cats compete with the native foxes?

Yes. Both cats and foxes prey upon the same vertebrates, (mice, birds, lizards), and therefore they are in direct competition for some food sources.

541. Is there a feral cat removal program on San Nicolas Island?

Yes. Cat eradication has been an ongoing, long-term endeavor. Most feral cat removal is accomplished by live trapping.

542. Are there marine mammals on San Nicolas Island?

Yes. The most abundant marine mammal is the California sea lion *(Zalophus californianus).* In addition, large numbers of Northern elephant seals *(Mirounga angustirostris)* and harbor seals *(Phoca vitulina)* are found here.

543. Which marine mammals are known to breed on San Nicolas Island?

California sea lions, Northern elephant seals, and harbor seals are all known to breed on San Nicolas Island.

544. Where are most of the marine mammals located on San Nicolas Island?

The marine mammals tend to use the southern shores of San Nicolas Island for hauling out and breeding.

545. Were sea otters known from San Nicolas Island?

Yes. Sea otter hunting on San Nicolas Island was particularly heavy in 1811 and again in 1815, when the Russian hunter Boris Tasarov was arrested on the island by Spaniards for hunting in Spanish waters. Tasarov and his Aluet companions had taken almost 1000 sea otters in seven months on San Nicolas Island.

The island night lizard is found only on San Nicolas, San Clemente and Santa Barbara islands.

546. Are there any snakes on San Nicolas Island?

No.

547. Are there any lizards on San Nicolas Island?

The island night lizard *(Xantusia riversiana)*, the side-blotched lizard *(Uta stansburiana)*, and the alligator lizard *(Elegaria multicarinatus)* are found on San Nicolas Island.

548. Are there any amphibians on San Nicolas Island?

No. No frogs or salamanders have been collected on San Nicolas Island.

549. Are there any insects endemic to San Nicolas Island?

Several insects on San Nicolas Island represent endemic taxa.

550. Do land mollusks occur on San Nicolas Island?

Yes. Four native and seven fossil species of land snails are known from San Nicolas Island. A new snail species *(Micrarionta opuntia)* was described from this island.

551. What land birds nest on San Nicolas Island?

osprey – former resident
bald eagle – former resident
American kestrel
burrowing owl
horned lark
barn swallow
northern raven – former resident
rock wren

northern mockingbird
European starling
orange-crowned warbler
house sparrow
western meadowlark
Brewer's blackbird
house finch
white-crowned sparrow

552. What shore and sea birds nest on San Nicolas Island?

black oystercatcher
western gull

snowy plover
Brandt's cormorant

553. Are there any endemic birds on San Nicolas Island?

Yes. The horned lark and the house finch are endemic Channel Islands races on San Nicolas Island.

554. Have any birds been introduced to San Nicolas Island?

Yes. In 1968, Navy personnel introduced Chinese ring-necked pheasants, which did not survive. Chukar, which were introduced by the California Department of Fish and Game in 1967, have a well-established population on San Nicolas Island.

555. How many different plants are known to occur on San Nicolas Island?

There are about 200 different plants which grow on San Nicolas Island.

556. How many Channel Islands endemic plants are found on San Nicolas Island?

Thirteen plants endemic to one or more California Channel Islands are found on San Nicolas Island.

557. Are there any plants endemic to only San Nicolas Island?

Four plants are restricted to San Nicolas Island: an undescribed species of *Malacothrix*, a member of the sunflower family; a phacelia *(Phacelia cinerea)*; a buckwheat *(Eriogonum grande timorum)*; and a box thorn *(Lycium verrucosum)*. The phacelia and the box thorn may now be extinct.

Coreopsis *and lupines grow almost to the water's edge on San Nicolas Island.*

558. What percentage of plants found on San Nicolas Island are introduced?

About 48 percent of the San Nicolas Island flora is introduced, a higher percentage than that found on any other California Channel Island.

559. Are there any ferns on San Nicolas Island?

Yes. Even though perennial streams and moist areas are scarce, three species of ferns have been found on San Nicolas Island.

560. When were all the introduced trees planted on San Nicolas Island?

Early ranchers may have introduced some trees on San Nicolas Island. Between 1965 and 1971, Felix Fernandez, a retired Navy barber, planted trees on San Nicolas Island to "beautify" it. In 1970, the Ventura Nurserymen's Association introduced 200 specimens of trees and shrubs to this island which they considered "barren." Plants native to Australia, New Zealand and Africa were among those introduced.

561. Are there any poisonous plants on San Nicolas Island?

Yes. Poison hemlock *(Conium maculatum)* occurs on San Nicolas Island, as does poison oak *(Toxicodendron diversilobum)*, nightshade *(Solanum nodiflorum)*, castor bean *(Ricinus communis)*, and tree tobacco *(Nicotiana glauca)*. There is no jimson weed on this island.

562. Was San Nicolas Island occupied by Indians?

Yes. Often referred to as Nicoleños, these Indians produced artifacts of exceptional quality, originality and elaborateness, indicating that they were somewhat culturally distinct from their island neighbors. Stone and wood sculpting were particularly well developed on San Nicolas Island. Steatite whales, fish, bowls and other vessels have been found on this island.

563. How many archaeological sites are there on San Nicolas Island?

At least 500 sites have been mapped. The San Nicolas Island sites lack the Spanish-Mexican trade good items found in historic sites on other islands, indicating that trade with Spanish settlements on the mainland was rare.

564. How many Indians lived on San Nicolas Island?

Population estimates indicate that as many as 300 Indians may have lived on San Nicolas Island at one time.

565. What happened to the Indian population on San Nicolas Island?

In 1811, an otter-hunting ship belonging to the Boston firm of Pope and Boardman, under the command of Captain Whitmore, brought to San Nicolas Island from Sitka a boat load of Kodiak hunters for the purpose of obtaining otter. These well-armed Kodiaks, when left upon the island, found the island women to their liking, and killed the men who tried to defend them. By the time the otters were nearly exterminated, so too were the Nicoleños.

566. What happened to the last of the Indians living on San Nicolas Island?

The last native inhabitants of San Nicolas Island were removed by boat in 1835. Franciscan mission fathers chartered the schooner *Peor es Nada* (Better than Nothing) to retrieve the last of the island Indians and bring them to the mainland for "missionization." Charles Hubbard, captain of the small vessel, and his crew conveyed to the Indians that they no longer needed to be subjected to the cruel forays of the otter hunters. The mainland offered a better way of life with plenty to eat. Twenty or so Indians were removed, but one lone woman remained.

567. When was the "lone woman" of San Nicolas Island rescued?

In 1853, Captain George Nidever and Carl Dittman visited San Nicolas Island and brought back with them the "lone woman." They had followed footsteps in the sand to a shelter atop a ridge where they found the woman had been living. She was not there at the time of their initial visit, but when the men returned the next day, she was inside her shelter roasting wild onions.

568. How did the "lone woman" react to her visitors?

According to George Nidever's account, she was startled, but she regained her composure and proudly offered the men the wild onions she was roasting. She then gathered her few possessions and left the island quite willingly. George Nidever brought her to Santa Barbara where she received the name Juana María.

569. Why didn't Juana María leave San Nicolas Island with the other Indians in 1835?

It is reported that Juana María did not leave the island when the others were removed because her baby had somehow been left behind. Once account states that, ironically, the child fell victim to the same feral dogs which were to become her only companions for the next eighteen years.

570. What is known about Juana María's life alone on San Nicolas Island?

Juana María lived in a hut constructed of whale ribs covered with brush and sea lion hides. Her only companions were a number of feral dogs and two pet ravens. She lived on a diet of birds, eggs, fish, abalone and seal blubber, augmented with whatever edible plants she could gather. Water was obtained from one of many springs.

571. What were Juana María's possessions?

Juana María's meager possessions included a knife made of a rusty piece of hoop, some bone needles and a bone knife, a few baskets and containers for food and water, fishing lines and cords for snaring seals, a limpet shell necklace, and a cormorant feather and bird skin dress. The dress was reportedly sent to the Vatican Museum in Rome, and there is no trace of any of her other possessions.

572. How did Juana María adjust to mainland life after eighteen years alone on San Nicolas Island?

Upon her arrival in Santa Barbara, Juana María was particularly amazed and delighted by the sight of men on horseback. It was said that she entered into her new life-style with "child-like zest." Her new clothes were her prized possessions, and she was particularly fond of new foodstuffs such as fruits and vegetables. For weeks she was the center of attention in Santa Barbara.

573. How did Juana María communicate?

Juana María communicated by elaborate hand signs and pantomime, since no one could be found who understood her language, although a few of the words she used were of the Shoshonean dialect. It has recently come to light that she may have been an Indian from a northern territory and not a native Nicoleño.

574. If Juana María was not a Channel Islands Indian, how did she end up on San Nicolas Island?

In an unpublished diary written three decades after the death of Juana María, the following was written by Emma Hardacre, researcher of Juana María: "There is a doubt in my own mind whether the woman was an Indian. There is a rumor that before the island was depopulated, a woman was cast ashore from a wreck, and that shortly after, she gave birth to a child. This information has reached me since the material was gathered for my article as originally published."

575. What happened to Juana María?

Six weeks after her arrival in Santa Barbara, where she lived with her rescuer, George Nidever and his family, she died. She is buried in the Santa Barbara Mission cemetery where a plaque commemorating her reads: "Juana María, Indian woman abandoned on San Nicolas Island eighteen years, found and brought to Santa Barbara by Captain George Nidever in 1853."

576. What happened to the feral dogs left behind on San Nicolas Island?

In about 1857, Captain Nidever returned to San Nicolas Island and shot the dogs so that the island could safely be stocked with sheep. According to Nidever's son, the dogs "were of the Alaskan breed."

577. Has anyone ever written about the life of Juana María?

Yes. Novelist Scott Odell fictionalized the story of the Lone Woman of San Nicolas Island in his novel, *Island of the Blue Dolphins,* which was later made into a major motion picture.

578. What 19th century archaeologists visited San Nicolas Island?

The first archaeologists were on San Nicolas Island less than twenty-five years after Juana María, the last Indian to leave the island. Artifact collectors included Gustav Eisen, Leon de Cessac, Paul Schumacher and Stephen Bowers, who removed over 1200 artifacts from San Nicolas Island. Other collections went to the Smithsonian and the Musee de L'Homme in Paris.

579. What 20th century archaeology has been conducted on San Nicolas Island?

The Southwest Museum in Pasadena has had a longstanding interest in San Nicolas Island archaeology, as has the Los Angeles County Museum of Natural History, and the University of California, Los Angeles, among others. Archaeologists continue to conduct field excavations on this island today.

580. Is there any rock art on San Nicolas Island?

San Nicolas Island is the location of the most detailed petroglyph found on a Channel Island, "Cave of the Killer Whales." Carved in sandstone are at least nine killer whales in both horizontal and vertical positions. A large piece of the cave wall is located at the Southwest Museum in Pasadena.

581. Who discovered and named San Nicolas Island?

Bartolome Ferrer, who took over on the Cabrillo expedition after Cabrillo's death, passed San Nicolas Island on his way southwest in February, 1543. December 6, 1602, Vizcaíno gave the island the name San Nicolas in honor of the saint of that day.

Martin Kimberly staked his claim and built a house at Corral Harbor, the former site of a Chinese abalone camp.

582. When was San Nicolas Island first surveyed?

W.E. Greenwell of the U.S. Coast and Geodetic Survey, made the first land survey of San Nicolas Island in 1858. Twenty-one years later, in 1879, the island was surveyed by Stehman Forney.

583. Did Chinese ever use San Nicolas Island for abalone fishing?

Yes. As early as the 1870s, Chinese abalone fishermen used the island as a source of supply of abalone, and camps were set up at Corral Harbor, which used to be called Chinese Harbor, and other spots.

584. Who was the first person to claim ownership of San Nicolas Island?

On October 1, 1858, five years after the "lone woman" was removed from San Nicolas Island, Captain Martin Kimberly filed a preemption claim in Santa Barbara County for 160 acres on San Nicolas Island. This claim for land in the vicinity of Corral Harbor was marked by several four-foot high white pine posts within which "a house and corral [were] erected by me."

585. What did Martin Kimberly do with his 1858 claim to San Nicolas Island?

On September 15, 1879, twelve years after his original claim, Kimberly recorded a deed selling "all houses, buildings, corrals, wells, and improvements thereon situate" on San Nicolas Island to Abraham Halsey and William Hamilton. It states that he "hath resided himself or his employees, and kept sheep, cattle, and horses for fourteen years past."

586. What did Abraham Halsey and William Hamilton do with San Nicolas Island after their 1870 purchase of Kimberly's interest?

William Hamilton died, leaving his interest in San Nicolas Island to his daughters Agnes, Alice and Maggie. They bought out Abraham Halsey's interest in San Nicolas Island for $2000 on January 22, 1872.

587. What did the Hamilton sisters do with their interest in San Nicolas Island?

On September 23, 1872, the Hamilton sisters sold their interest in San Nicolas Island to the Pacific Wool Growing Company for $8000. In that same year, the Pacific Wool Growing Company also acquired interests on San Miguel and Anacapa islands.

588. What were the conditions on San Nicolas Island during the tenure of the Pacific Wool Growing Company?

Archaeologist Paul Schumacher visited San Nicolas Island in 1875 and in 1877 and wrote: "The vegetation on the island is like that of San Miguel, ruined by overstocking it with sheep, which are here found in like starving condition . . . The shifting sand has almost buried the adobe house, and its old inmate, the superintendent of the stock-raising Company."

589. Who had an interest in San Nicolas Island following the Pacific Wool Growing Company's interest?

The Pacific Wool Growing Company sold its assets in the 1880s. An 1897 deed records the sale of San Nicolas Island from J.V. Elliott to Peter Cages for $8000. Although it is not known how Elliott acquired his interest in San Nicolas Island, this same year he also sold his interests in Anacapa Island, which he had acquired in 1882 by quit claim deed.

590. What were the conditions on San Nicolas Island in 1897?

Botanist Blanche Trask visited San Nicolas Island in 1897 and reported: "There is an old house built of stones yet standing, half snowed-in by sand, at Corral Harbor. At the east end there are a cabin, a barn, shearing sheds, a cistern, and a platform which drains its rainwater into a reservoir. All these improvements are due to the once ambitious ranchmen who seem now to have abandoned the sheep; about 500 are occasionally seen."

591. To whom did the U.S. Government lease San Nicolas Island?

1902–1907	W.J. McGimpsey
1907–1909	D.R. Weller
1909–1914	J.G. Howland
1914–1919	J.G. Howland
1919–1924	E.N. Vail
1924–1929	E.N. Vail
1929–1934	E.N. Vail

592. What did W.J. McGimpsey do with San Nicolas Island?

McGimpsey owned a fishing company, and for awhile he placed fishermen on the island. In 1904 he sublet the island to D.R. Weller, incorporator of the San Nicolas Development Company.

593. Who had the second lease on San Nicolas Island, from 1907–1912?

D.R. Weller, President of the San Nicolas Development Company, was the successful bidder for the second five-year lease on San Nicolas Island. In 1909 however, with Weller's consent the Government declared the lease as abandoned, and a new lease was issued.

594. Who obtained the San Nicolas Island lease in 1909?

After the San Nicolas Development Company defaulted on its lease, the Government leased the island to J.G. Howland. He also held the lease on Santa Barbara Island (1909–1914). Howland received the San Nicolas Island lease again from 1914–1919.

595. Who was the successfu bidder for the San Nicolas Island lease in 1919?

E. N. Vail secured the leases for San Nicolas Island until 1934. During this time, sheep continued to be raised on the island. In 1926 Vail requested a 25-year lease be granted to him. He cabled

Superintendant Rhodes of the Lighthouse Bureau: "Missed you in San Francisco. Between droughts. Resting and regrowing pasture. Building landing facilities, developing cisterns. Refencing and attendant heavy transportation costs. The short five year Island lease is not tenable. . . ." Although a 25-year lease was not granted, Vail continued to lease San Nicolas Island until 1934. He continued to run Vail & Vickers operation on Santa Rosa Island, which began there in 1902.

596. What happened in 1933 when the administration of San Nicolas Island was transferred to the Navy?

Lessee E.N. Vail gave his consent to allow an airplane landing field to be established on the island, along with a weather station. Future lessees were made subject to the Navy's maintenance and use of this facility.

597. Was E.N. Vail the last one to run sheep on San Nicolas Island?

No. Roy Agee and L.P. Elliott raised sheep on San Nicolas Island from the early 1930s until 1941 when the Navy revoked the lease. They operated without a Government lease. In 1939 Agee bought out Elliott's island interests.

598. What happened on San Nicolas Island during World War II?

During World War II, San Nicolas Island was designated a Naval Auxilary Air Station, and was used to train Carrier Air Support units and Acorn units. Acorn units were special Naval construction units designed to build and operate airfields in remote Pacific locations.

599. Have there been any ships wrecked on San Nicolas Island?

There have been both private boat wrecks as well as Navy shipwrecks on San Nicolas Island. In 1936 during the last years of ranching operations on San Nicolas Island, Alvin Hyder's sheep-hauling boat, *Nora II,* was lost in a storm at San Nicolas Island. Hyder and his son Buster were hauling sheep at the time. Although Buster Hyder was able to swim to shore, his father was lost at sea in the accident. On April 10, 1949, a 15,000 ton freighter S.S. *Steel Chemist* went aground on San Nicolas Island in a heavy fog. She was enroute to the Orient with a full cargo of sugar, rubber, and tin valued at over a million dollars. It took 160 men and six tug boats to salvage the cargo and tow the disabled ship back to the mainland. In 1986, two divers survived 18 hours in the waters off San Nicolas Island, and a third was lost at sea when their boat sank in heavy seas.

600. Have any deaths been recorded on San Nicolas Island in historic times?

Yes. On January 3, 1911, Charles Peterson, a fisherman staying on San Nicolas Island, died of pneumonia. San Clemente Wool Company employee Horace Linton was tending sheep on San Nicolas Island at the time, and came across the body. On February 23, 1930, fisherman Steve Semerenko was shot and killed for poaching sheep on the island. There have been several historic and recent drownings of people swept off the island or lost in fishing and boating accidents nearby.

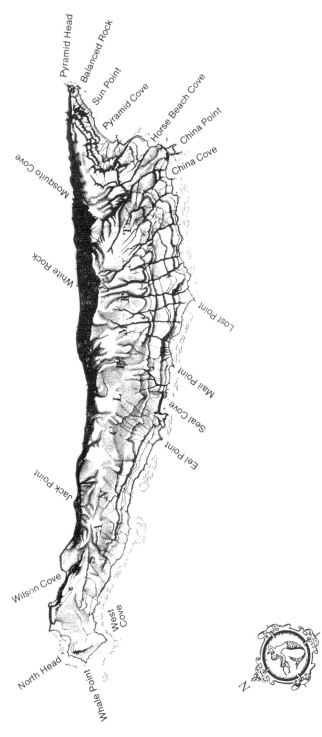

Pyramid Head

Balanced Rock

Sun Point

Pyramid Cove

Horse Beach Cove

China Point

China Cove

Mosquito Cove

White Rock

Lost Point

Mail Point

Seal Cove

Eel Point

Jack Point

Wilson Cove

West Cove

North Head

Whale Point

N

SAN CLEMENTE ISLAND

SAN CLEMENTE ISLAND

601. How large is San Clemente Island?

San Clemente Island is 56 square miles and ranks fourth in size. It is 21 miles long and from two to four miles wide.

602. In what county is San Clemente Island?

San Clemente Island is in Los Angeles County.

603. How far from the mainland is San Clemente Island?

San Clemente Island is second farthest from the mainland at 41 miles, and is the southernmost of the Southern California Islands. Santa Catalina Island is 21 miles to the north.

604. What is the highest point on San Clemente Island?

Mount Thirst, 1965 feet in elevation, is the highest point. The conspicuous white radar dome once located here was demolished in 1996 and replaced with a new structure.

605. What is the physiography of San Clemente Island?

San Clemente Island consists of a rugged coastline and precipitous cliffs, especially on the east side and at Seal Cove on the west. A series of about 20 spectacular marine terraces dominates the island's western portion. Geologically young canyons dissect the island's coast, and there are only a few sandy beaches, the largest of which is on the southern part of the island. The western shore is dotted with offshore rock islets. Two large offshore rocks on the north end are named Bird Rock and Castle Rock.

151

606. What is the geology of San Clemente Island?

This island is largely composed of volcanic rocks, chiefly andesite, formed during the Miocene Era. Miocene shales, cherts, and limestone are also present. Interbedded with the volcanics are sedimentary rocks dating through the Pliocene in which fossils have been found.

607. What fossils have been found on San Clemente Island?

Fossil sharks, whales, fishes, and seaweeds are among those which have been discovered from the Miocene to Pliocene deposits. Thus far, all of the fossils found are from former marine seas.

608. Did anyone apply to remove minerals from San Clemente Island?

Yes. As early as 1805, an application was received to quarry rocks on San Clemente Island, followed by another request in 1898. In 1901 Healy, Tibbits & Co. applied for permission to quarry and remove stone for use in extending the Government jetty in San Diego and to build a breakwater at San Pedro. This request was later dropped in favor of stone from Santa Catalina Island. In 1926, F.L. Wilcox applied for a 99-year lease to remove

1939 view of the "Fuller's Earth" deposit, Chalk Canyon, San Clemente Island.

1986 view (47 years later) of Chalk Canyon, San Clemente Island.

diatomaceous earth from Chalk Canyon on the island's back side. "Fuller's Earth," as it was called, was used in oil refining operations as well as in the manufacture of cement and waterproofing products. The Law and Property division of the Department of Commerce eventually decided it did not have the authority to grant such a lease.

609. What is the climate of San Clemente Island?

The island is classified as semi-arid. Its southern location results in a drier climate than the other Channel Islands. Prevailing winds are from the west or northwest. Due to the influence of marine air, humidity is high, even during the summer. Frost is unknown on this island.

610. What is the average rainfall on San Clemente Island?

This island usually receives less than six inches of rain a year. Most of the precipitation occurs during major winter storms between December and April. Thick fogs often blanket the island during summer months.

611. Is there any fresh water on San Clemente Island?

The availability of fresh surface water is extremely limited. Most springs and seeps are not potable. Early ranchers con-

Fog surrounding the eastern coastline of San Clemente Island.

structed dams and dug wells powered by windmills to provide enough water for sheep ranching.

612. Who owns San Clemente Island?

San Clemente Island is owned by the U.S. Government, and has been administered by the U.S. Navy since 1934. In 1977 the Naval Air Station (NAS), North Island, San Diego took over administrative duties for the island. Until 1934, it was controlled by the Department of Commerce and leased for sheep ranching.

613. Can one visit San Clemente Island?

No. San Clemente Island is not open to the public. It is restricted by the U.S. Navy.

614. Have any fires occurred on San Clemente Island?

Yes. Several fires are reported during sheep ranching days. In 1980, a large arson-caused fire covered much of the island's mesa grasslands. As a result of this fire and the costs involved in fighting it, the Navy decided to institute a controlled burn program to reduce the fire hazard on certain portions of the island. Priority burn areas were established, and controlled burns are set annually. Between 1993 and 1996, several large unintentional fires resulted from military operations.

615. Are there any boat anchorages on San Clemente Island?

Yes. The most frequented anchorages are at Northwest Harbor, Wilson Cove, Mosquito Cove and Pyramid Cove. Wilson Cove is the major military anchorage for supplies and equipment. Pyramid Cove, also known as Smuggler's Cove, is used during shore bombardment exercises. Pleasure boaters may use any anchorage on San Clemente Island which is not in use during bombardment, except Wilson Cove.

616. Are there any wharfs or piers on San Clemente Island?

Yes, three. There is a fuel pier at Lighthouse Point, a pier which is currently condemned at Wilson Cove, and a third pier in Ben Weston Cove built by the Naval Ordnance Test Station and hence called NOTS Pier. All three are for military use only.

617. Can one obtain a landing permit for San Clemente Island?

No. Landing is restricted to Naval and authorized personnel only. Except in the gravest emergency, no facilities are available to the public.

618. What Naval activities now occur on San Clemente Island?

Among other things, the island is used for missile testing, and research and development of naval weapons by the Navy Research, Development, Test and Evaluation (RDT&E) department. It is also used for aircraft carrier flight training, and land troop and amphibious training. Shore bombardment from ships is a part of target practice exercises.

619. Do these military activities have an impact on the ecology of the island?

Yes. Degrees of impact differ throughout the island. In 1973 a Natural Resources Management Plan was implemented cooperatively by the U.S. Navy, California Department of Fish and Game, and the U.S. Fish and Wildlife Service to monitor, protect, and reestablish as closely as possible the island's native ecological conditions.

620. Where are the main Naval facilities located on San Clemente Island?

Wilson Cove on the island's northeast is the location of the main military installation for the Navy's activities on the island. Buildings include civilian, enlisted, and officer barracks, a security building, maintenance shops, transportation motor pool, administration building, galley, library, operations building, dispensary, barber shop and servmart.

621. Is the Navy the only military branch that uses San Clemente Island?

No. Although the island is administered by the Navy, other branches of the military use the island. The Marine Corps, Air Force, and Army periodically use San Clemente Island for exercises and special training programs, as do various branches of military reserve units.

622. How many people are stationed on San Clemente Island?

Between 250 and 300 people are stationed on the island. Depending upon various operations, numbers will fluctuate. Time on the island is considered the equivalent of sea duty, and it has become an attractive place to station female Naval personnel since there are restrictions on the kinds of ships to which women can be assigned. Approximately 35 percent of the Naval personnel stationed on the island are women.

623. Are there any recreational facilities on San Clemente Island?

Yes. There is a bowling alley, gymnasium, television room, recreation room, racketball court, tennis court, volleyball/basketball court, and bar, the "Salty Crab Club." A closed television cable system offers movies each night. Some service men also spend spare time fishing and diving.

624. Are there military facilities anywhere other than at Wilson Cove?

Yes. The BUDS Camp (Basic Underwater Demolition and Seal Training facility) is located at Northwest Harbor. This facility is used as the second phase of a three phase course for training Navy Seal (Sea, Air and Land) personnel for special forces. In addition, there is an observation post (OP) overlooking the Naval gunnery and bombing range of the Shore Bombardment Impact Area (SHOBA) on the south end of the island. Naval Research and Development (NRaD, formerly known as NOSC/Naval Ocean Systems Center) has variously located test and camera facilities, some of which are operated by civilian contractors.

625. Is there a medical facility at Wilson Cove?

Yes. An island dispensary is manned by hospital corpsmen on a rotating basis. This facility, equipped with an ambulance, is set up primarily for stablizing someone who is injured or seriously ill, and preparing the person for evacuation by aircraft to a mainland facility.

626. Who operates the different facilities on San Clemente Island?

Most of the support functions on the island, the food preparation, operation of the club and recreational facilities, maintenance and custodial work are operated by private contractors under contract with the Navy. Motor vehicles, the power plant, and the fresh water system are maintained by the Naval Public Works Center, San Diego.

627. What happens to all of the garbage on San Clemente Island?

The island has a central dump which is operated largely as a land fill. The Public Works operates a truck which collects refuse in dumpsters placed at island facilities. The dump site is burned weekly, and periodically refuse is covered with surrounding dirt by heavy equipment. In the past, a lot of little dumps were used, evidence of which can still be found today.

628. What non-military activities take place on San Clemente Island?

The North Island Command entered into an agreement with the San Diego Council of Boy Scouts of America which allows Boy Scout troops to camp in a designated area during the summer vacation period. Troops come out on weekends, arriving Fridays and leaving Mondays.

629. How do non-military and military personnel get to and from San Clemente Island?

Most people come and go by plane. A regularly scheduled air-charter service runs weekday flights from the Naval Air Station, North Island, San Diego, to San Clemente Island. A private airline company has the current contract with the Navy to provide this service.

630. What type of airport is on San Clemente Island?

A 9500-foot runway for military use only was completed in 1960. It is located on the island's north end, and has an air traffic control tower, a small airport terminal, and a fire station next to it.

631. Are there any aircraft flying restrictions around San Clemente Island?

Aeronautical charts warn that San Clemente Island lies within a warning area in which National Defense Area Operations may be hazardous to the flight of aircraft within this area. Before flying in the vicinity of the island, the Notice to Airmen should be consulted for up-to-date restriction information.

632. Is there a fire station on San Clemente Island?

Yes. There are two fire stations on San Clemente Island, one at the airport and another one at Wilson Cove. The one at the airport deals primarily with aviation problems, while the one at Wilson Cove is for structural fires, wildfires, and prescribed burns. They are a part of the Federal Fire Department, San Diego, manned by civilian personnel.

633. How does the island receive its fuel supplies?

Diesel, gasoline and aviation fuel are barged to the island on a regular schedule and offloaded on a special fuel pier into storage facilities.

634. How does the island receive enough fresh water to support all of the facilities on the island?

Water is barged to the island weekly in 250,000–300,000 gallon increments. It is pumped to two million-gallon storage tanks atop the hill at Wilson Cove. From here, a recently installed pipeline distributes the water to each facility.

635. How is electrical power supplied on San Clemente Island?

Electricity is provided by a power plant located near the beach at Wilson Cove. The generators are powered by diesel which is stored in the nearby fuel farm. Power service extends the length of the island to the Observation Post located at the island's south end. Other facilities receive power along the way. Waste heat energy produced as a steam byproduct is piped to living quarters at Wilson Cove as a source of heat. The power lines on the island run above ground on poles and are very conspicuous against the otherwise stark mesa landscape.

636. Are there any telephones on San Clemente Island?

In addition to an internal military phone system, phones within the 310 area code are located at both Wilson Cove and at the airport terminal.

637. What happens to the sewage at San Clemente Island?

There is a sewage treatment facility at Wilson Cove that secondarily treats materials and discharges them into the ocean. At some point in the future, it is hoped that some of the treated water can be recycled on the island for irrigation purposes. In the past, the military had a saltwater sewage system which discharged untreated material directly into the ocean.

638. What type of road system is on San Clemente Island?

The northern third of the island contains the main paved driving system, leading from the airport to Wilson Cove. Roads are paved for about six miles south of Wilson Cove to the site of the old airfield area, near the entrance to the middle portion of the island. Parking spaces are marked in the Wilson Cove area, and traffic is policed by island security personnel who issue both parking and moving violation citations. The island roads on the middle, southern and western portions are dirt, and often require four-wheel-drive vehicles.

639. Is the entire island open to military personnel?

No. The island is divided into three basic zones. The northern third of the island contains the airport, Wilson Cove with the living quarters, and most of the facilities. The second third of the island is a buffer zone area, which is marked at its northern boundary by the "Stone" gate and at its southern boundary by the "Range" gate. South of the Range gate is the Shore Bombardment Impact Area (SHOBA) of the island. Live ordnance can be found here, and this area is considered extremely hazardous. Within each of these three zones, certain areas are off limits to various personnel.

640. What happens to live ordnance?

Specially trained explosive ordnance disposal (EOD) personnel conduct live ordnance disposal. As one travels south on the island, the amount of live ordnance increases due to the proximity of the gunnery and bombing range. The island buffer zone is occasionally hit by shells which skip up island after being fired.

641. What are the accommodations for civilian scientists and researchers on San Clemente Island?

Archaeologists, botanists, biologists and other scientists interested in the natural resources of the island stay at a field station provided by the Navy for approved research projects. Accommodations include kitchen facilities, living/lab space, sleeping quarters, a bathroom, and a separate lab/storage building. Water is hauled to the facility and kept in a storage tank nearby. Electrical and telephone power is provided by distribution from Wilson Cove. A small library and herbarium is available for research.

642. From what are many of the San Clemente Island place names derived?

Located throughout the island are a series of precisely located camera pads operated by Naval Research and Development for the filming of various operations. Many island place names are of recent origin and correspond with these pad areas. Some of the more historic names refer to early U.S. Coast and Geodetic Survey marks, or are derived from the Shoshonian dialect of the peoples once occupying the island.

643. Are there any native mammals on San Clemente Island?

Two native terrestrial mammals, the island fox *(Urocyon littoralis clementae)* and the deer mouse *(Peromyscus maniculatus clementis)* occur here. Both are endemic subspecies found only on San Clemente Island.

644. Are there bats on San Clemente Island?

Four species have been collected: the fringed myotis *(Myotis thysanodes)*, the California myotis *(Myotis californicus)*, Townsend's big-eared bat *(Plecotus townsendii)*, and the Brazilian free-tailed bat *(Tadarida brasiliensis)*. It is not known if any of these species breeds on the island.

645. What non-native mammals are found on San Clemente Island?

Accidental introductions of the western harvest mouse *(Reith-rodontomys megalotis longicaudus)*, and the California vole *(Microtus californicus sanctidiegi)*, occurred with shipments of hay during ranching times, although it is not currently known if either species still lives on the island. Accidental introductions of the house mouse *(Mus musculus)* and black rat *(Rattus rattus)* still persist.

646. What feral animals live on San Clemente Island?

Currently there are feral cats on the island. Under the Endangered Species Act of 1973, it became the Government's responsibility to protect species threatened by feral animal populations. The implementation of feral animal removal programs successfully eliminated former populations of goats and pigs.

647. How did goats get to San Clemente Island?

Evidence suggests that goats were introduced more than once. In 1875 an early island resident claims to have brought a pair of goats to this island from Santa Catalina. Later, ranchers brought additional goats to San Clemente Island. Left unchecked, their population flourished to extreme numbers.

648. When did goat removal programs begin?

In 1972, with the establishment of the Natural Resources Management Plan, the feral goat population was estimated at 12,000–15,000 animals. By 1977, through herding, trapping and sport hunting, the population was reduced to an estimated 1500 animals. By 1979 a temporary injunction as a result of a suit by the Fund for Animals, stopped a proposed shooting program. The removal program was allowed to continue however, and by using helicopters, the last of the feral goats on San Clemente Island was shot in 1991.

649. How did pigs get to San Clemente Island?

Pigs were intentionally introduced sometime around 1950 from Santa Catalina Island stock. They have since been eliminated.

650. Are there deer on San Clemente Island?

No. Deer, which are considered introduced exotic animals as opposed to feral animals, were introduced to San Clemente Island twice. In 1954 black-tailed mule deer *(Odocoileus hemionus columbianus)* were introduced to the Wilson Cove area. In 1962 California mule deer *(Odocoileus hemionus)* were also imported. Both species were removed by sport hunting.

651. Do any pinnipeds breed at San Clemente Island?

Yes, three species. The California sea lion *(Zalophus californi- anus)* and the harbor seal *(Phoca vitulina)* have bred here for many years. More recently, the Northern elephant seal *(Mirounga angustirostris)* has established a breeding colony on the island's west side near Seal Cove.

652. Are there any snakes on San Clemente Island?

No.

653. Are there any lizards on San Clemente Island?

Two species, the island night lizard *(Xantusia riversiana)* and the side-blotched lizard *(Uta stansburiana)* occur here.

654. Are there any amphibians on San Clemente Island?

No. No frogs or salamanders have been collected.

655. Do land mollusks occur on San Clemente Island?

Yes. There are at least eight species of recent and two species of fossil snails here. All but two of them are endemic to either San Clemente or the Southern California Island system.

656. What land bird nesting records are known for San Clemente Island?

osprey – former (1927)	rock wren
bald eagle – former (1927)	Bewick's wren
red-tailed hawk	northern mockingbird
peregrine falcon – former (1915)	loggerhead shrike
American kestrel	European starling
mourning dove	orange-crowned warbler
barn owl	sage sparrow
burrowing owl	Western meadowlark
white-throated swift	house finch
Allen's hummingbird	house sparrow
horned lark	
barn swallow	
northern raven	

657. Of these, which are San Clemente Island endemic races?

    Bewick's wren – now thought to be extinct

    loggerhead shrike – very uncommon

    sage sparrow – very uncommon

658. Why are so many of these bird races thought to be extinct?

The loss of some breeding bird species can be attributed to the reduction of brushy vegetation caused by introduced herbivores such as sheep and goats. Feral cats also prey upon birds and impact their populations.

659. What shore and sea bird nesting records are known for San Clemente Island?

    Brandt's cormorant

    black oystercatcher

    western gull

    Xantus' murrelet

660. What exotic birds have been introduced to San Clemente Island?

In about 1912 ten dozen Gambel's quail were introduced from Banning, California. In 1960 the California Department of Fish and Game introduced 176 chukar. Both have established breeding populations. Historic records indicate a 19th century introduction of California quail, though they no longer occur.

661. What plant communities occur on San Clemente Island?

Seven plant communities cover the island, the largest of which is the grassland community covering about 45 percent of the island. Maritime cactus scrub is second, covering about 35 percent of the island's surface. Island woodland, coastal bluff, coastal strand/dunes, coastal sage scrub and salt marsh communities occur over the remaining 20 percent.

62. How many different plants occur on San Clemente Island?

Approximately 330 different native and introduced plants have been collected on San Clemente Island. This island has the highest proportion of endemism for any Southern California Island.

663. What are the dominant native species?

Bunchgrasses, pricklypear cacti, cholla and velvet cacti are common. Native trees and shrubs are essentially restricted to steep cliffs and canyons away from the reach of feral goats.

664. What plants are endemic to San Clemente Island?

Fourteen plants are endemic to San Clemente Island: *Brodiaea kinkiensis, Triteleia clementina, Eriogonum giganteum formosum, Delphinium kinkiense, Delphinium variegatum thornei Lithophragma maximum, Astragalus nevinii, Lotus argophyllus adsurgens, Lotus dendroideus traskiae, Malacothamnus clementinus, Camissonia guadalupensis clementina, Castilleja grisea Galium catalinense acrispum,* and *Munzothamnus blairii.*

665. Which of these are listed by the Federal Government a Endangered Species?

San Clemente Island broom *(Lotus dendroideus traskiae),* San Clemente Island larkspur *(Delphinium kinkiense),* San Clemente Island bush mallow *(Malacothamnus clementinus),* and San Clemente Island Indian paintbrush *(Castilleja grisea)* are currently listed as endangered.

Steve Junak

Munzothamnus blairii *found only on San Clemente Island, and is endemic at the genus level.*

The former San Clemente Island "National Forest" of introduced Eucalyptus trees is now gone.

666. What is *Munzothamnus*?

Munzothamnus is an endemic genus of plant in the sunflower family found only on San Clemente Island and nowhere else. This represents the only plant genus restricted to a California Channel Island.

667. What is the Navy doing to protect native vegetation of San Clemente Island?

In addition to feral animal removal programs, the Navy has entered into a contract agreement with a native plant nursery to gather seeds and cuttings from the island, propagate them on the mainland, and return them to San Clemente Island for planting. A small nursery facility serves as a holding area for reintroduced seedlings until they can be planted in the appropriate island areas. The island nursery is located several miles south of Wilson Cove.

668. What was the San Clemente Island National Forest?

Along the roadside on top of the island were about five very wind-pruned, introduced Eucalyptus trees. Signs were posted at each end of the "forest," announcing that one was either "Now Entering" or "Now Leaving" San Clemente Island National Forest. These were the only conspicuous trees on top of the island, and all have now died.

165

669. Was San Clemente Island occupied by Indians?

Yes. Evidence of Indian occupation is indicated by the presence of over 3000 prehistoric archaeological sites.

670. What did the island Indians call San Clemente Island?

San Clemente Island was called Kinkipar.

671. What is the last documented evidence of Indian occupation on San Clemente Island?

The last historic account of Indians living on San Clemente Island comes from the diary of an Anglo named Richard Cleveland, who kept notes while aboard the ship *Leila Byrd* in 1803. He remarks: "In this miserable domicil (a cave), resided eleven persons, men, women, and children; and though the temperature was such as to make our woolen garments requisite, they were all in a state of perfect nudity."

672. What happened to the last of the San Clemente Island Indians?

No one knows what happened to the last Indians on San Clemente Island. It is thought that they abandoned the island as opposed to having been removed. Mission San Gabriel has baptismal records between 1776 and 1832 of Indians who claim to have come from this island.

An Indian bowl excavated and reconstructed on San Clemente Island.

673. What 19th-century archaeologists worked on San Clemente Island?

The first archaeological collections were made on San Clemente Island in about 1877 by Paul Schumacher for the Smithsonian and Peabody museums. The U.S. Fish Commission steamer *Albatross* expedition collected artifacts in 1887–1888. In the summer of 1895, famous fisherman Charles Holder and a friend, J. Neal Plumb, also collected a few artifacts, as did botanist Blanche Trask sometime between 1895 and 1910.

674. What 20th-century archaeologists worked on San Clemente Island?

Artifact collecting continued in the 20th century by both private individuals as well as institutions. The Museum of the American Indian, Heye Foundation, visited this island in 1922–1923. Private collector and island resident, Theodore Murphy, spent considerable time between 1926 and 1944 amassing artifacts, as did several other individuals. In 1939 the Los Angeles County Museum of Natural History sponsored Phil Orr. The San Diego Museum of Man, San Diego State College, UCLA, the Southwest Museum, and the Los Angeles County Museum of Natural History have all conducted research on San Clemente Island. In 1983 Clement Meighan of the UCLA Department of Anthropology began conducting summer field research in cooperation with the Navy on San Clemente Island.

675. How old are the oldest known Indian occupation sites?

Radiocarbon-14 dates indicate habitation on the island at least as long ago as 9300 years before present.

676. Who discovered and named San Clemente Island?

Juan Rodríguez Cabrillo passed San Clemente Island in 1542, although no mention of the island appears in surviving records from the expedition. In 1602, Sebastian Vizcaíno named the island. On March 15, 1769, the ship *San Antonio* of the Portolá expedition landed at Pyramid Cove on the island's south end. It was recorded that Indians in plank canoes came out to greet the vessel, and gave them two otter skin robes.

677. When was San Clemente Island first surveyed?

The U.S. Coast and Geodetic Survey worked on San Clemente Island in the early 1860s. An 1874 survey of San Clemente Island reported the location of four good harbors or landing places: "North Harbor, Shubrick Harbor, Mosquito Harbor, and Smugglers Cove." Today Shubrick Harbor is called Wilson Cove, and Smugglers Harbor is called Pyramid Cove.

678. Who occupied the island after the Indians?

Various fishermen, sea mammal hunters, Chinese abalone fishermen and ranchers occupied the island through the end of the 19th century. Chinese occupation is evidenced by opium tins and pieces of porcelain found in recent archaeological investigations along the island's west side. Before official leasing began, S.S. Hubbell used the island for grazing sheep and goats, and Walter Vail brought cattle and sheep to the island for a number of years for himself and others. Both men commented on the lack of available water on the island. As late as the 1930s, whale boats anchored in Pyramid Cove to process whale meat for shipment to the Dr. Ross dog food factory in Los Angeles County. Official Government leases first appear in 1901.

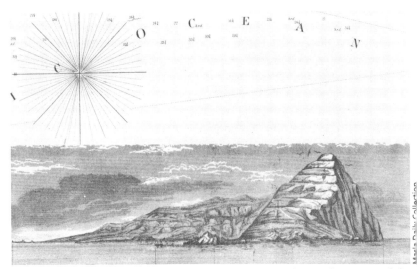

The southeast end of San Clemente Island by the Hydrographic Party of the U.S. Coast Survey, 1856. Note the marine terraces.

679. Was San Clemente Island reserved for lighthouse purposes?

Yes. By order of the President, in 1854 the entire island was reserved for lighthouse purposes.

680. Are there any lighthouses on San Clemente Island?

Although there are no lighthouses on San Clemente Island, there are several pyramidal structures supporting navigational lights. Clockwise from the north, they are located at Northhead, Lighthouse Point, one at each side of Wilson Cove, Jack Point, Pyramid Head, and China Point. There are also navigational range lights used for entering a harbor, located at Wilson Cove. A light once located in Pyramid Cove no longer exists.

681. To whom did the Government lease San Clemente Island?

1901–1905	San Clemente Wool Company
1906–1909	San Clemente Wool Company
1910–1934	San Clemente Wool/Sheep Company

In 1918, this lease was transferred, with the Government's permission, to the San Clemente Sheep Company. The lease agreement forbade the removal of minerals of any kind from the island.

682. Who formed the San Clemente Wool Company?

In 1905 the directors of the San Clemente Wool Company were: A.C. Harper, President; R.S. Howland, Vice President; Charles T. Howland, Secretary and Manager; S.A. Howland, Treasurer. Charles Howland, attorney, answered correspondence, signed leases, etc. According to the 1906 lease agreement, the San Clemente Wool Company was to pay annual rent of $1000. In addition, $5000 was to be spent in 1906 for the development of water supplies and in the construction of reservoirs. No permanent buildings were to be constructed. In 1914 Charles Howland was listed as Company president. In 1916 this changed to E.G. Blair.

683. What improvements did the San Clemente Wool Company place upon the island?

Several dams for storing water were constructed, as per the terms of the lease agreement. At Wilson Cove (also known as Gallagher's), they built one house 65 feet long with eight rooms, a bunkhouse 40 feet long, wool sheds, shearing pens, shearing

Buster Hyder Collection

The Casa Blanca, built by the San Clemente Wool Company at Gallagher's (now Wilson Cove). Photo c. 1920s.

sheds, corrals, a blacksmith shop, a barn, and a small wharf. Six tanks were placed about the buildings for catching rainwater that fell from the roofs. On the island's northerly end, two wells, a windmill and a bunk house were constructed. At a point called Ocean Spring, a two-room house, windmills, three tanks, corrals and large well were built. At Red Canyon (now called Chinetti Canyon) the Company placed a small room, corrals, well, tank and windmill. At Russell's, a house, well, windmill, tank and corrals cost the company about $1000. A four-and-a-half-mile-long fence was placed across the middle of the island. In addition, an estimated fourteen miles of wagon roads were built by 1905.

684. How many men ran the San Clemente Wool Company?

During most of the year, about seven men and a schooner worked for the Company. For the six-week period of round-up and shearing, as many as 65 men lived and worked on San Clemente Island. During road and dam construction, additional temporary labor was required.

685. How many sheep were kept on the island during this time?

The San Clemente Wool Company kept about 11,000–12,000 sheep on the island.

686. How were sheep rounded up?

The sheep were rounded up by men on horseback and on foot. Animals were gathered from the south and herded north to turning fences above Wilson Cove, then called Gallagher's. Here they were shorn, and the wool was bailed for shipment to the mainland. The average sheep yielded about 6.5 pounds of wool at shearing.

687. How did the San Clemente Wool Company obtain a 25-year lease in 1909?

An Act of Congress was required to change the lease period from five to 25 years. Senate Bill 4856 was introduced and passed in 1909 authorizing the Secretary of Commerce to lease San Clemente Island for 25 years for $1500 a year plus $1000 a year in developments. The new lease to the San Clemente Wool Company became effective January 1, 1910.

688. Did anyone oppose the granting of a 25-year lease?

Several people wrote letters of protest, including Lew Wallace, secretary of the Newport Beach Chamber of Commerce, who wrote to President Theodore Roosevelt: "We believe that it ought to be

View of Gallagher's (Wilson Cove) as it existed in the 1920s.

Buster Hyder Collection

brought to your personal attention that some five or six years ago San Clemente Island was covered with a heavy growth of underbrush and trees. This Company, in order to increase the grass area, burned over San Clemente Island from one end to the other three separate times, almost completely destroying the tree growth . . . Our main objection to a lease of any longer period is that as soon as the Panama Canal is completed this island will have additional value to the American people at large . . . as a pleasure resort . . . as now exists on Catalina Island." A second letter urged that the island be explored for oil potential rather than leased as a sheep ranch again. Protests were ignored and the 25-year lease was granted, adding great value to the San Clemente Wool Company. This is the only long-term lease granted by the Government on a Channel Island.

689. What happened to the island's fishermen?

Severe conflicts arose between the San Clemente Wool Company and the fishermen living on the island's shores. The former claimed the latter were poaching sheep and livestock, and the Company asked for Government intervention. In an attempt to solve the problem, revocable fishing licenses were granted to applicants for camping and fishing along the shoreline. A clause prohibiting the shooting or killing of birds and marine mammals was incorporated into the agreement, along with a clause prohibiting the shooting of any Company livestock. Five-year licenses cost $5.

690. Who formed the San Clemente Sheep Company?

E.G. Blair was the largest stockholder, president and manager. Seven directors governed the corporation: A.J. Huneke, F. Pierce, B.M. Stansbury, W.B. Merwin, G.W. Parsons, C.S. Gilbert, and F.E. Bennett. Capital stock was $250,000 divided into 2500 shares to be sold or disposed of as the Board determined.

691. When did the San Clemente Sheep Company take over from the San Clement Wool Company?

In order for the lease to be reassigned, permission from the U.S. Government was required. E.G. Blair incorporated the San Clemente Sheep Company in 1916 for the express purpose of buying the lease and assets from Charles Howland and the San Clemente Wool Company. In 1918, the lease was reassigned to the San Clemente Sheep Company.

692. When did sheep operations end on San Clemente Island?

In 1934, the leasing of San Clemente Island by the U.S. Government was discontinued. Sheep operations ended and the Navy's administration of the island began. The Navy began development on the island with the construction of an airplane landing field, which was then expanded to include development of a cantonment area and shore bombardment area during World War II.

693. What evidence is left of sheep ranching days?

Three reservoir areas constructed during the sheep ranching era remain. Also, on the south end of the island where the ground was too hard to place fence posts, posts were supported by piles of rock held in place by wire baskets. A line of these posts remains. In the area of Middle Ranch are a few foundations and a brick fireplace. No evidence is left of Casa Blanca, the main ranching facility once located in Wilson Cove. Military construction and development covers this area. Offshore there is a large cement block exposed in shallow water which once supported the ranch wharf.

694. What happened to San Clemente Island after World War II?

From 1951 to 1961, a U.S. Air Force radar station was in service. During the 1950s, the island was used extensively for shore and underwater missile and rocket research, development and testing. Torpedos and depth charges were tested in island waters. Naval Ordnance Test Station (NOTS), China Lake, administered the island in the 1950s and 1960s.

695. What was the island used for in the 1960s and 1970s?

The old airfield and World War II facilities on the middle of the island were abandoned in the early 1960s, with the construction of the new airfield on the north end. The U.S. Air Force radar station was deactivated in 1961, and fleet training, ordnance disposal and storage, and missile tesing was continued. The administration of the island changed periodically, with the most recent transfer occurring in 1977 to the Naval Air Station, North Island, San Diego.

696. What happened to the World War II airport and Air Force facilities on the middle of the island?

The pavement of the airstrip was torn out and removed. The

Home of longtime island resident Chinetti, who died in his cabin in 1919. The cabin no longer exists, although a canyon is named in Chinetti's honor.

abandoned buildings remain, and are painted in camouflage colors. Occasionally they are used in ground maneuver exercises.

697. Have there been any plane wrecks on San Clemente Island?
Yes. Around 1960 a military reserve group was killed when its plane crashed into the island in a dense fog. A propellor from this wreck is placed on the roadside near Mount Thirst. In the late 1970s another plane crashed which was not found for over a year. Its single occupant was smuggling marijuana and did not survive the crash.

698. Are there any deaths recorded on San Clemente Island since Indian occupation?
Several people died on the island in the late 19th and early 20th centuries. In 1890, a whaler, John Innes, was buried in the area of Seal Point. In 1919, a long-time resident by the name of Chinetti was found dead of natural causes in his cabin at the south end of the island. He was 74 at the time of his death. Chinetti Canyon was named after him. Sometime around 1930, a quail hunter was shot and killed on San Clemente Island. Circumstances surrounding his

death remain a mystery. None of the thirty quail hunters on the island at the time could account for the accident.

699. Are any deaths recorded on San Clemente Island since the Naval occupation of the island in 1934?

In addition to the deaths caused by plane accidents, several other people have died on the island. In the early 1960s, two people were killed in a vehicle accident when their truck rolled over on the hill leading to Eel Point. In 1978, Navy L.C. D.R. Maycumber, a former officer-in-charge at the island, died of a heart attack shortly after jogging several miles. The main road on the island is named Maycumber in his honor. Also in the late 1970s, a man slipped in wet weather and fell to his death in Burns Canyon, which is named after him. In 1993, PFC Anthony Dye was killed in an equipment accident while repairing a road in upper Horse Canyon.

700. Are there any major shipwrecks on San Clemente Island?

Several large shipwrecks are evident on San Clemente Island. In 1972, the Navy towed the 376 foot World War II destroyer USS *Gregory* to the back side of San Clemente Island below Mail Point, where she became a target used for air attack practice. In 1968, the Liberty ship *White Eagle* went aground north of Eel Point, also on the island's west coast. In 1976 the Navy lost a YFU Landing Craft to the east of Northwest Harbor. Pieces of all of these ships are still evident today.

Wreckage of the White Eagle *north of Eel Point. Note the marine terraces in the background.*

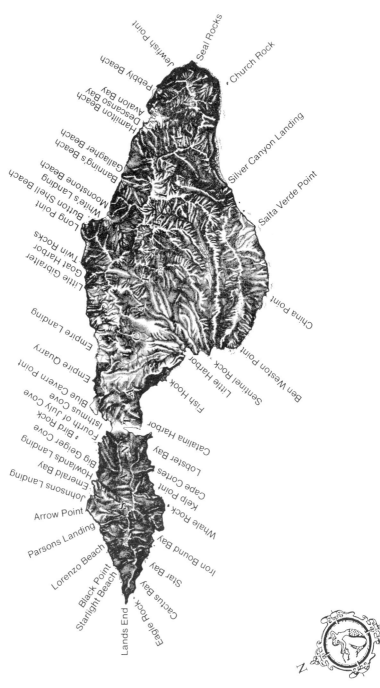

Seal Rocks
Jewish Point
Church Rock
Pebbly Beach
Hamilton Beach
Descanso Bay
Avalon Bay
Gallagher Beach
Banning's Beach
Moonstone Beach
White's Landing
Button Shell Beach
Long Point
Goat Harbor
Twin Rocks
Little Gibralter
Empire Landing
Empire Quarry
Blue Cavern Point
Isthmus Cove
Fourth of July Cove
Bird Rock
Big Geiger Cove
Cherry Cove
Howlands Landing
Emerald Bay
Johnsons Landing
Arrow Point
Parsons Landing
Lorenzo Beach
Black Point
Starlight Beach
Lands End
Eagle Rock
Cactus Bay
Star Bay
Iron Bound Bay
Whale Rock
Kelp Point
Cape Cortes
Lobster Bay
Catalina Harbor
Fish Hook
Sentinel Rock
Little Harbor
Ben Weston Point
China Point
Salta Verde Point
Silver Canyon Landing

N

SANTA CATALINA ISLAND

SANTA CATALINA ISLAND

701. How large is Santa Catalina Island?

Santa Catalina Island is approximately 75 square miles in size and ranks third largest of the California Channel Islands, falling after Santa Cruz and Santa Rosa islands. It is 21 miles long and up to eight miles wide, with 47,884 acres. There are 54 miles of coastline.

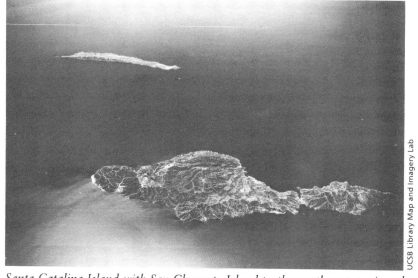

Santa Catalina Island with San Clemente Island to the southwest as viewed from a U2 aircraft at 65,000 feet.

UCSB Library Map and Imagery Lab

702. In what county is Santa Catalina Island?

Santa Catalina Island is in Los Angeles County.

703. How far is Santa Catalina Island from the mainland?

Santa Catalina Island is 19.7 miles from the nearest mainland at the Palos Verdes Peninsula. The nearest neighboring island is San Clemente, 21 miles to the south.

704. What is the highest point on Santa Catalina Island?

Mt. Orizaba, which reaches an elevation of approximately 2070 feet, is the highest point. Mt. Black Jack at 2006 feet in elevation is a close second.

705. What is the average rainfall on Santa Catalina Island?

Annual rainfall averages about 12 inches a year, with some years much drier, and others much wetter. On this island, there are local variations as well.

706. What is the climate on Santa Catalina Island?

Santa Catalina Island is dominated by a mild, Mediterranean-type climate, very similar to that found on the adjacent Southern California mainland. Due to its maritime environment, offshore breezes, and westerly winds, however, Santa Catalina Island has better air quality than any other part of Los Angeles County. Only during Santa Ana wind conditions does smog blow out to this island. On the island, there are microclimates which vary with altitude and topography.

707. What is the physiography of Santa Catalina Island?

Rugged mountains and canyons interwoven with rolling hills and pasturelands cover much of Santa Catalina Island. Sandy and cobbled coves and pocket beaches occasionally break the boldness of the otherwise generally rugged coastline. Toward the island's northerly end, it narrows to less than $1/4$ mile across at the isthmus.

708. What is the geology of Santa Catalina Island?

Santa Catalina Island, like the other Channel Islands, is composed of a variety of rock types of differing geological ages. Metamorphic rocks, 119–165 million years old, are interspersed with Miocene volcanics more recent in age. The western two-thirds of Santa Catalina contains primarily metamorphic rocks,

Chaparral-covered hills meet the sea on Santa Catalina Island.

Terry Martin

while the eastern end is composed of igneous rocks. This is the only Channel Island on which steatite, a type of soapstone coveted by prehistoric peoples, is found.

09. Has there ever been any mining on Santa Catalina Island?

More people have searched for their fortunes on this island than on any other California Channel Island, and its mining history is extensive. As early as the 1830s, nebulous reports of island gold deposits leaked throughout mainland California. By the early 1860s, Santa Catalina Island had become the scene of an "island gold rush," during which time several hundred fortune-seekers hiked the hills and valleys of the island in search of instant fortune. Gold prospecting activities were halted, however, when Union Army troops occupied the island during the Civil War. Only small amounts of gold were ever found. Other ores, including lead, zinc and silver, have been mined post-Civil War.

10. What types of rock quarries are on Santa Catalina Island?

The oldest quarry, which was used prehistorically for thousands of years, is a steatite quarry at Empire Landing. Indians formed this soft stone into various utensils, implements and adornments. Historically, steatite was mined for building facades and ornamentation. Other non-precious island rock has been and continues to be quarried, providing building materials and fill for such projects as the San Pedro breakwater, the Santa Barbara breakwater, and improvements in the city of Long Beach.

711. Who owns Santa Catalina Island?

Eighty-six percent of Santa Catalina Island is privately owned and managed by the Santa Catalina Island Conservancy, a private, non-profit foundation. The city of Avalon, located on the island's leeward southern portion, falls under Los Angeles County government.

712. What is the Santa Catalina Island Conservancy?

In 1972, the Santa Catalina Island Conservancy was formed "with the specific and primary purposes . . . to preserve native plants and animals, biotic communities, geological and geographical formations of educational interest, as well as open space lands used solely for the enjoyment of scenic beauty . . ." An easement agreement was signed with Los Angeles County in 1974, ensuring limited public use of the island, and in 1975 the Santa Catalina Island Conservancy received 86 percent of the island from the Wrigley family through the Santa Catalina Island Company. This gift totaled 42,135 acres—approximately 66 square miles of land. The Santa Catalina Island Conservancy is an independent organization which depends on revenues from public contributions.

713. What is unique about Santa Catalina Island?

Unlike any other California Channel Island, Santa Catalina Island is the only island with an area of extensive urban development—the city of Avalon. Avalon provides a variety of recreation and outdoor educational opportunities for a major segment of Southern California. Santa Catalina is internationally known as a mecca for travelers. It is more accessible to the public than any other Channel Island.

714. What public transportation is available to Santa Catalina Island?

Santa Catalina Island is the only California Channel Island to which there are several daily boat methods of transportation. Public ferries and boats run from San Pedro Harbor, Long Beach Harbor, Huntington Harbor, and Newport Beach on regularly scheduled runs to either the city of Avalon or to Two Harbors at the island's isthmus. In addition, Santa Catalina Island is equipped with an airport and heliports to accommodate both fixed-wing and helicopter services. (See directory).

715. Where is the airport on Santa Catalina Island?

The Airport-in-the-Sky, owned and maintained by the Santa Catalina Island Conservancy, is located about ten miles from the city of Avalon. Named for its 1602 foot elevation, it was constructed by leveling two mountain tops. It is open to the flying public, and over 20,000 landings are made here annually. Shuttle bus service is currently available between the airport and Avalon through the Catalina Conservancy. Shuttle service from the airport to Two Harbors is offered on a seasonal basis and provided by Catalina Safari Shuttle.

716. What is the population of Avalon?

The resident population of Avalon differs with the season. The year-around population is about 3500 people, with a summer population often in excess of 10,000 daily. Over a million people

Over a million people a year visit Santa Catalina Island.

a year visit Santa Catalina Island, most of whom go to Avalon, a city of only one square mile in size.

717. What transportation is available in Avalon?

In the city of Avalon, electric cars and bicycles are available for rent, however their use is restricted to within city limits. Walking is the most popular method of getting around in this small city, although taxis are also available here.

718. Does Avalon receive services from Los Angeles County?

Yes. The Los Angeles County Health, Fire, and Building Inspection departments provide services in Avalon. The L.A. County Sheriff's Department offers police protection. Local government consists of a mayor, a city council, and a city manager.

719. Is there a jail in Avalon?

Yes. In addition to a jail, there is also a small courthouse. The judge comes from the mainland.

The city of Avalon, one square mile in size, is the only urban development on any California Channel Island.

720. Is there a cemetery in Avalon?

Yes. The cemetery, located near Avalon, now has hundreds of occupants, most of whom were Santa Catalina Island residents. The graves date back to the 19th century. This is the only public cemetery on a California Channel Island.

721. How is the city of Avalon supplied with its utilities?

Since 1962, the Southern California Edison Company has been responsible for providing fresh water, gas and electricity to the city of Avalon. Natural gas is shipped in tankers after which it is offloaded and stored at a facility located at Pebbly Beach. The gas is vaporized and compressed before distribution to Avalon residents. Electricity is provided by five diesel generators capable of supplying 6200 kilowatts of power. Almost a million and a half gallons of diesel fuel are required annually to run the generators. Diesel fuel is also delivered by boat, and stored by Pebbly Beach. Southern California Edison owns the island's water rights as well.

722. How is fresh water provided to the residents of Avalon?

Much of the island's water system is dependent upon rainfall for fresh water. Ground water and surface water are scarce. Rainwater is captured at Middle Ranch Reservoir (built in 1920), and piped over the east summit through various pumping stations to a holding reservoir—Wrigley Reservoir. From there it is gravity fed to Avalon residents. The isthmus requires a different pipe system, and the water there is supplied by a well at Howland's Landing. The Santa Catalina Island water system includes at least six wells, nine springs and tunnel sources, twenty-three storage tanks, and a series of reservoirs. The sewage system and fire department hoses are supplied with salt water to flush toilets and extinguish fires.

723. What other types of facilities are found in Avalon?

Avalon has all of the practicalities one would expect to find in any small city in the United States, including a Chamber of Commerce and Visitors Bureau, where one can obtain further information about Avalon. In addition, the Avalon business community includes two local weekly newspapers, a wide variety of hotels, a few markets, several laundromats, one drug store, one bank, a post office, a choice of fishing and diving stores, and a myriad of curio and souvenir shops and restaurants.

724. What water sport activities are available from Avalon?

Rental paddle boards, motorboats, fishing equipment, and snorkeling and diving gear are all available at Avalon. Harbor, sunset and coastal cruises and trips on glass-bottom boats originate in Avalon Harbor. An underwater park, created in 1965, is located off Casino Point. This is the only area within city limits where diving is permitted. Other water sports include pedal boats, ocean kayaking, ocean rafting, jet skiing, swimming, para-sailing and fishing.

725. What on-island activities are available at Avalon?

Avalon and its vicinity is supplied with a museum, botanic garden, several art galleries, two game arcades, a movie theater, and a night club. Horseback riding stables, a golf course, miniature golf and tennis courts are also available, as are bicycle and golf-cart rentals, volleyball and basketball courts, sightseeing tours, hiking and camping.

726. How can one see the island's interior?

Catalina Safari Bus has scheduled service from Avalon and Two Harbors and makes stops at the Airport-in-the-Sky and at camp sites and trail heads. The Santa Catalina Island Conservancy offers half-day, full-day and two-hour Jeep-Eco tours to the interior.

727. Is there a hospital on Santa Catalina Island?

Yes. Avalon Municipal Hospital is located on Falls Canyon Road. It is equipped with an emergency room, an intensive-care unit, X-ray facilities, and a laboratory. Ambulance service is available on the island. In addition, helicopter Medivac service to the mainland is on call.

728. Are there telephones on Santa Catalina Island?

Yes. Today's phone link is via microwave, and Santa Catalina Island is within the Los Angeles area code. The first island-mainland communication was provided by carrier pigeons in 1894. In 1902, the Pacific Wireless Company placed a station on the island, and in 1912 the island was linked to the mainland for the first time by an airplane. In 1920, a radio-telephone system was opened by the Pacific Telephone Company, and in 1923 cables were placed on the ocean floor between San Pedro and Santa Catalina Island. The island's manual switchboard system was replaced in 1978 with a computerized advanced electric switching system. Public payphones are available at various locations.

729. What is the road system on Santa Catalina Island?

Road building began on the island in 1897 with construction of a road from Avalon to the island's isthmus. Today, roads are paved within most of the city of Avalon and to the airport. However, as one leaves town, dirt roads are on the island's interior, often requiring four-wheel-drive vehicles. Road-use permits are available from the Santa Catalina Conservancy for vehicles entering the island's privately owned interior. Bicycle permits are required. Visitors cannot bring their own vehicles to the island, and there is an eight-year waiting list to own a car on the island. Golf carts, taxis, bikes, and walking are the most common modes of transportation.

730. Is hiking allowed on Santa Catalina Island?

Large parts of the island are open for hikers, and several day trails are located in the vicinity of Avalon and Two Harbors. Permission to enter some of the areas is required. (See directory).

731. How can one go camping on Santa Catalina Island?

There are five improved campgrounds on this island that include toilets, fire rings, showers and barbeque pits: Hermit Gulch, Black Jack, Little Harbor, Little Fisherman's and Parsons Landing. The Santa Catalina Island Conservancy handles Hermit Gulch Campground in Avalon. Camping reservations for interior campsites are made through Doug Bombard Enterprises. Camping is permitted in designated campgrounds only.

732. What is El Rancho Escondido?

El Rancho Escondido, built by Philip K. Wrigley, is a privately owned 700-acre Arabian horse ranch located on the island's ocean side. Some island tours offer a visit to El Rancho Escondido, where one can view Arabian horses and some of the elaborate bridles, saddles, and historic island photographs in the Wrigley tack room. Discovery Tours offers a visit to El Rancho Escondido.

733. What is Middle Ranch?

Middle Ranch, located in the island's largest interior valley, is a part of the Santa Catalina Island Conservancy. Here housing

Avalon Harbor provides moorings on a space-available basis for visiting boaters.

and maintenance facilities are provided for the Conservancy's personnel and equipment. Visiting scientists and student interns conducting various island research stay here as well. Farm animals and a pony club are also located at Middle Ranch. The surrounding land contains 80 acres of dry-farmed oat hay, and the Thompson reservoir.

734. What is Eagle's Nest?

Eagle's Nest, located near Middle Ranch, was once a stop for the stagecoach as it traveled from Avalon to Little Harbor. It was built as an inn by the Bannings in 1894 and managed by O.T. Fellows. Goat hunters often stayed here. Once an eagle's nest was located in a cottonwood tree here.

735. What boat facilities are available on Santa Catalina Island?

There are eighteen coves around the island, which are provided with moorings, some of which are leased to private concerns and others of which charge a use fee. In additon, a number of coves provide adequate shelter and anchorage for small boats.

186

Further information is available at Two Harbors, or from the Harbor Master at Avalon (see directory).

736. What is located at Two Harbors?

Two Harbors, located at the island's isthmus, is second in commercial development after Avalon. Here the resident population is about 150, increasing to about 250 during the summer. Fishing, diving, kayaking, hiking and camping are common activities. There is a general store here for supplies, and the University of Southern California's Santa Catalina Marine Science Center is within walking distance.

737. What is located at Descanso Bay?

Descanso Bay, originally named Bannings Cove and directly to the north of Avalon Harbor, was the site of the luxurious Hotel Saint Catherine, built in 1918 by the Bannings. In a much expanded form, the hotel was torn down in the 1960s. Open to the public, Descanso Beach Club, the only privately owned beach in Avalon, operates a full-service restaurant and bar, as well as barbeque facilities. A large lawn area terraces down to a stage with live entertainment in the summer months. Other amenities include a children's play area, a volleyball court, bathrooms, showers, and beach chair and umbrella rentals. Kayak and snorkeling gear rental are also available.

738. What is located at Hamilton Cove?

Hamilton Cove, two coves north of Avalon Harbor, was once the location of a pre-war seaplane terminal. In the 1970s, the hillside above the beach was severely graded and altered to make way for an extensive condominium construction project. Today, private villas are offered both for sale and for rent.

739. What is located at Goat Harbor?

Goat Harbor, midway between the isthmus and Avalon, is a beautiful cove and safe anchorage. Steep cliffs, deep canyons, and talus-covered slopes make hiking dangerous here, however. Ironwoods, oak woodland, bald eagles, red-tailed hawks and ravens add to its scenic beauty.

740. What is the Santa Catalina Island Marine Science Center?

The Marine Science Center was founded in 1963 when Philip

The Santa Catalina Island Marine Science Center, located just north of Two Harbors at Big Fisherman's Cove, is the site of marine research and education.

K. Wrigley and his family donated 45 acres at Big Fisherman's Cove to the University of Southern California for the development of a marine science facility. An additional 180 surrounding acres were set aside as a buffer zone, giving the Center a mile of coastline. In 1967, a 30,000-square-foot laboratory building was completed, which includes a library, classrooms, laboratories and offices. Other features of the site include a dormitory and dining facilities, and a diving support complex complete with small boats and a hyperbaric chamber.

741. Is there a yacht club on Santa Catalina Island?

Yes. This is the only California Channel Island which has an official yacht club, the Santa Catalina Yacht Club, which has a facility in Avalon Harbor. In addition, many other clubs lease harbors: Newport Harbor Yacht Club leases Moonstone Beach; 4th of July Yacht Club leases 4th of July Cove; Corsair Yacht Club leases part of Emerald Bay; Balboa Yacht Club has a facility on leased land at the west side of White's Landing; King Harbor Yacht Club leases part of Little Fisherman's Cove with the Channel Cruising Club; the Offshore Cruising Club leases Big Geiger Cove; the Los Angeles Yacht Club leases part of Howland's; Del Rey and California yacht clubs lease facilities at

Catalina Harbor; and the Isthmus Yacht Club leases the old Civil War barrack building at Two Harbors.

742. What scouting and family organizations have facilities on Santa Catalina Island?

The Boy Scouts of America had their first lease at Emerald Bay in 1925, where today there is a Scout Camping Consortium. Boy Scout camps are located at Cherry Cove and Steadman Cove. Catalina Island Camps operates at Howland's Landing; Catalina Sea Camp is at Toyon Bay as a part of the Catalina Island Marine Institute; Campus by the Sea, a Christian camp, is located at Cherry Cove; YMCA camps are located at Button Shell Beach and at White's Landing.

743. Are there any lighthouses on Santa Catalina Island?

Although there are no lighthouses on Santa Catalina Island, there are navigational lights located at West End, Ship Rock, Long Point, Avalon, East End, and at Catalina Harbor.

744. What native terrestrial mammals are found on Santa Catalina Island?

There are five native terrestrial mammals found on Santa Catalina Island: the ornate shrew *(Sorex ornatus willetti)*; the California ground squirrel *(Spermophilus beecheyi nesioticus)*; the western harvest mouse *(Reithrodontomys megalotis catalinae)*; the deer mouse *(Peromyscus maniculatus catalinae)*; and the island fox *(Urocyon littoralis catalinae)*.

745. What is known about Santa Catalina Island's rare shrew?

The Santa Catalina Island shrew is known only from two collections (1941 and 1983), and five sight reports of this rare animal. It was given its own island subspecies status based on its apparent larger size and darker color than its mainland counterpart. Shrews have been captured and released twice this decade, in 1991 and again in 1993.

746. What is known about island foxes on Santa Catalina Island?

On Santa Catalina Island, the endemic fox population has been adversely affected by overgrazing of large herbivores, as well as competition with introduced feral cats for food resources. The greatest known mortality factor, interestingly enough, is from cars.

747. What feral animals are found on Santa Catalina Island?

Currently, there are populations of feral goats, pigs, and cats on Santa Catalina Island.

748. Why and how are feral goats controlled?

Feral goats have a severe impact on vegetation because they will eat a greater variety of plants and shrubs than most other herbivores. Organized goat-control programs began with fencing measures in 1956, and the elimination of goats from Middle and Bulrush canyons, and the upper Grand Canyon drainage. In the later 1950s, there was additional fencing and removal of animals in the Salta Verde region. The most severe grazing today occurs in Silver Canyon, lower Grand Canyon, the channel slope by Twin Harbors, and the area west of the isthmus. Periodic hunting and trapping help keep population numbers down. They have lived on Santa Catalina Island at least since the mid-1800s.

749. How did pigs get introduced to Santa Catalina Island?

Pigs were intentionally introduced to Santa Catalina from Santa Rosa Island in the early 1930s in hopes that they would eliminate some of the rattlesnake population. Today, pigs are hunted for sport, and there is an ongoing trapping program.

750. What large non-feral animals occur on Santa Catalina Island?

Horses, bison, mule deer, and black buck antelope have been placed on Santa Catalina Island. All domestic cattle have been removed.

751. How did bison get to Santa Catalina Island?

Fourteen bison were brought to Santa Catalina Island in 1924 for the filming of Zane Grey's novel *The Vanishing American*. When the film crew departed, the animals were left behind. Their population was supplemented in 1934 with the introduction of 30 additional animals from Colorado, and in the 1970s with animals from Montana. Today's population is maintained at levels between 400 and 500 animals. The herd is periodically culled, and occasionally "buffalo burgers" are sold at various island restaurants.

752. Where do mule deer occur on Santa Catalina Island?

Mule deer, which are hunted for sport by rifle, can be found throughout the island. The last census, which was in the 1980s, estimated a population in excess of 2000 animals. There is no current population estimate.

753. When were black buck antelope placed on Santa Catalina Island?

In 1973, two females and one male Asian black buck antelope were introduced to Santa Catalina Island. Less than 20 animals are now thought to live in various Black Jack Peak drainages.

754. What rodents have been accidentally introduced to Santa Catalina Island?

Santa Catalina Island is home to introduced black rats *(Rattus rattus)*, brown rats *(Rattus norvegicus)*, and house mice *(Mus musculus)*.

755. What species of snakes are found on Santa Catalina Island?

With five species of snakes, Santa Catalina Island supports a larger variety than that found on any other California Channel Island. They are: the ringneck snake *(Diadophis punctatus similis)*; the gopher snake *(Pituophis melanoleucus annectens)*; the California king snake *(Lampropeltis getulus californiae)*; the two-striped garter snake *(Thamnophis couchii)*; and the Southern Pacific rattlesnake *(Crotalus viridis helleri)*.

Terry Martin

Bison were first brought to Santa Catalina Island in 1924.

191

756. Where are rattlesnakes found on Santa Catalina Island?

Rattlesnakes are widespread on Santa Catalina Island. Dry rocky hillsides and brushy canyons are the habitats in which they are most common. They are least common in woodlands and wet places. An awareness of their habitats and a knowledge of their potential presence should be remembered as a precaution during hiking on Santa Catalina Island.

757. What species of lizards are found on Santa Catalina Island?

Three species of lizards are known to occur on Santa Catalina Island; the side-blotched lizard *(Uta stansburiana)*; the western skink *(Eumeces skiltonianus skiltonianus)*; and the alligator lizard *(Elegaria multicarinatus webbi)*. One record for the desert night lizard *(Xantusia vigilis vigilis)* occurred in 1952 when it was collected at the Wrigley Botanic Garden. It was an isolated individual brought in with plants for the garden.

758. Which amphibians are found on Santa Catalina Island?

Two species of salamanders and three species of frogs have been collected on Santa Catalina Island: the garden salamander *(Batrachoseps major)*; the arboreal salamander *(Aneides lugubris)*; the Pacific tree frog *(Hyla regilla)*; the California toad *(Bufo boreas halophilus)*; and the bullfrog *(Rana catesbeiana)*. The California toad and the bullfrog are considered alien species, and the toad is not recently reported.

759. What species of bats have been collected on Santa Catalina Island?

Five species of bats have been collected on this island: the pallid bat *(Antrozous pallidus)*; the big-eared myotis *(Myotis evotis)*; the California myotis *(Myotis californicus)*; the lump-nosed bat *(Plecotus townsendii)*; and the Yuma myotis *(Myotis yumanensis)*.

760. What marine mammals breed on Santa Catalina Island?

Today, Santa Catalina Island is used by seals and sea lions primarily as a haul-out area rather than a breeding area, although as many as 150 harbor seals may be born here each year. Animals can be seen regularly in the area between China Point and Ben Weston Point and around Seal Rock. For a number of years after the turn of the century, a legendary sea lion, "Old Ben" resided in Avalon Harbor, where today he is commemorated in bronze.

761. Are there any unusual marine habitats on Santa Catalina Island?

Yes. Santa Catalina Island is the only California Channel Island which supports a shallow mud habitat. Here mud flat invertebrates such as fiddler crabs *(Ura crenulata)*, mud shrimp *(Upogebia pugettensis)*, and ghost shrimp (*Callianassa* sp.) occur.

762. What land birds nest on Santa Catalina Island?

bald eagle (former resident/reintroduced)

osprey – former resident	horned lark
peregrine falcon	barn swallow
red-tailed hawk	northern raven
American kestrel	bushtit – former resident
Catalina quail	Bewick's wren
black oystercatcher	rock wren
American coot	northern mockingbird
mallard	Swainson's thrush
killdeer	phainopepla
rock dove	loggerhead shrike
mourning dove	European starling
barn owl?	Hutton's vireo
burrowing owl	orange-crowned warbler
long-eared owl	house sparrow
saw-whet owl	western meadowlark
white-throated swift	hooded oriole
Anna's hummingbird	house finch
Allen's hummingbird	gold finch
common flicker	lesser goldfinch
acorn woodpecker	rufous-sided towhee
black phoebe	chipping sparrow
Lazuli bunting	Brewer's blackbird
great blue heron	western flycatcher

763. Which marine birds nest on Santa Catalina Island?

western gull
pelagic cormorant
Xantus' murrelet

764. Which birds are Channel Islands endemic subspecies on Santa Catalina Island?

There are ten endemic Channel Islands subspecies of birds on Santa Catalina Island, three of which are Santa Catalina Island subspecies endemics: Catalina quail, Bewick's wren and Hutton's vireo.

Catalina quail	loggerhead shrike
Allen's hummingbird	orange-crowned warbler
western flycatcher	house finch
horned lark	rufous-sided towhee
Bewick's wren	Hutton's vireo

765. What is the bald eagle reintroduction program?

The goal of the bald eagle reintroduction is to reestablish a breeding base of birds on Santa Catalina Island. The last bald eagle nesting record occurred around 1950. In 1980, a hacking release platform was built, and three eaglets were placed on the island. Since then, scores of introductions of the birds now enable one to see eagles flying about Santa Catalina Island once again. Place names such as Eagle Reef, Eagle Rock, and the stage stop Eagle's Nest attest to their former presence.

766. What birds have been intentionally introduced to Santa Catalina Island?

Carrier pigeons were used on Santa Catalina Island in the late 1800s as mainland-island messengers. For many years, the Wrigley

The former Wrigley Bird Park is now the site of a campground.

Chaparral, meadows, and oak woodlands meet on Santa Catalina Island.

Terry Martin

Bird Park housed thousands of exotic birds. Various domestic fowl such as chickens have been kept through the years, and in 1979, the California Department of Fish and Game released wild turkeys in the hopes of establishing a resident population. Chukars, pheasants and peafowl have also been introduced.

67. What was the Wrigley Bird Park?

Prior to the World War II era of island development, William Wrigley dismantled the original octagonal Sugerloaf Casino and had its steel frame moved into Avalon Canyon to become a large birdcage. It was expanded into the extensive Wrigley Bird Park, and served as such until its closure in 1966. The birds became the nucleus of the Los Angeles County Zoo aviary, and the island site became the location of Bird Park Campground.

68. What are the different plant communities found on Santa Catalina Island?

Santa Catalina Island supports a wide variety of plant communities, ranging from those found in Northern Baja California to those found in San Luis Obispo County. They include: southern coastal dunes, coastal bluffs, coastal sage scrub, maritime cactus scrub, island chaparral, valley and foothill grasslands, southern coastal oak woodlands, island woodlands, southern riparian woodlands, and coastal marsh communities.

769. How many different plant species are found on Santa Catalina Island?

There are over 600 different plant species which occur on Santa Catalina Island, about two-thirds of which are native.

770. How many plants on Santa Catalina Island are endemic to the California Channel Islands?

There are 24 species and subspecies of plants which are restricted to Santa Catalina Island and one or more of the California Channel Islands.

771. Which plants are endemic only to Santa Catalina Island?

There are four species and four subspecies of plants restricted to Santa Catalina Island:

Catalina manzanita *(Arctostaphylos catalinae)*
Trask's mahogany *(Cercocarpus traskiae)*
Catalina dudleya *(Dudleya hassei)*
Trask's monkeyflower *(Mimulus traskiae)* – probably extinct
Trask's yerba santa *(Eriodictyon traskiae traskiae)*
St. Catherine's lace *(Eriogonum giganteum giganteum)*
Catalina ironwood *(Lyonothamnus floribundus floribundus)*
Catalina bedstraw *(Galium catalinense catalinense)*

Terry Martin

Trask's mahogany, found only on Santa Catalina Island, is known from only a few adult trees.

196

772. When was Catalina ironwood first discovered?

Catalina ironwood *(Lyonothamnus floribundus floribundus),* was first discovered in 1874 by Gustav Eisen, a naturalist and plant lover who sent specimens of this tree to Europe, where its significance was overlooked for a decade. In 1884, William Lyon, California's first State Forester, sent specimens to botanist Asa Gray, who described and named this "new" tree genus *Lyonothamnus* in honor of William Lyon.

773. Where can one see many of the native and endemic plants of Santa Catalina Island?

The Wrigley Memorial and Botanical Garden, located at the head of Avalon Canyon, is the site of Santa Catalina Island's botanical showcase. In addition to many introduced non-native succulents and Mediterranean-type plants, there are examples of many of Santa Catalina's native flora. An herbarium of dried specimens is available for scientific study by advance appointment. The garden is open daily from 8 A.M. until 5 P.M. Admission for adults is $1.00 and children under 12 are free. The Santa Catalina Island Conservancy is also developing a botanical garden of only native species at the Airport-in-the-Sky.

774. Did Indians occupy Santa Catalina Island?

Yes. Gabrieliño Indians and their predecessors once lived on Santa Catalina Island. At the time of Spanish contact, there were several hundred people living in villages scattered throughout the island.

775. What was the Indian name for Santa Catalina Island?

Historic records indicate that this island was known as Pimu to the Gabrieliños.

776. How many archaeological sites are there on Santa Catalina Island?

It is estimated that there are at least 2000 archaeological sites on Santa Catalina Island, about half of which have been mapped, described or studied.

777. What archaeological investigations occurred on Santa Catalina Island?

Early archaeological investigations were conducted for the Smithsonian Institute by Paul Schumacher in the 1870s. Ralph

Glidden, representing the Museum of the American Indian, Heye Foundation, New York, amassed an extensive artifact collection. Other early collectors included Charles Holder, Luella Trask and A.A. Carraher, each of whom sought Indian relics from this island. Twentieth century work has emphasized a more scientific approach than just artifact collecting, and this island has hosted much in-depth study.

778. Where can one see Indian relics from Santa Catalina Island?

In Avalon, the Santa Catalina Island Museum Society was incorporated in 1953 by a group of people who wished to preserve the unique cultural heritage of the island. Today, the Santa Catalina Island Museum is located in the Casino building, and one can see many relics from Santa Catalina Island's past. Admission to the museum is free. The Santa Catalina Island Conservancy also has an exhibit at their Nature Center located at the Airport-in-the-Sky.

779. What happened on Santa Catalina Island during the Spanish period (1542–1821)?

Historic records indicate that several expeditions visited Santa Catalina Island during the Spanish period of California. In 1542, the Cabrillo expedition reported when they arrived: "There issued a great quantity of Indians from among the bushes and grass." In 1602, the Vizcaíno expedition was greeted here by Indians who made "demonstrations of joy in proof of their happiness...." of the guests' arrival. In the late 18th century and continuing into the early 19th century, Russian and Aleut sea otter hunters and early trading vessels visited Santa Catalina Island. This period represents a rapid decline in Santa Catalina Island native inhabitants.

780. How was Santa Catalina Island named?

First named San Salvador in 1542 by the Cabrillo expedition, the name was changed in 1602 by the Vizcaíno expedition. Santa Catalina was chosen as the name in honor of the Feast Day of Saint Catherine, November 25.

781. What happened on Santa Catalina Island during the Mexican period (1821–1848)?

During the Mexican period, the last of the Indians left Santa

Catalina Island, some of whom were baptized at San Gabriel Mission. In 1846, American Thomas Robbins of Santa Barbara received Santa Catalina Island from Mexican Governor Pio Pico by grant. Robbins owned the island until 1850. Although he was the first individual to own the island, he was not the first to build a house or to live there. Hunters, squatters, and concessionaires made free use of the island before Robbins' time and after.

782. Who was the first non-Indian to build a house on Santa Catalina Island?

Samuel Prentiss of Rhode Island was the first non-Indian known to build a house on Santa Catalina Island. Built in the 1820s at Johnson's Landing, it was where Prentiss was to spend the better part of 30 years until his death in 1854. He was buried on a hill above Emerald Bay.

783. Who owned Santa Catalina Island after Thomas Robbins?

In 1850, Thomas Robbins sold the island to José María Covarrúbias for $10,000. He, in turn, conveyed it to Albert Packard of San Francisco in 1853. The island then went through a series of ownership changes and divisions, separating it into various undivided interests until the coming of James Lick in 1864.

784. What happened on Santa Catalina Island during the Civil War?

January 1, 1864, the Fourth Infantry of California Volunteers took military possession of Santa Catalina Island, setting up headquarters, complete with a twelve-pound gun at Two Harbors.

785. Who was living on the island at the time of the Civil War occupation?

November 26, 1863, Lieutenant James F. Curtis reported: "The population of the island is about 100, one half of whom are miners, who perhaps with much reason entertain highly exalted views of the vastness of its mineral wealth." Curtis also estimated the sheep population at 15,000 and the goat population at 7000–8000. Named residents included: brothers Charles and John Johnson, 10-year residents; Francisco Guerrero, 8 years; William Howland, 6 years; Spencer Wilson, 5 years; the Whittley family since 1856; Benjamin Weston, Juan Cota, and D.B. Dietz.

786. Who was James Lick?

James Lick, Pennsylvania manufacturer and philanthropist, began buying interest in Santa Catalina Island in 1864, and by 1867 he managed to merge the ownership back to one person. In 1874, two years before his death, Lick created a three million dollar trust with trustees taking title to the island. Lick's son contested the trust, and in 1887 new trustees sold the island to George Shatto for $200,000. The Lick years span from 1867 to 1887 on Santa Catalina Island.

787. How did Avalon receive its name?

George Shatto's sister-in-law Etta named the harbor after a line from a Tennyson poem, "Idylls of the King": ". . . to the island valley of Avalon, where falls no hail, or any snow nor ever winds blow loudly. . . ." During Indian occupation of the island, it had been called the Bay of the Seven Moons, and under Lick's ownership it was called Timm's Harbor after a sea captain who frequented here.

788. Who was George Shatto?

George Shatto, 1887 buyer of Santa Catalina Island, subdivided the area in which the city of Avalon was created. He laid out streets and auctioned lots for $150 to $2000 where people pitched tents or built summer cottages. Shatto himself built the once magnificent Hotel Metropole, gathering place for many "who's who" of the era. His two steamers shuttled people back and forth from the mainland, setting Avalon's future course as a tourist attraction. Four years after his purchase, however, Shatto was unable to keep up with his debts, and the trustees of the Lick Trust foreclosed on Shatto, reselling the island to William Banning. The Shatto years spanned from 1887 to 1892.

789. Who was William Banning?

William Banning, son of the stagecoach king Captain Phinneas Banning, purchased Santa Catalina Island in 1892 for $128,740. In 1896 he transferred the title to the newly formed Santa Catalina Island Company. Its stock was owned by three Banning brothers and two Banning sisters. By the turn of the century, Avalon was a tent city with a summer population of up to 3000, and a permanent population of about 100. By 1909, the residents had increased to about 500, with as many as 10,000 summer visitors. Thwarted by a lack of capital and a destructive fire in

Avalon in 1915, the major portion of the company stock was sold to William Wrigley, Jr. in 1919 for three million dollars.

790. What did William Wrigley, Jr. do with Santa Catalina Island?

After purchasing complete interest in the Santa Catalina Island Company, William Wrigley, Jr. invested huge amounts of money into various buildings and recreational activities for which Santa Catalina Island today is world renowned. His developments and changes included the construction of an enormous ballroom Casino, an exotic bird park, and a baseball field where his Chicago Cubs came for spring training. In 1921 he built his summer home atop Mt. Ada, named for his wife. Wrigley died in 1932, whereupon his son Philip became director of the Santa Catalina Island Company.

791. Who owns the Wrigley mansion today?

The seventeen-room summer family home atop Mt. Ada, known as the Wrigley Mansion, was given to the University of Southern California by the Santa Catalina Island Company in 1978. In 1985, the University of Southern California, the Santa Catalina Island Conservancy, and private parties entered into a 30-year landlordship agreement which operates the house as a bed-and-breakfast establishment called Inn on Mt. Ada.

792. What was Sugarloaf?

A large rock named Sugarloaf once stood at the northwest end of Avalon Harbor where, in the 1890s, a stairway led to its top. A tunnel leading through the rock for access to neighboring Descanso Bay collapsed in 1906, thus altering Sugarloaf from one rock structure into two: Big Sugarloaf and Little Sugarloaf. In 1917 Big Sugarloaf was blasted away to make room for the first Sugarloaf Casino, built in 1920 and removed in 1928. In 1929, well-weathered Little Sugarloaf was also removed.

793. What is the history of the Casino at Avalon?

A major project undertaken by William Wrigley, Jr. in 1928 was the construction of a larger, more elaborate casino than that which he had already built at Sugarloaf Point. The new hemispheric Casino, designed by Los Angeles architects Weber and Spaulding, is 140 feet high with an outside diameter of 178 feet. It was built as both a movie theatre and a place for live music and ballroom dancing. The Casino today still serves as a major attraction to Avalon, just as Wrigley had envisioned.

794. How many people does the Casino hold?

Movie theater seating capacity is 1184, and ballroom dancing capacity is 2000.

795. What is the history of the Holly Hill House at Avalon?

Holly Hill House, adroitly perched atop the south end of Avalon Harbor, is one of the oldest houses in Avalon. Its constructor, Peter Gano, purchased the land from George Shatto in 1888 for $500. That same year, Gano began his 19th century engineering feat of building his dream castle, "Look Out Cottage." It was finished in 1890, and contained 3000 square feet on three floors, with a conspicuous cupola atop. In 1921 the house was sold to the Giddings family, who changed its name to Holly Hill House. The Giddings owned the house for the next 40 years. Today the house has its fourth private owner.

The Avalon Casino, opened in 1929, has become the landmark that identifies Avalon.

Marla Daily

The privately owned Holly Hill House sits as sentinel above Avalon Harbor.

796. What is the history of the Tuna Club?

In 1898, noted author and fisherman Charles Frederick Holder and seven friends set down the rules and membership qualifications of what was to become one of the most well-known fishing clubs in the world, the Tuna Club. The club's first building, constructed at Avalon Harbor at the turn of the century, burned in the 1915 Avalon fire. The present structure, built in 1916, is still a place where gentlemen anglers gather and protect the honor of their sport.

797. When was the first church built on Santa Catalina Island?

In 1889, a Congregational Church was built in Avalon, where today it is known as the Community Congregational Church. In the 20th century, churches of many denominations followed, including Catholic, Episcopal, Christian Science, and Seventh-Day Adventist, among others.

798. When was the first school built on Santa Catalina?

School history began on the island in 1891 with the appointment of the first teacher, Mrs. Morris, who held classes in the Congregational Church. In 1901, a two-room school was built in Avalon. Today, Santa Catalina Island has both a public elementary and a high school combined, and is a part of Long Beach Unified School District. A small school for elementary grades was placed at Two Harbors in 1987.

799. Is there a regular newspaper on Santa Catalina Island?

The *Catalina Islander* newspaper is published weekly in Avalon, and has been in operation for almost 75 years.

800. Have any fires occurred on Santa Catalina Island?

A major fire destroyed most of Avalon on November 19, 1915, and today buildings and events are spoken of in terms of before or after "the fire." There have been a number of small localized fires, including one which started by lightning, and a 400-acre fire in 1983 which burned at Catalina Harbor. The Santa Catalina Island fire policy is one of suppression accompanied by the construction and maintenance of fire breaks where the soil is treated with sterilants. A "let burn" policy exists in the event of a fire on Santa Catalina Conservancy land when no structures or significant features are threatened.

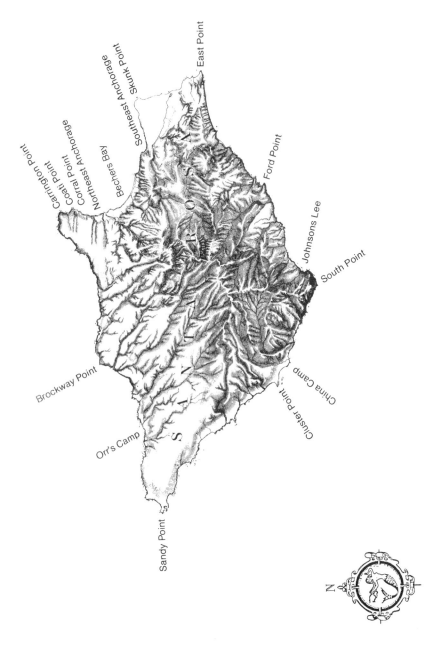

East Point

Southeast Anchorage

Skunk Point

Ford Point

Carrington Point

Coati Point

Corral Anchorage

Northeast Anchorage

Bechers Bay

Johnsons Lee

South Point

Brockway Point

China Camp

Cluster Point

Orr's Camp

Sandy Point

S A N T A   R O S A

N

SANTA ROSA ISLAND

SANTA ROSA ISLAND

801. How large is Santa Rosa Island?

Santa Rosa Island is 84 square miles in size and ranks second largest of the eight California Channel Islands. It is about 15 miles long and 10 miles wide.

802. In what county is Santa Rosa Island?

Santa Rosa Island is in Santa Barbara County.

803. How far is Santa Rosa Island from the mainland?

Santa Rosa Island is 26.5 miles from the nearest mainland. It is situated three miles east of San Miguel Island and six miles west of Santa Cruz Island. It is 30 nautical miles from Santa Barbara Harbor to Bechers Bay on Santa Rosa Island.

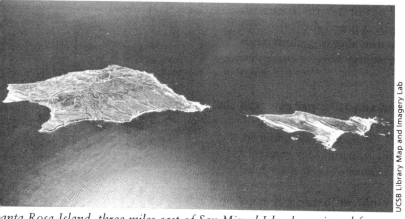

Santa Rosa Island, three miles east of San Miguel Island, as viewed from a U2 aircraft at 65,000 feet.

207

804. What is the highest point on Santa Rosa Island?

An unnamed peak, 1589 feet in elevation, is the highest point. Soledad Mountain, about a mile to the east, is a close second at 1574 feet.

805. What is the climate on Santa Rosa Island?

Santa Rosa Island has a Mediterranean climate with dry and sometimes foggy summers and cool rainy winters. Strong prevailing winds are from the northwest.

806. What is the rainfall on Santa Rosa Island?

Average rainfall on Santa Rosa Island is about 15 inches a year, with extreme years of droughts as well as exceptionally wet years.

807. Is there any fresh water on Santa Rosa Island?

Yes. Santa Rosa Island has many permanent springs. Nine canyons have year-around water. Both springs and wells are developed for animal husbandry and domestic use. Although some of the water is brackish and of poor potability, Clapp Spring has water of exceptionally good quality.

808. How did Clapp Spring get its name?

According to Santa Rosa Island lore, one of the island old timers, who had a chronic case of gonorrhea, swore that drinking water from that particular spring either cured or helped him. It has been called Clapp Spring ever since, and no one has bothered to change the name. In recent history, tests of the water quality of Clapp Spring showed this water to be far superior to any other water tested on the island.

809. What is the physiography of Santa Rosa Island?

Unlike any other northern Channel Island, Santa Rosa Island is blanketed predominantly with gentle rolling hills and grasslands. High mountains with deeply cut canyons are limited. The northeastern shore consists of well-developed marine terraces where cliffs abut the ocean. The southern sector of the island is steeper and more rugged. The island's coastline is quite variable, with broad sandy beaches on the northwest, northeast and southwest.

Grassland slopes on the eastern sector of Santa Rosa Island face the south-western section of Santa Cruz Island in the distance.

810. What is the geology of Santa Rosa Island?

The structure of Santa Rosa Island is that of an uplifted block deformed by folding and faulting. This island has a larger area of Tertiary sedimentary non-volcanic rocks than any other Channel Island. Tertiary sandstones, siltstones, shales and volcanics on the northern half of the island are covered with a thick layer of Quaternary (Pleistocene era) deposits. The oldest Cretaceous rocks are on the south side, along with a complex series of Eocene, Oligocene, and early Miocene shale and sandstones interbedded with early Miocene volcanics, consisting of basalts, breccias, and conglomerate rocks.

811. Are there any geological faults on Santa Rosa Island?

A well-defined fault runs in an east-west direction from north of Skunk Point to just south of Sandy Point. The rocks to the north of the fault are younger than those to its south.

Winds can carve unique sandstone sculptures on Santa Rosa Island.

812. Have any earthquakes been reported on Santa Rosa Island?

Yes. The 1812 earthquake, which destroyed much of the Santa Barbara Mission, had its epicenter near Santa Rosa Island. A rift 1000 feet long, 100 feet wide, and 50 feet deep, opened on the island in the vicinity of Lobo Canyon. Indians living on the island at the time of this earthquake were sufficiently scared to want to leave Santa Rosa Island for a life on the mainland. Today this fault is still quite evident.

813. Are there any fossil beds on Santa Rosa Island?

Yes. Pleistocene fossil beds are particularly well developed on Santa Rosa Island. The thick Quaternary deposits on the island's northern sector have all yielded fossil evidence of mammoths, giant mice, whales, sea otters, and an extinct flightless goose.

814. Has anyone explored for oil on Santa Rosa Island?

Yes. Santa Rosa Island has had more exploration for oil than any other Channel Island. In 1932, Standard Oil drilled for oil, followed by Signal-Honolulu in 1949–50, and Mobil Oil in the early 1970s. A total of twelve wells were drilled, all of which were dry.

An Imperial mammoth tooth is excavated on Santa Rosa Island. Fossil evidence of mammoths is more common on this island than on any other California Channel Island.

315. Have there been any fires on Santa Rosa Island?

There have been no major wild fires on Santa Rosa Island recorded in historic times. In 1968, a ranch building burned to the ground. In 1994, the National Park Service accidentally started a fire while building a fence on the island's east end. It burned about 10 acres.

316. What are the "fire areas" that occur on Santa Rosa Island?

Bright red lenses of soil found in Quaternary sediments on Santa Rosa Island have been called "fire areas" by some researchers. Over 100 such areas occur, and a number of hypotheses explain their origins.

317. What are some of the explanations for the occurance of "fire areas" on Santa Rosa Island?

One explanation for these reddened areas of soil is that they were former barbeque pits of early Indian inhabitants. Another theory suggests these areas were caused by tree-stump burning as a result of wild fires. A third hypothesis, the "ground water hypothesis," suggests that these areas were caused by a boggy or wet situation in which chemical reactions occurred over a period of time, changing the soil color by microbial and geological processes rather than by heat. Oxidations of iron and manganese are thought to cause the red coloring.

818. Who owns Santa Rosa Island?

Santa Rosa Island is owned by the United States Government. From 1902 until 1987 however, the island was owned by Vail & Vickers. Until the purchase of this land by the government, Santa Rosa Island was a privately owned inholding within the boundaries of the Channel Islands National Park.

819. Why was Santa Rosa Island not purchased by the government in 1980 with the passing of the Channel Islands National Park bill?

Although President Carter signed the bill that created the Channel Islands National Park, funds were not appropriated by his administration for the purchase of privately owned lands within the Park boundaries. The bill did state however, that Santa Rosa Island was to be purchased as a priority, before the east end of Santa Cruz Island could be purchased.

820. Once funds were appropriated for the purchase of Santa Rosa Island, why was the island not purchased immediately?

Title to Santa Rosa Island became clouded in 1985 when a lawsuit was filed on behalf of the Chumash Indians who claimed ownership of this and Santa Cruz Island. Purchase was delayed pending outcome of the lawsuit and title clearance. In early 1987, the legal actions ceased, thus clearing title to the island.

821. How much did the United States government pay for the purchase of Santa Rosa Island?

The selling price of Santa Rosa Island was $29,850,250. The deed was signed in December 1986, pending the island's title clearance. The sale was announced to the public on February 9, 1987.

822. Does the National Park Service have any facilities on Santa Rosa Island?

Currently there are temporary Park Service facilities on Santa Rosa Island. Elaborate plans to renovate the abandoned Air Force complex located on the island's south side at Johnson's Lee were abandoned and the facility torn down. New plans are completed for an eight-unit development complex to the southeast of Vail & Vickers ranch.

823. How many people live on Santa Rosa Island?

Since Santa Rosa Island has been privately owned, very few people have lived on the island. The number of people on the island at any one time depended upon the cattle and hunting activities, although under Vail & Vickers ownership there were about six to eight permanent residents.

824. What are the activities on Santa Rosa Island?

Santa Rosa Island has been operated as a cattle ranch by Vail & Vickers since 1902. Tenant groups have included the U.S. Air Force, the U.S. Navy, several oil companies, and a private hunting operation. Today, the private hunting operation continues under Vail & Vickers, and the National Park Service has opened Santa Rosa Island to public camping and day trips.

825. What type of ranching operation has been run on Santa Rosa Island?

Vail & Vickers operates as a cattle "stocker" operation, as opposed to a cow/calf operation. Young animals shipped to the island will be raised, fattened, and sent to market. In addition, horses are bred, raised and broken on the island for ranch use.

826. Who operates Vail & Vickers?

Twin brothers A.L. Vail and N.R. Vail, Jr., oversee the company operations. Their central office is located in Santa Barbara.

827. Does Vail & Vickers have a registered brand?

Yes. Their brand is VR placed on the left ribs of the animal. It is a brand formerly used by Vails ranching in Arizona.

828. How many cattle are on Santa Rosa Island?

The number of cattle on the island at any one time will vary with the annual rainfall, the available feed, and the cattle market. As many as 6500 head may be kept on the island during a good year. In the drought of 1948, all the cattle were moved off the island.

829. How are cattle transported to and from Santa Rosa Island?

Vail & Vickers owns and operates a 65-foot wooden hull cattle boat, the *Vaquero II*. She was built in Santa Barbara by Lindwall Boatworks and launched in 1959. At the time, she was the largest boat ever built in Santa Barbara.

830. Was there a *Vaquero I*?

Yes. The first *Vaquero* was a 130-foot motor vessel built in 1913, and used to transport cattle, personnel, and supplies to Santa Rosa Island. In 1943, during the Second World War, she was acquired by the U.S. government for use in Army transport operations.

831. What types of animals are hunted on Santa Rosa Island?

Historically, stocked elk, deer, and pigs were hunted on Santa Rosa Island as game animals. The feral pig population was eradicated by the National Park Service in 1994, and deer and elk continue to be hunted. For hunting trophies, elk are graded according to the number of points on their antlers.

832. How many ranches are there on Santa Rosa Island?

The main ranch on Santa Rosa Island is located at Bechers

Horses are bred, raised and trained on Santa Rosa Island for island use.

The Vaquero II *transports cattle and supplies to Bechers Bay.*

William B. Dewey

Bay. This island does not have major outposts such as those found on neighboring Santa Cruz Island. Line camps are located in Wreck Canyon, Arlington Canyon and at China Camp.

833. How many airstrips are there on Santa Rosa Island?

There is one well-developed dirt airstrip near the main ranch facility at Bechers Bay. This runway is used both by Vail & Vickers privately and by Channel Islands Aviation, airplane concessionaire to Channel Islands National Park.

834. Are there any good anchorages or boat facilities on Santa Rosa Island?

There are only a few spots along the island's coast where small boats anchor. Unlike many of the other Channel Islands, there are no all-weather, well-sheltered coves on Santa Rosa Island.

835. Is there public transportation to Santa Rosa Island?

Public boat transportation to Santa Rosa Island is offered by park concessionaire, Island Packers, Inc. Airplane transportation is offered by Channel Islands Aviation (see directory).

The main ranch on Santa Rosa Island is located at Bechers Bay.

Bechers Bay is one of the few boat anchorages on Santa Rosa Island.

836. What is the road system on Santa Rosa Island?

A dirt road system requiring four-wheel-drive vehicles circles and crosses this island. The only paved road is one built in connection with the former Air Force facilities at Johnson's Lee.

837. How does Santa Rosa Island receive its fuel and other supplies?

Since there is no good landing beach on Santa Rosa Island suitable for landing crafts, fuel such as diesel, gasoline and propane and other supplies must be off-loaded in manageable quantities onto the wharf near the main ranch.

838. Are there any telephones on Santa Rosa Island?

There are no conventional telephones on Santa Rosa Island. Comunication with the mainland is via marine radio or cellular phone.

839. What are the native terrestrial mammals found on Santa Rosa Island?

There are three native terrestrial mammals found on Santa Rosa Island: the island fox *(Urocyon littoralis santarosae),* the spotted skunk *(Spilogale gracilis amphialus),* and the deer mouse *(Peromyscus maniculatus sanctaerosae).*

840. What bats have been collected on Santa Rosa Island?

Only the California myotis *(Myotis californicus)* has been collected here. However, with increased collecting efforts, other species are expected to be found.

841. What is the status of feral pigs on Santa Rosa Island?

Feral pigs, hunted for decades as a game animal on Santa Rosa Island, were eliminated by the National Park Service in 1994.

842. Are there any feral animals on Santa Rosa Island?

No. Although elk and deer remain on the island, they are considered introduced, not feral, animals.

843. What animals have been introduced to Santa Rosa Island other than cattle and horses?

Both elk and deer have been stocked on Santa Rosa Island.

844. When were elk introduced?

In about 1913, elk were placed on Santa Rosa Island to form a breeding herd. Supplemented by additional animals in 1930, today the elk herd is numerous enough to cull by hunting.

845. When were deer introduced?

In the late 1920s, several shipments of mule deer from the Kaibab Forest in Arizona were sent to Santa Rosa Island. Today, deer are hunted as a game animal on this island.

846. What pinnipeds breed on Santa Rosa Island?

Harbor seals haul out (lie ashore) and breed on Santa Rosa Island. The first record of an elephant seal birth on this island occurred in 1985. Although California sea lions haul out here, they are not known to breed on Santa Rosa Island.

847. Are there any snakes on Santa Rosa Island?

Yes. There is one species of snake, the gopher snake *(Pituophis melanoleucus)*, on Santa Rosa Island.

848. What lizards are found on Santa Rosa Island?

The alligator lizard *(Elegaria multicarinatus)*, and the western fence lizard *(Sceloporus occidentalis becki)*, are found here. These two species also occur on the neighboring island of San Miguel to the west and Santa Cruz Island to the east.

849. What amphibians are found on Santa Rosa Island?

The Pacific tree frog *(Hyla regilla)* and the slender salamander *(Batrachoseps pacificus)* are found on Santa Rosa Island.

850. What land birds nest on Santa Rosa Island?

bald eagle – former resident	barn swallow
peregrine falcon – former resident	northern raven
red-tailed hawk	Bewick's wren
American kestrel	northern mockingbird
Catalina quail	loggerhead shrike
snowy plover	European starling
killdeer	Hutton's vireo
black oystercatcher	orange-crowned warbler
mourning dove	song sparrow
common barn owl	chipping sparrow

white-throated swift
Allen's hummingbird
black phoebe
western flycatcher
horned lark

rufous-sided towhee
western meadowlark
lesser goldfinch
house finch
chukar

851. What marine birds nest on Santa Rosa Island?
Brandt's cormorant
pelagic cormorant
western gull
pigeon guillemot

852. What birds endemic to the California Channel Islands are found on Santa Rosa Island?

Allen's hummingbird
western flycatcher
horned lark
Bewick's wren
loggerhead shrike

orange-crowned warbler
house finch
rufous-sided towhee
song sparrow
Catalina quail – introduced

853. How did quail and chukar get to Santa Rosa Island?
The Santa Catalina variety of California quail was intentionally introduced to Santa Rosa Island in the early 1930s. Chukar were introduced in 1985.

854. What plant communities are found on Santa Rosa Island?
A diverse array of plant communities is found on Santa Rosa Island, including coastal strand, coastal bluffs, grasslands, coastal sage scrub, chaparral, woodlands, pine forests, riparian and marsh communities.

855. What types of pine forests are there are on Santa Rosa Island?
There are stands of the Bishop pine-Santa Cruz Island pine complex *(Pinus muricata-P. remorata),* as well as a stand of Torrey pines *(Pinus torreyana)* on Santa Rosa Island.

856. Where is the Torrey pine forest on Santa Rosa Island?
Torrey pines are found on the northeast sector of Santa Rosa Island on the northwest-facing slopes to the east of Bechers Bay. They grow at elevations between about 200–500 feet. This is the

only native stand of Torrey pines on any Channel Island. They occur naturally at only one other location on the southern California coast, just south of Del Mar in San Diego County.

857. Where are the Bishop pine forests on Santa Rosa Island?

Bishop pines are found at elevations between 600-1000 feet above sea level on the north- to west-facing slopes of the northeastern part of Santa Rosa Island.

858. How many different plant species occur on Santa Rosa Island?

There are about 500 different native and introduced plants which occur on Santa Rosa Island.

859. How many Channel Islands endemic plants occur on Santa Rosa Island?

About 36 different species of plants on Santa Rosa Island are endemic to the California Channel Islands.

860. Are any plants endemic to only Santa Rosa Island?

There are four plants restricted to Santa Rosa Island: live-forever *(Dudleya blochmanae insularis)*, manzanita *(Arctostaphylos*

Torrey pines are found only on Santa Rosa Island and in San Diego County.

Island oak trees, found on Santa Rosa Island, are endemic to the California Channel Islands.

confertiflora), gilia *(Gilia tenuiflora hoffmannii)*, and the variety of Torrey pine *(Pinus torreyana insularis)*.

861. Are there any poisonous plants on Santa Rosa Island?
Santa Rosa Island has poison oak *(Toxicodendron diversilobum)*, chaparral zygadene *(Zygadenus fremontii)*, and several species of nightshade *(Solanum* sp.), each of which has some toxic properties.

362. Is there jimson weed on Santa Rosa Island?
Yes. Jimson weed *(Datura* sp.) is found on Santa Rosa Island.

863. What did the Chumash Indians call Santa Rosa Island?
The Chumash Indians called this island Wima.

864. What 19th-century archaeology occurred on Santa Rosa Island?
Little archaeological work was conducted on Santa Rosa Island in the 1800s. In 1876, Rev. Stephen Bowers and Lorenzo Yates collected artifacts for the Smithsonian Institution, followed by Gustav Eisen, who excavated some island burials for skeletal material in 1897.

221

865. What 20th-century archaeology occured on Santa Rosa Island?

In 1901, Philip Mills Jones conducted archaeological work on Santa Rosa Island for the University of California at Berkeley, a project financed by Phoebe A. Hearst. His collections are housed in the Lowie Museum in Berkeley. David Banks Rogers visited this island several times in the late 1920s for the Santa Barbara Museum of Natural History, followed by Arthur Woodward of the Los Angeles County Museum of Natural History in 1941. Beginning in the 1940s, Phil Orr of the Santa Barbara Museum of Natural History conducted the most extensive and prolonged archaeological examinations ever undertaken on Santa Rosa or any other California Channel Island.

866. When did archaeologist Phil Orr work on Santa Rosa Island?

In 1941 and 1945, Phil Orr flew over Santa Rosa Island several times, laying the groundwork for his future island study. In March 1947 the first expedition began, which was the forerunner of 20 years of field work. Orr was interested not only in archaeology, but also in geology and paleontology.

867. Where was Phil Orr's camp located?

Phil Orr built his three camp buildings just west of Skull Gulch, in a deep gully out of the prevailing winds. Although today the camp is in a very deteriorated condition, it represents the determined occupation and research of 20 years (1947–1967) in the life of Phil Orr. His research efforts culminated in the publication of *Prehistory of Santa Rosa Island.*

868. Is there any rock art on Santa Rosa Island?

Yes. In 1901, Philip Mills Jones recorded several pictographs and petroglyphs located in a deep canyon on Santa Rosa Island.

869. Why is Santa Rosa Island considered by some to be the burial place of Juan Rodríguez Cabrillo?

Philip Mills Jones recovered a stone slab in 1901 that bears several incised designs, including the initials "JR," a simple cross and a headless stick figure. In 1972, anthropologist Robert Heizer hypothesized that this 13.5-inch-long stone slab could have been the stone which marked Cabrillo's grave after his death in 1543. Others remain skeptical.

The remains of Phil Orr's camp can still be seen just west of Skull Gulch.

870. To whom was Santa Rosa Island granted during the Mexican era?

On October 3, 1843, Governor Micheltorena granted Santa Rosa Island to José Antonio Carrillo and Carlos Carrillo. In January 1839, an order had been issued authorizing the Carrillo brothers to be granted this island, but Governor Alvarado had vied politically with the Carrillos and granted the island to José Castro instead. When Micheltorena took office, the Carrillos petitioned for the upholding of the original order. After paying José Castro some restitution, they secured the grant.

871. What did José Antonio and Carlos Carrillo do with Santa Rosa Island?

On November 2, 1843, a month after the Carrillo brothers received Santa Rosa Island, they assigned their rights to Carlos Carrillo's two daughters, Manuela and Francisca. These sisters were married to two Americans, John Jones and Alpheus Thompson, who entered into partnership to occupy and operate the island.

872. What did John Jones and Alpheus Thompson do with Santa Rosa Island?

In 1844, Thompson occupied Santa Rosa Island, taking with him 270 head of Carlos Carrillo's mainland cattle, several horses, and a flock of fifty-one ewes and two rams. In 1846, Jones and his family moved to Boston, leaving his affairs in the hands of his friend and financial advisor, Alfred Robinson. The island ranching operations continued to flourish. By 1857, it was reported that there were 8000 head of cattle and 2000 head of sheep on the island.

873. What happened to the Jones-Thompson partnership?

Brothers-in-law Jones and Thompson, who had been in business together as co-owners of several ships engaged in transporting goods from Mexico to California, had a falling out over their Santa Rosa Island affairs. A bitter legal battle ensued in the mid-1850s over money matters. In 1859 a part of Alpheus Thompson's interest in the island was sold to pay debts. T. Wallace More purchased this interest for $3000. Jones died in 1861, and

The two-story house at the main ranch dates back to the More occupation of Santa Rosa Island. The single story is a later addition.

his interest in Santa Rosa Island was purchased from his heirs by
Alexander P. More, brother of T. Wallace More.

874. What were the first improvements built on Santa Rosa Island?

In 1844, Alpheus Thompson built a small, 24-foot-long, 15-
foot-wide, 9-foot-high plank house with one door and one window. Several corrals were built, and the ranch prospered. By
1855, Thompson had built a second, larger ranch house.

875. What happened to T. Wallace More's interest in Santa Rosa Island?

T. Wallace More traded his interest in Santa Rosa Island to his
brother, A.P. More, in exchange for property located on the
Rancho Sespe. A.P. More eventually became the sole owner of
Santa Rosa Island, and remained as such until his death in 1893.

876. Did any of the Mores occupy the island in the late 1850s?

In 1859, a voting "Precinct of the Islands" was established on
Santa Rosa Island at the "Camp of T. Wallace More" by the
Santa Barbara County Board of Supervisors. It is not known how
many people were to be served by such a precinct.

877. What did the More brothers do with Santa Rosa Island?

During the More tenure (1858–1902), Santa Rosa Island was
used primarily as a sheep ranch. At one point, over 100,000 sheep
were said to be on the island. The greatest prosperity occurred during and just after the Civil War, when wool was in great demand.

878. How long did the boom of the sheep market continue?

In 1876 the wool market collapsed. In an effort to curb losses,
a large sheep slaughter was held on the island. About 1200 sheep a
day were killed, boiled until their bones softened, and then pressed
for tallow. The pressed meat was fed to the pigs, and the tallow
and skins were sold, making it a slightly profitable undertaking.

879. Which of the More brothers took the most active interest in Santa Rosa Island?

Alexander P. More possessed and managed the island from
1881 until his death in 1893. He had been a controversial hot-
tempered man. In 1886, More caught a Chinese cook trying to
defect from the island by stowing away on a boat, so he shot and

killed him. Since the murder took place over water, there was a legal jurisdiction problem, and More was acquitted.

880. What happened to Santa Rosa Island after Alexander P. More's death in 1893?

John More, youngest of the twelve More children, managed the island's affairs as the executor of his brother's estate. After he was caught for embezzling $80,000 from the estate, he was fired and fined. In 1902, the estate was sold.

881. Who purchased Santa Rosa Island in 1902?

Walter L. Vail and J.V. Vickers entered into a partnership and purchased Santa Rosa Island from the heirs of A.P. More. This partnership, still in effect today as Vail & Vickers, is in its third generation.

882. What did Vail & Vickers do with Santa Rosa Island?

After Vail & Vickers purchased Santa Rosa Island, they converted it from a sheep ranch to a cattle ranch. All of the sheep were removed.

Two wooden barns on Santa Rosa Island date back to the More era on Santa Rosa Island.

883. Was there ever a school house on Santa Rosa Island?

Yes. A little white building of early, but unknown origin, is located at the main ranch complex at Bechers Bay. During the Vail & Vickers period, this building was used as a school house before it was converted into the residence it is today.

884. Did Chinese abalone fishermen occupy Santa Rosa Island?

Yes. On the south side of Santa Rosa Island there is a structure still known as "China Camp," which may date back to the More ownership of Santa Rosa Island and a period of Chinese squatters.

885. What is China Camp used for today?

China Camp is used as an outpost of the main ranch. In the four-room wooden house, a sign hangs on the wall above the stove with the name "Rita," the mythical China Camp occupant. Cowboys today repeat the island lore that they hope Rita will have hot coffee awaiting their arrival after their long, hard ride to China Camp.

886. What activities occurred on Santa Rosa Island during World War II?

In 1943, the U.S. Army established a radar station on the island's south side. A small base of four or five houses was located near Pecho Peak to service this radar station. Today some of the foundations, a water tank, and some piles of wood remain.

887. What was the development at Johnson's Lee?

The large development which dominated the landscape at Johnson's Lee is an abandoned military base. In the early 1950s, the Air Force leased and developed about ten acres of land on the south side of Santa Rosa Island. It operated as an Air Control and Warning Station in response to the the threat of attack during the Cold War. It was manned from 1951 to 1963 and was officially abandoned in 1965.

888. What facilities were developed at Johnson's Lee?

Military structures consisted of seven two-story barracks, a mess hall, a powerhouse, a pier, three maintenance buildings, seven administrative support buildings, two water tanks, an incinerator, and a number of small sheds. The facility was surrounded

227

by a fence, with a paved road leading to a radar installation on top of the highest, unnamed point on this island.

889. Did the Air Force have all of its facilities confined to Johnson's Lee?

No. An operations building, power house, radar tower foundation, and wooden maintenance building were placed atop the island's highest peak. Two other smaller units were built to the southeast and northwest of the facilities at Johnson's Lee.

890. How many people were stationed at Johnson's Lee?

During peak occupancy, approximately 300 men were stationed here.

891. How did military personnel get to and from Johnson's Lee?

Transportation of personnel and supplies was provided by the U.S. Navy from the Port Hueneme Naval Base, using 85-foot crash boats similar to the ones presently used to supply other military bases on the Channel Islands.

The Air Force facilities at Johnson's Lee, abandoned since 1965, were torn down in the early 1990s under the direction of Channel Islands National Park.

892. How did Johnson's Lee receive its water?

Fresh water was barged to Johnson's Lee, where it was stored in four 20,000-gallon storage tanks. A nearby well did not have an adequate yield to supply the base. An early desalinization plant proved inadequate for the facility.

893. What is the status of the military complex at Johnson's Lee today?

Abandoned since 1965, the military station at Johnson's Lee underwent major widespread vandalism and natural deterioration. The pier collapsed, and some buildings were recycled to other parts of the island. In the early 1990s, most of this facility was torn down by the National Park Service after they abandoned their elaborate plans for its use as an admininstrative and visitor center.

894. For whom is Johnson's Lee named?

Johnson's Lee is named after William M. Johnson, United States Coast Survey employee in charge of Channel Islands topographic surveys compiled in 1855, 1859 and 1860. It is the only harbor on the south side of Santa Rosa Island.

895. Are there any lighthouses on Santa Rosa Island?

Although there are no lighthouses on Santa Rosa Island, there is one navigational light on the island's south side.

896. Are there any major shipwrecks on Santa Rosa Island?

Yes. Some of the more significant shipwrecks include: the *Golden Horn* (1893); the *Crown of England* (1894); the *Magic* (1899); the *Dora Bluhm* (1910); the *Thornton* (1910); the *Aggie* (1915); the *Aristocratis* (1949); the *Patria* (1954); and most recently, the *Chickasaw* (1962).

897. What happened to the *Chickasaw*?

The *Chickasaw*, an Alabama-registered freighter, ran aground on the south side of Santa Rosa Island between Cluster Point and South Point. She was enroute from Japan to Wilmington with a load of toys and optical supplies. Today a few large pieces of her broken hull still remain in view.

898. How did Wreck Canyon gets its name?

Wreck Canyon, on the island's south side, is named after the

1894 wreck of the British ship *Crown of England*. A large piece of machinery marks the spot from where she was salvaged.

899. Have there been any deaths on Santa Rosa Island during historic times?

Yes. In 1886, island owner A.P. More shot and killed his Chinese cook, who was trying to leave the island. Influential More was acquitted. In 1914, Dede Pepper, the 23-year-old wife of island foreman Frank Pepper, committed suicide "during a moment of temporary mental aberration." In the 1930s, a cowboy died as a result of a fall from his horse, and a bulldozer operator was killed in an accident in 1950. In 1968, an island employee died in the fire in which the bunk house/kitchen burned to the ground, and in 1980, a hunter died of a fatal heart attack.

900. Have there been any plane wrecks on Santa Rosa Island?

Yes. During construction of the facility at Johnson's Lee in the early 1950s, a plane servicing the contractors crashed, killing one of three persons aboard. On the island's south side, some poachers landed illegally to hunt game, but their plane got stuck in the mud in a usually dry lakebed, where today parts of the plane remain.

The freighter Chickasaw *ran aground on the south side of Santa Rosa Island in a heavy rainstorm in 1962.*

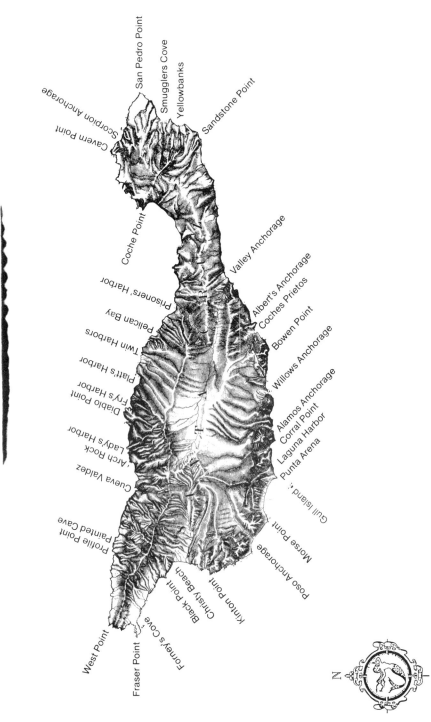

San Pedro Point
Smugglers Cove
Yellowbanks
Sandstone Point
Scorpion Anchorage
Cavern Point
Coche Point
Valley Anchorage
Prisoners' Harbor
Albert's Anchorage
Coches Prietos
Pelican Bay
Bowen Point
Twin Harbors
Willows Anchorage
Platt's Harbor
Fry's Harbor
Diablo Point
Alamos Anchorage
Corral Point
Laguna Harbor
Punta Arena
'Arch Rock
Lady's Harbor
Cueva Valdez
Gull Island
Profile Point
Painted Cave
Morse Point
Poso Anchorage
Black Point
Christy Beach
Kinton Point
West Point
Fraser Point
Forney's Cove

N

SANTA CRUZ ISLAND

SANTA CRUZ ISLAND

901. How large is Santa Cruz Island?

Santa Cruz Island is the largest of the Southern California Islands. It is 96 square miles or about 62,000 acres, and is approximately 22 miles long, and between two and six miles wide. (This island is larger than the District of Columbia, and over four times the size of Manhattan!) It is the largest privately owned island in the continental United States.

Aerial view of Santa Cruz Island with Santa Rosa Island to the west taken at an oblique angle from a U2 aircraft flying at 65,000 feet. 1972.

UCSB Library Map and Imagery Lab

902. In what county is Santa Cruz Island?

Santa Cruz Island is in Santa Barbara County.

903. How far is Santa Cruz Island from the mainland?

The closest mainland is 19 miles from the island's east end. The entire island lies about 22–25 miles off the adjacent mainland coast between Ventura and Goleta.

904. What is the highest point on Santa Cruz Island?

Picacho Diablo, at 2434 feet in elevation, is the highest point. Several other peaks surpass the 2000 foot mark on the island's rugged north side.

905. How was Santa Cruz Island named?

The 1769 expedition of Portolá, led by Juan Peréz, is credited with the naming of the island. A walking staff topped by a small iron cross was left on the island by a priest and returned the next day by island Indians. The name "Santa Cruz" or "Holy Cross" is said to have resulted from this incident.

906. Why does Santa Cruz Island have a different boundary than the other California Channel Islands?

Santa Cruz Island is the only California Channel Island which is owned to the water's edge at all times. It was stated in the original grant of 1839 that the island had "for its boundaries the water's edge." There are about 77 miles of shoreline, depending on the tide. The other seven Southern California islands are owned to mean high tide.

907. What type of weather is there on Santa Cruz Island?

The entire island has a Mediterranean climate—cool, rainy winters and warm, dry summers. Due to the island's large size and varied topography, a number of microclimates exist. The coastal areas are mild throughout the year with little or no frost. Temperature records, which have been kept for over 80 consecutive years, show that coastal areas rarely have temperatures above 85°F or below 35°F, while the central valley may reach over 100°F during the summer. Winter in the central valley brings temperatures of 20°F or less. Often, while the coastal areas of the island are shrouded in fog, the central valley will have bright sunshine.

View to the west from Picacho Diablo, the highest point on Santa Cruz Island. It was said to have been connected to the mainland by a rainbow bridge according to Chumash legend.

908. What is the annual rainfall on Santa Cruz Island?

Rainfall records have also been kept for over 80 years. The average annual rainfall is about 20 inches at the main ranch head-quarters in the central valley. Extreme years vary between 6.5 inches and 60 inches of rain.

909. Does it ever snow on Santa Cruz Island?

Yes. Occasionally snow will fall on the northern mountain range of the island, particularly around the Picacho Diablo area. In February 1949 the entire island was blanketed in snow. Such snowfall at lower elevations is extremely rare.

910. Is there any water on Santa Cruz Island?

Yes. Santa Cruz Island has many permanent springs and a few permanent streams, though most of the water courses are dry much of the year. Both springs and wells have been developed for use at the various ranches and other island facilities.

911. What is the physiography of Santa Cruz Island?

Santa Cruz Island is the most topographically diverse of the Southern California islands. It is rough and mountainous with deep canyons, and large areas of flat land are limited. Much of the northern shore is bold and rugged, with cliffs dropping to the sea and interspersed with small pocket beaches at the mouths of canyons. Longer stretches of beach are found along the western and southern shores. A large central valley is nestled between two mountain ranges for much of the island's length. Access into this valley is through a narrow, winding, stream-filled canyon, three miles long.

912. What is the geology of Santa Cruz Island?

The geology is greatly varied on Santa Cruz Island. The oldest rocks are schists and other metamorphosed sedimentary rocks of pre-Cretaceous period, intruded by Cretaceous and Jurassic quartz diorites. These are found on the island's south side. The northern side of the island contains primarily Miocene volcanic rocks. Pliocene rocks are missing. Limited Pleistocene deposits are

Aerial photography from west to east, looking down the volcanic spine of Santa Cruz Island.

particularly well developed at Potato Harbor and on the island's east end.

913. Are there any fossil beds on Santa Cruz Island?

Yes. There are both Miocene and Pleistocene fossil deposits on Santa Cruz Island.

914. Where is the fumarole on Santa Cruz Island?

In the past, several fumarole vents have been active along the shale slopes of China Harbor. In the recent past, boaters have reported these smoking vents as fires. This is the only Southern California island on which fumaroles have occurred in recent times.

915. Has anyone explored for oil on Santa Cruz Island?

Yes. Both the east end and the western portion of the island have had oil exploration. In the 1950s Richfield Oil drilled two exploratory wells on the western portion of the island, none of which yielded oil. An exploratory well on the east end of the island yielded water instead of oil.

916. Are there any rock quarries on Santa Cruz Island?

Yes. Fry's Harbor, located on the north side of the island, was the site of a quarry created in the 1920s to provide stone for the Santa Barbara breakwater. It was operated by Merritt-Chapman and Scott, a New York-based firm. The quarried rocks were towed across the channel on large barges. The first paystone was placed in the breakwater in 1927. In 1930, the operations were abandoned. Today, remains of this defunct operation can still be seen at Fry's Harbor.

917. What are the rockpiles that can be seen on the east end of Santa Cruz Island, above Valley Anchorage and near Fraser Point?

During the ranching and farming days of Justinian Caire, workers cleared stones from the fields by hand, and placed them in large piles which still can be seen today.

918. What is Painted Cave?

Painted Cave, located near the western end of the island's north side, is an erosional feature carved in a steep volcanic cliff by powerful waves and wind action. It is the largest known sea cave in California, measuring 1215 feet in length, the size of more than four football fields. The entrance, located in 30 feet of water, reaches upward 160 feet above the water level to its ceiling, and is almost 100 feet wide. The name "painted" is derived from naturally occurring colors created by various rock types, lichens and algae. Marine organisms, harbor seals, sea lions, and several species of birds inhabit this cave.

919. Why does Santa Cruz Island have a central valley?

The central valley on Santa Cruz Island is due to the Santa Cruz Island fault, a major geologic feature extending the length of the valley. This is the only Southern California island which has such a central valley/fault system.

920. Who owns Santa Cruz Island?

This island is divided into two different ownerships. The western 54,381 acres (approximately 90 percent of the island) today are owned by The Nature Conservancy. From 1937 to 1987, this western portion of the island was owned by the Santa Cruz Island Company. With the December 8, 1987, death of the company president, Dr. Carey Stanton, the land and company assets were

A fault system runs the length of the central valley on Santa Cruz Island.

transferred to The Nature Conservancy. The eastern 6,264 acres of the island are owned by Channel Islands National Park. They had been owned jointly by descendents of Justinian Caire since 1925. Three of the four owners sold their interests to the National Park Service in the early 1990s, and the fourth had his 25 percent ownership interest taken from him by Legislative Taking in 1996. The western portion of the island is often called the Stanton property, while the east end is referred to as the Gherini property.

21. How many people live on Santa Cruz Island?

Since the western portion of Santa Cruz is privately owned by The Nature Conservancy, very few people live on this part of the island. Full-time rangers are stationed at Scorpion and Smugglers ranches on the east end of the island owned by the National Park Service, where public visitation is heavy.

22. What are the activities on the east end of Santa Cruz Island—the Gherini property?

The former Gherini property, now owned by Channel Islands National Park, is used by the public for day trips and for camping. Kayaking is also allowed.

23. What are the activities on the western portion of Santa Cruz Island—the Stanton property?

This part of the island had been operated by the Santa Cruz Island Company primarily as a cattle ranch. In December of 1987 when the land was transferred to The Nature Conservancy, the cattle were sold and ranching operations ceased. Today the island is being managed, protected and preserved by The Nature Conservancy with limited public access. Scientific research is conducted on the island through the University of California's Santa Cruz Island Reserve.

24. What type of ranching operation was run by the Santa Cruz Island Company?

The western nine-tenths of the island were run as a cattle ranch, and Polled Herefords were raised. The island was divided into various pastures to accommodate bulls, cows, calves, and animals of varying age or sex.

925. Who operated the Santa Cruz Island Company?

Carey Stanton was the company president until his death on the island December 8, 1987. In 1957, twenty years to the day after his parents bought the western nine-tenths of the island, Carey Stanton moved to the island to begin managing company affairs. He was graduated from Stanford University School of Medicine and worked in internal medicine and pathology for about ten years, after which he returned to live and work on the island. April 10, 1987, marked the fiftieth anniversary of the Stanton family on Santa Cruz Island.

926. Did the Santa Cruz Island Company have a registered brand?

Yes. The company's first brand was registered in 1869 with the formation of the Santa Cruz Island Company. It was an "S" over a cross enclosed in a circle. In 1918, the brand was altered to an "S" followed by a cross, without the circle, to be placed on the animal's left hip. It was designated as brand #1840 in the State Registry, which now has over 50,000 brands. This brand was transferred to Edwin Stanton in 1937. It remained the active brand of the Santa Cruz Island Company until December 1987 when The Nature Conservancy assumed ownership of the company's assets, and cattle ranching operations were discontinued. The brand continues to be registered by the Santa Cruz Island Foundation.

927. How were cattle sent to market?

The cattle were sent to the mainland by cattle boat. Vail & Vickers on neighboring Santa Rosa Island owns a cattle boat, *Vaquero II,* which the Santa Cruz Island Company hired as needed.

928. How long have horses been on Santa Cruz Island?

The first record of horses having been introduced was in 1831. Ranch manager J.B. Shaw introduced additional horses twenty years later. From this time forward, horses have played an important role in the island's cultural landscape.

929. What is The Nature Conservancy?

The Nature Conservancy is a national, private, non-profit conservation organization devoted to the purchase and protection of ecologically significant land. In 1975, Dr. Carey Stanton, president of the Santa Cruz Island Company, met with The Nature Conservancy about a possible joint conservation effort to ensure the future preservation of Santa Cruz Island. On September 15, 1978, 12,000 acres were sold in fee to The Nature Conservancy and leased back to the Santa Cruz Island Company. The remainder of the Santa Cruz Island Company's holding passed to The Nature Conservancy on December 8, 1987, with Dr. Carey Stanton's death.

930. What is the Santa Cruz Island Foundation?

The Santa Cruz Island Foundation is a non-profit organization founded by Carey Stanton several years before his death to protect, preserve and promote the cultural and historical aspects of Santa Cruz and the other Channel Islands. Foundation assets include archives of island photographs, early ranch wagons, winemaking equipment, and memorabilia covering a century of history and occupation of Santa Cruz Island. Santa Cruz Island Foundation activities have included: installation of a small archaeology museum in Pete's House at the Main Ranch on Santa Cruz Island in 1989; restoration and seismic upgrading of the chapel on Santa Cruz Island for its centennial celebration in 1991; installation of a visitors' center on Santa Barbara Island in 1993; and restoration of Campo del Norte on Santa Cruz Island in 1996. In addition, the foundation publishes a series of *Occasional Papers,* eight to date, which deal with cultural aspects of California's Channel Islands.

931. When was the University of California research facility established on Santa Cruz Island?

The establishment of a research station on Santa Cruz Island began with field geology courses held by the University of California at Santa Barbara during the summers of 1964 and 1965. Formal agreement was reached between the Santa Cruz Island Company and the University in 1966. Today the Santa Cruz Island Reserve is the largest of 24 reserves within the University of California's Natural Land and Water Reserve System, now called the Natural Reserve System

932. What are the facilities of the Santa Cruz Island Reserve field station?

The main building includes a kitchen, dining and limited work space as well as a screened porch with accommodations for about

20 visitors. An adjoining building has a carport for station vehicles, lavatory-shower rooms, and a laundry facility. East of these is a decked trailer complex which includes a laboratory. The entire facility has electricity, running water, and a propane stove. Four-wheel-drive vehicles and a Boston Whaler are available for researchers' use, along with a reference library, herbarium, and insect collection. The field station facilities are located about one-half mile west of the main ranch complex.

933. What does the U.S. Navy do on Santa Cruz Island?

The U.S. Navy leases an area of land on top of the eastern portion of Santa Cruz Island Company land where they have an installation operated under the command of the Pacific Missile Range out of Point Mugu. Lights surrounding the Navy facilities can be seen from the mainland on clear nights.

934. Can one camp on the western nine-tenths of Santa Cruz Island?

No. The Nature Conservancy currently does not allow camping.

935. What facilities does the National Park Service have on the east end of Santa Cruz Island?

The National Park Service owns both the historic Scorpion and Smugglers ranches. Thirty-five primitive campsites and several outhouses are available to the general public in Scorpion Canyon. Other campsites may be available in the future.

936. What transportation is there to and from Santa Cruz Island?

Transportation differs for various travelers. Island Packers, concessionaire to Channel Islands National Park, provides boat transportation to the entire island. Channel Island Aviation provides air service.

937. How many airstrips are there on Santa Cruz Island?

There are five dirt strips that are currently used on the island. Three are on The Nature Conservancy portion of the island, and two are on the Gherini eastern end of the island. Their use is restricted.

938. Can boaters visit Santa Cruz Island?

Yes. To land on the private property of The Nature Conservancy, one must obtain a permit in advance in Santa Barbara.

Permits are $50 a calendar year, or $15 for any consecutive 30-day period. No permits are issued on the island or in The Nature Conservancy office. They are processed through the mail only. Permit applications may be requested by phone or mail. They allow daytime landing and list strict rules governing activity on the island. Private boaters may visit the east end of Santa Cruz Island at any time without a permit from the National Park Service. Public boat transportation to the east end is arranged through Island Packers, concessionaire to Channel Islands National Park.

939. What is the road system on Santa Cruz Island?

No paved roads exist on the island. The western nine-tenths of the island has a well-developed dirt-road system which allows access to the entire length of the central valley, the length of the southern mountain range, and out to the island's west end, Fraser Point. From the southern ridge road, several side roads drop down to canyons and beaches along the south side of the island. In general, conditions require four-wheel-drive vehicles. On the east end of the island, the dirt-road system is currently used by four-wheel-drive all-terrain cycles and not vehicles, although in the past, cars and trucks operated here. No roads connect the Gherini property with The Nature Conservancy property.

940. How does Santa Cruz Island receive its fuel?

The western portion of the island receives diesel, propane and gasoline by tanker trucks brought to the island aboard landing crafts, which land at Prisoners' Harbor on an irregular schedule. The eastern end of the island receives fuel in small quantities either by plane or boat. They currently have no wharf or boat landing facility.

941. Are there any telephones on Santa Cruz Island?

Yes. With advances in technology, cellular phones work from many parts of the island. The former microwave system which connects the island with the mainland is still active, however the century-old on-island phone system was abandoned by The Nature Conservancy in 1987.

942. What are the native terrestrial mammals on Santa Cruz Island?

There are only four native terrestrial mammals which occur on

Santa Cruz Island: the island fox *(Urocyon littoralis santacruzae)*, the spotted skunk *(Spilogale gracilis amphialus)*, the deer mouse *(Peromyscus maniculatus santacruzae)*, and the western harvest mouse *(Reithrodontomys megalotis santacruzae)*.

943. What bats have been collected on Santa Cruz Island?

Of the following nine species of bats which have been collected, breeding records exist only for the first three species:

California myotis *(Myotis californicus caurinus)*
lump-nosed bat *(Plecotus townsendii)*
pallid bat *(Antrozous pallidus)*
big-eared bat *(Myotis evotis)*
big brown bat *(Eptesicus fuscus)*
silver-haired bat *(Lasionycteris noctivagans)*
hoary bat *(Lasiurus cinereus)*
red bat *(Lasiurus borealis)*
Brazilian free-tailed bat *(Tadarida brasiliensis)*

944. Are there any feral animals on Santa Cruz Island?

Yes, there are both feral pigs and sheep on Santa Cruz Island.

945. What is the status of feral sheep on Santa Cruz Island?

The exact date of the introduction of sheep is unknown. However, it is known that by 1853 a large herd of sheep was being managed. By 1870 a U.S. Department of Agriculture census reported 50,000 animals on the island, and in 1877, 24,000 sheep were slaughtered to reduce the enormous flock. Annual round-ups, called *corridas,* were conducted during which time sheep were either sheared and released or sent to market. Shortly after 1937, when Edwin Stanton purchased the western 90 percent of the island, almost 30,000 sheep were sent to market. In 1981, The Nature Conservancy began its feral sheep removal program on the western portion of the island, and sport hunting programs continued to eliminate feral sheep until 1985. Sheep remaining on the eastern end of the island will be removed by Channel Islands National Park.

946. What is the status of feral pigs on Santa Cruz Island?

Although the first written record for the presence of pigs on the island is 1853, it is not known if a feral population existed before then. Elimination of feral pigs on Santa Cruz Island is a

Justinian Caire Collection

Sheep shearing on Santa Cruz Island was all done by hand, with the use of island-wrought shears.

goal of both The Nature Conservancy and of Channel Islands National Park.

947. Are there any marine mammal breeding rookeries on Santa Cruz Island?

This island lacks the large rookeries found on some of the nearby islands, although California sea lions and harbor seals are commonly found in the adjacent waters or hauled out on rocky ledges. Occasionally elephant seals are sighted, particularly along some of the small pocket beaches of the island's southwestern quarter.

948. Are there any snakes on Santa Cruz Island?

Yes. There are gopher snakes *(Pituophis melanoleucus pumilis)* and racers *(Coluber constrictor)* on Santa Cruz Island. One collection record from 1939 exists for the night snake *(Hypsiglena torquata).*

949. What lizards occur on Santa Cruz Island?

Three species are known to occur on Santa Cruz Island: the side-blotched lizard *(Uta stansburiana),* the western fence lizard *(Sceloporus occidentalis),* and the alligator lizard *(Elegaria multicarinatus).*

950. What amphibians are found on Santa Cruz Island?

Two slender salamanders *(Batrachoseps pacificus pacificus)* and *(B. nigriventris)* and the Pacific tree frog *(Hyla regilla)* occur on this island. In 1919 three specimens of the red-legged frog *(Rana aurora draytoni)* were collected near Pelican Bay. None has been collected since then.

951. Are there any fresh water game fishes on Santa Cruz Island?

No. Attempts in the past to introduce brown trout failed because they washed out after heavy rains. Goldfish have been placed in some of the cattle troughs.

952. How did the scale insect cochineal (*Dactylopius* sp.) get to Santa Cruz Island?

In 1938, Edwin Stanton estimated that as much as 40 percent of the rangeland on the island was infested with prickly pear

The racer, Coluber constrictor, *is a harmless snake found on Santa Cruz Island. This is the only California island on which it occurs.*

The cochineal insect was intentionally introduced to Santa Cruz Island to control prickly-pear cacti.

cacti, and he was interested in a biological way of controlling it. With the help of Professor Harry Smith of the Riverside Experimental Station, between the years of 1940 and 1960 several introductions of the cactus-eating scale insect cochineal were attempted. By the mid 1950s, the insect established itself on the island and cactus populations decreased. It was introduced on the Gherini property in 1960. This is the insect from which red dye is made in Mexico.

953. Which land birds nest on Santa Cruz Island?

bald eagle – former resident	barn swallow
peregrine falcon – former resident	northern raven
red-tailed hawk	Santa Cruz Island jay
American kestrel	bushtit
Catalina quail	red-breasted nuthatch
snowy plover	rock wren
killdeer	Bewick's wren
American oystercatcher	blue-grey gnatcatcher
black oystercatcher	northern mockingbird
mourning dove	loggerhead shrike
common barn owl	European starling
Northern saw-whet owl	Huttons' vireo

white-throated swift
Anna's hummingbird
Allen's hummingbird
acorn woodpecker
red-shafted flicker
western flycatcher
black phoebe
ash-throated swift
horned lark
house finch

orange-crowned warbler
black-headed grosbeak
song sparrow
chipping sparrow
rufous-crowned sparrow
rufous-sided towhee
red-winged blackbird
western meadowlark
lesser goldfinch

954. Which birds are endemic Channel Islands subspecies or races?

Allen's hummingbird
western flycatcher
horned lark
Santa Cruz Island jay (species)
Bewick's wren

loggerhead shrike
orange-crowned warbler
house finch
rufous-sided towhee
Catalina quail – introduced

955. Why is the Santa Cruz Island jay special?

The Santa Cruz Island jay *(Aphelocoma insularis)* is a species found on no other island, and none has ever been found on the mainland. Its bright blue color, larger size and heavier bill distinguish it from its mainland counterpart. This bird represents a case of island gigantism. Lack of competition and predators has allowed this island species to utilize resources generally unavailable to mainland jays.

956. Which marine birds nest on Santa Cruz Island?

ashy storm petrel
double-breasted cormorant
Brandt's cormorant
pelagic cormorant
tufted puffin – former resident
California brown pelicans nest on offshore rocks.

pigeon guillemot
Xantus' murrelet
Cassin's auklet
western gull

957. What birds have successfully been introduced to Santa Cruz Island?

Quail, turkeys, and peafowl have been successfully introduced to Santa Cruz Island. California quail were brought to this island from Santa Catalina stock in 1947. Wild turkeys were introduced in 1975 by the California Department of Fish and Game, and there have been several different introductions of peafowl. Breeding populations of all three species have been established.

958. Have Pleistocene plant remains been found on Santa Cruz Island?

Yes. In Cañada de los Sauces, various fossil plant remains, including huge logs, have been recovered from Pleistocene deposits. Among the more notewothy of these are the Douglas fir *(Pseudotsuga menziesii)*, Bishop pine *(Pinus muricata)*, and Gowen cypress *(Cupressus goveniana)*. In 1930 paleobotanists Ralph Chaney and H.L. Mason reported that at some time during the Pleistocene, Santa Cruz Island supported a much richer arboreal flora, not unlike that found in the Fort Bragg area of California today.

959. What plant communities are found on Santa Cruz Island?

Due to the large size and topographic and geologic complexity of Santa Cruz Island, this island supports a large variety of plant communities. Coastal strand, coastal bluffs, valley and foothill grasslands, coastal sage scrub, chaparral, island and oak woodland, pine forests, southern riparian woodlands, and marsh communities are all present. Introduced cultivated plants occur as well.

960. What type of pine trees are there on Santa Cruz Island?

Bishop pines *(Pinus muricata)*, which are relics left from the Pleistocene age, compose most of the pine forests on Santa Cruz Island. Some plant taxonomists believe this species has split and formed a separate Santa Cruz Island pine *(Pinus remorata)* species. Italian stone pines on the island are introduced ornamentals.

961. How many different plant species are there on Santa Cruz Island?

There are over 650 different plants on Santa Cruz Island, including both native and introduced species.

962. How many Channel Islands endemic plants grow on Santa Cruz Island?

About 42 Channel Islands endemics are found on Santa Cruz Island.

963. Which plants are found only on Santa Cruz Island?

Island lace pod *(Thysanocarpus conchuliferous)*, live-forever *(Dudleya nesiotica)*, island manzanitas *(Arctostaphylos insularis,*

A. viridissima and *A. tomentosa subcordata),* silver lotus *(Lotus argophyllus niveus),* island mallow *(Malacothamnus fasciculatus nesioticus),* gooseberry *(Ribes thacherianum),* and monkey flower *(Mimulus brandegei)* are Santa Cruz Island endemics.

964. Is jimson weed found on Santa Cruz Island?

Yes. Jimson weed *(Datura* sp.) is commonly seen about many canyons and streambed areas on Santa Cruz Island.

965. Are there any other poisonous plants on Santa Cruz Island?

Yes. In addition to poison oak *(Toxicodendron diversilobum),* there is poison hemlock *(Conium maculatum)*—the plant that killed Socrates—and chaparral zygadene *(Zygadenus fremontii),* a close relative of death camas. Several species of nightshade *(Solanum* sp.) have toxic berries. Tree tobacco *(Nicotiana glauca)* is found on the island's east end.

966. When were the eucalyptus trees planted on Santa Cruz Island?

Early ranch records indicate that eucalyptus trees were planted on the island as early as 1884. The blue-gum eucalyptus *(Eucalyptus globulus)* are among the oldest and tallest in the state of California. On the island, eucalyptus trees were planted in both groves and along lanes in areas of habitation. Some groves, such as Rincón Papal, the Bosque Maño, the Bosque Cabrillo and La Selva, still retain their names from early ranching days.

967. How many Indians lived on Santa Cruz Island?

At the time of Spanish contact in 1542, it is estimated that no more than 2000 Indians occupied Santa Cruz Island. In 1805 Father Tapis wrote that there were an estimated 1800 natives occupying both Santa Cruz and Santa Rosa islands that year.

968. What did the Indians call Santa Cruz Island?

Santa Cruz Island was called Limu.

969. How many archaeological sites are there on Santa Cruz Island?

A 1973–1974 survey of Santa Cruz Island by the University of California at Santa Barbara Department of Anthropology placed the number of sites somewhere around 3000, many of which were just temporary. At least a dozen well-developed village sites existed at the time of the Spanish contact.

970. Is there any rock art on Santa Cruz Island?

Although there are a few rock art sites on Santa Cruz Island, none is well developed. Most of the art in rock shelters consists of ocher or hematite blobs or spots in no apparent pattern or design. Only one cave has more developed art, containing both pictographs and petroglyphs. These take the form of lines, dots, and rake figures.

971. What 19th-century archaeological work was conducted on Santa Cruz Island?

In 1875, Paul Schumacher conducted work on the island for the Smithsonian Institution, followed in 1877 by Leon del Cessac, who made collections for the Musée de L'Homme in Paris. The Rev. Stephen Bowers also made collections on the island in the latter part of the 19th century.

972. What 20th-century archaeological work has been conducted?

In 1916, U.C. Berkeley sponsored Leonard Outhwaite to locate and record sites on Santa Cruz Island. He mapped 86 sites and collected artifacts now in the Lowie Museum in Berkeley. David Banks Rogers and Ronald Olson worked on the island in 1927 for the Santa Barbara Museum of Natural History and U.C. Berkeley. In 1932 Richard Van Valkenburgh excavated areas of Forney's Cove, where he and his crew spent a month. After the war in the late 1950s and 1960s, Phil Orr made several trips collecting artifacts and gathering data. Since the 1960s, there has been a strong resurgence of interest in Santa Cruz Island archaeology.

973. What happened on Santa Cruz Island during the Spanish period from 1769–1822?

As early as 1770, the Spanish government in Mexico proposed the building of a mission on the island to "bring the gospel to the inhabitants of the Channel Islands." The plan did not receive approval of the viceroy, and so it was set aside for 30 years. The building of a mission was again proposed in the early 1800s by Father Tapis. A measles epidemic depleted the Indian population on Santa Cruz and Santa Rosa islands, however, and in 1807 the plan to build an island mission was abandoned.

974. When did the last Indians leave Santa Cruz Island?

According to mission baptismal records, most of the last

remaining Indians on Santa Cruz Island were baptized on the mainland between 1812–1815. In 1824, a few islanders temporarily returned to Santa Cruz Island, but eventually returned again to the mainland.

975. Who was the first individual owner of Santa Cruz Island?

Andrés Castillero was the first to own Santa Cruz Island. On May 22, 1839, during the Mexican era in upper California, Santa Cruz Island was granted by Juan Bautista Alvarado, governor of California, to Andrés Castillero. With this grant, Castillero became the first private individual to own the island. California was ceded to the United States in 1848, and the title of Castillero was confirmed by the U.S. Supreme Court in 1864. In the meantime, Castillero had sold Santa Cruz Island.

976. What is the first record of a structure on Santa Cruz Island?

A deed in the Santa Barbara County Court House dated November 12, 1852 records the following: "... I, Thomas Jeffries of Santa Barbara . . . in consideration of the sum of $10 . . . do hereby sell, remise, release and forever quit claim unto said Charles Fernald . . . a certain frame house situated on the Island of Santa Cruz . . . near the beach fronting that part of the Island, known as Prisoners' Harbor." Nothing further is known about this house or transaction. It occurred during Castillero's ownership of Santa Cruz Island, and presumably was an unauthorized transaction.

977. What is the next record of a structure on Santa Cruz Island?

The first view of a house on Santa Cruz Island appears in a watercolor painted by James Madison Alden, dated 1855. Entitled "Central Valley, Santa Cruz Island," this painting shows a one-and-a-half-story house, a man on horseback, and some hay stacks, thus establishing both animal husbandry and agricultural practices on the island by 1855.

978. What did Andrés Castillero do with Santa Cruz Island?

Not a great deal is known about Castillero's involvement with the island during his 18-year ownership from 1839–1857. After California became a state in 1850, several people tried to claim parts of the island, as recorded in deeds filed in the Santa Barbara County courthouse, though none was later recognized as valid. James Barron Shaw, Santa Barbara physician, managed the island

An 1855 watercolor by James Madison Alden entitled "Central Valley, Santa Cruz Island" shows the first known view of an island structure.

for Castillero beginning in the early 1850s. By 1855, a ranch house had been constructed in the island's central valley.

979. To whom did Castillero sell Santa Cruz Island?

William E. Barron, by a deed dated June 21, 1857, bought Santa Cruz Island. In the following year, it was advertised for sale in the *Daily Alta* newspaper:

> For sale: An island containing about 60,000 acres of land, well-watered and abounding in small valleys of the best pasturage for sheep. There are no wild animals on it that would interfere with livestock. There is a good harbor and safe anchorage.

James Barron Shaw continued to manage the island through Barrons' 12-year ownership (1857–1869). Adobe and wooden buildings formed the nucleus of a main ranch complex. To date, it is not known if James Barron Shaw and William E. Barron were related.

980. What happened to Santa Cruz Island in 1869?

Ten men (Gustave Mahé, Camilo Martin, Alexander Weill, T.

Lemmen Meyer, Nicolas Larco, Adrien Gensoul, Giovanni B. Cerruti, Justinian Caire, Thomas J. Gallagher, and Pablo Baca) bought Santa Cruz Island on February 16, 1869. On March 29, 1869, they incorporated to form the Santa Cruz Island Company with a capital stock of $300,000.

981. Did all of the incorporators in the Santa Cruz Island Company actively participate in island affairs?

No. In 1873 the company reincorporated, adding J.V. Delavega and H. Ohlmeyer as stockholders, and dropping Nicolas Larco, Pablo Baca, and T.J. Gallagher. Capital stock was increased to $500,000. By 1880, Justinian Caire had become the major stockholder, and in that year he decided to pay his first visit to Santa Cruz Island to survey his holdings.

982. What did Justinian Caire do with Santa Cruz Island?

Under Caire's direction, a variety of agricultural and ranching endeavors were developed. Buildings including several ranch houses, bunk houses, barns, wineries, a chapel, mess hall, blacksmith shop and saddle shop were constructed. Wherever possible, native island materials were used. Kilns were built for the manufacture of bricks and limestone mortar. Stones were quarried and cut to shape on the island. A resident blacksmith forged wrought-iron fittings, railings and hinges used on many of the buildings. Employees included masons, carpenters, dairymen, team drivers, vintners, a wagon maker, cobbler, butcher, seasonal grape pickers and sheep shearers, a sea captain and sailors to run the company's 60-foot schooner. Hay, vegetables, and over a dozen varieties of grapes were grown, in addition to almond, walnut and other fruit and ornamental trees. Sheep, cattle, horses and pigs were raised. Justinian Caire ran a very efficient and almost entirely self-contained operation on Santa Cruz Island.

983. Where did Justinian Caire build other ranches on the island?

In addition to the development of the main ranch in the island's central valley, nine other areas were developed. Caire expanded an existing ranch at Christy, located at the west end of the central valley. New ranches and outposts included those of La Playa at Prisoners' Harbor; Rancho Punta West at Forney's Cove; Buena Vista which was a wooden outpost; Portezuela in the central valley; and Rancho Sur at the east end of the central valley.

Justinian Caire Collection

The main ranch on Santa Cruz Island was developed in the island's central valley. Many of the buildings date back to the 19th century.

Rancho Nuevo, located midway between Christy Ranch and Rancho Punta West, was constructed later by Justinian Caire's sons after Rancho Punta West was dismantled. On the east end of the island, out-ranches were developed at both Scorpion and Smugglers.

84. What was the purpose of these other ranches and outposts?

The island was too large to manage from just one ranch, so various other facilities were built. Prisoners' Harbor was the main point of entry on the island, so the ranch located here included a large magazine in which supplies were stored to await shipment to or from the island. Scorpion Ranch was the major out-ranch used to handle activities on the island's east end. Lesser ranches such as those at Portezuela, the west end, and Smugglers, controlled farming or ranching activities in the immediate area.

85. How did the island become partitioned?

Justinian Caire and his wife Albina had six surviving children: Delphine, Arthur, Amelie, Aglae, Frederic and Helene. Justinian Caire died in 1897, leaving his stock in the Santa Cruz Island Company to his wife. Some stock was distributed to Caire's chil-

255

Justinian Caire developed an out-ranch at Smugglers Cove in 1889. Today the buildings on either side of the two-story adobe are no longer standing.

Justinian Caire and his daughter Delphine on Santa Cruz Island taken from a broken glass plate negative.

dren in varying amounts by his widow. In 1910, a $5 corporation renewal fee was not paid, and the company was legally dissolved. Extensive litigation between Caire family members ensued, and the island was partitioned seven ways. The eastern two parcels (#6–7) containing the Scorpion and Smugglers ranches, are today owned by Channel Islands National Park. The western parcels #(1–5) were reunited to form the Santa Cruz Island Company, and sold in 1937 to Edwin Stanton. In 1987 they passed to The Nature Conservancy

986. What happened to the Santa Cruz Island winery?

A variety of wines, including Zinfandel, Chablis, Muscat, Pinot Noir, Reisling, and Burgundy, were produced under the direction of Justinian Caire. The first grape slips were planted on the island in 1884, imported from Caire's native country, France. Wine was shipped in bulk to San Francisco where it was then bottled. After Caire's death, the wine business was carried on by his two sons,

The two Santa Cruz Island winery buildings as they stood among the vineyards. Both buildings were gutted by a fire in 1950 and reroofed.

Several hundred acres were planted with a variety of grapes in the island's central valley.

Arthur and Frederic. Prohibition stopped the production of wine, but grapes continued to be grown and sold to local Santa Barbara markets. Eventually, the business became too unprofitable to continue, and the hand-watered and hand-sprayed vines were removed from the island's central valley. Today furrow lines from the vineyards can still be seen. No bottle of island wine is known to exist.

987. When did the western nine-tenths of Santa Cruz Island sell?

In 1937, after the western nine-tenths of Santa Cruz Island had been on the market for over a decade, Los Angeles businessman Edwin Stanton purchased the land offered for sale.

988. What did Edwin Stanton do with Santa Cruz Island?

For the first two years of his ownership, Edwin Stanton tried to revive and improve the sheep business. Domestic sheep were brought to the island to mix with the feral population, but soon they too became unmanageable on the island's rugged terrain. Thirty thousand sheep were sent to market, and ranching emphasis was switched to cattle, the mainstay of ranching operations through 1987. The last of the cattle were shipped off the island by The Nature Conservancy on April 10, 1988, 51 years to the day after Edwin Stanton purchased the western nine-tenths of Santa Cruz Island.

989. When was Rancho del Norte built?

In 1950, Rancho del Norte was built on the northeast quarter of Santa Cruz Island to act as a center for cattle activities on that part of the island. It was restored in 1996 by the Santa Cruz Island Foundation.

990. Have there been any plane wrecks on Santa Cruz Island?

There have been several plane accidents on Santa Cruz Island. As early as Prohibition, a rum-running plane wrecked on Christy Beach. Today only the wheels remain. Remnants of a World War II plane are scattered about the east end of the island. In 1949, a Marine flier was killed when his plane crashed into the island during a storm. Seven people were killed in two separate plane accidents on March 9, 1966, when two planes owned by Santa Paula Aviation crashed the same day. In the early 1970s, a Navy pilot fatally flew into Picacho Diablo. In 1978, a single-engine plane with two occupants flew too close to the water at Poso Beach where a wave caught the plane and turned it over in the surf. Both people survived, and the plane washed in on the beach where parts of it remain today. Another non-fatal single-engine plane accident occurred on the east end of the island several years ago. The wreckage recently has been removed. In 1985, a single-engine plane used for fish spotting crashed into the island's southeast side when the pilot was looking the other way. He survived, and the plane was removed by helicopter.

991. Are there any lighthouses on Santa Cruz Island?

There are no lighthouses or navigational lights on Santa Cruz Island. There is one automated light located on top of Gull Island, three-quarters of a mile off the southern coast. Legally, however, Gull Island is considered a part of Santa Cruz Island. It rises 65 feet from the water and is actually composed of several rocks. The light, which flashes every four seconds, is housed in a white pyramidal structure.

992. Are there any wharfs on Santa Cruz Island?

Currently there is one wharf on Santa Cruz Island located at Prisoners' Harbor. Evidence of a former wharf can be seen near Forney's Cove. It was used during the early 1950s to facilitate oil exploration in the area. A wharf once located at Scorpion has rusted and fallen into the ocean.

993. How did Prisoners' Harbor receive its name?

In February 1830, the Mexican government sent a shipload of convicts out of Acapulco to Alta California, where the criminals were to be off-loaded. The ship *Maria Ester* arrived in San Diego only to be told she must keep going. A second attempt was made by the ship's captain in Santa Barbara to unload his passengers, but again permission was denied. Frustrated and low on supplies, the captain took matters into his own hands and released the men on Santa Cruz Island. The anchorage where the prisoners were dropped off and abandoned now bears the name "Prisoners' Harbor." According to legend, these men fashioned rafts and floated back to the mainland, where they assimilated into the Santa Barbara-Carpinteria area.

994. Did fishermen ever live on the shores of Santa Cruz Island?

Yes. Fish camps were established during the Caire ownership of Santa Cruz Island, and a small rental fee was charged. Camps were built at Coches Prietos, Willows, Morse Point, Gull Island, Dick's Harbor, Chinese Harbor, Scorpion, and various other coastal locations. Many of the fishermen changed locations seasonally, moving from one cove to another. In the 1930s this system diminished, until World War II when fishing boats no longer made pick-ups on the island.

Prisoners' Harbor is the main port of entry on Santa Cruz Island.

The ruins at Pelican Bay are the site of a once active resort run by Ira and Margaret Eaton.

995. What are the ruins at Pelican Bay?

Ira Eaton and his wife Margaret ran a resort at Pelican Bay from 1910 to 1937. Today, various foundations and ornamental plantings are all that remain of this once flourishing resort. *Diary of a Sea Captain's Wife: Tales of Santa Cruz Island* by Margaret Eaton, edited by Janice Timbrook (Santa Barbara: McNally & Loftin, 1980) offers information in some detail about this former operation.

996. Have there been any major fires on Santa Cruz Island?

Several fires have occurred on Santa Cruz Island in historic times. The first recorded fire was in 1830 when a fire burned the Prisoners' Harbor area. An 1871 newspaper article reported: "It is generally believed Santa Cruz Island is on fire. There is a great smoke out that way." Fires again occurred in the Prisoners' Harbor-Pelican Bay area in 1918–1919, 1927, and 1931. The 1931 fires destroyed several tents in Ira Eaton's Pelican Bay resort. On June 11, 1950, a fire destroyed the Santa Cruz Island Company's main ranch house, dining room and kitchen, and a part of both wineries. In 1979, 200 acres above San Pedro Point burned. In 1987 a small lightning-caused fire burned near Pelican Bay. The Nature Conservancy now conducts control burns. In

1995 their annual burn got out of control and burned the pine forest above China Harbor on the island's north side.

997. Have any movies been filmed on Santa Cruz Island?

Yes. From sometime around 1910 and continuing through the 1920s, Santa Cruz Island was a popular location for the filming of silent pictures. Companies were accommodated at Ira Eaton's Pelican Bay resort, a convenient north shore location. Films with alluring titles such as *Heart of My Heart* (1912), *Diamond in the Sky* (1917), *Pearls of Paradise* (1916), *Sirens of the Sea* (1917), *Battle of Hearts* (1918), and *Adam and Eve* (1918) resulted. In 1919, Gloria Swanson, then an unknown aspiring actress, played in Paramount Pictures' *Male and Female.* Herbert Brenon's *Peter Pan* (1924), was followed by *The Devil Master* (1926), starring Janet Gaynor and George O'Brien. In 1928, a film based on Joseph Conrad's novel *The Rescue,* starring Ronald Coleman and Lily Damita, was shot in part at Prisoners' Harbor.

998. Has anyone died on Santa Cruz Island in the last century?

Yes, over 30 people have died on this island since 1885. Ranch records show at least three 19th-century island employees were killed, including one who drowned, one who was killed by a fall from his horse, and one who was run over by a cart. Twentieth-century deaths include a fatal hunting accident, a fatal vehicle accident, three fatal falls from cliffs, several deaths by heart attack, and several deaths by plane accident—all males. On December 8, 1987, Carey Stanton, president of the Santa Cruz Island Company, died in his island home. Innumerable people have died in boating accidents around Santa Cruz Island.

999. Is there a cemetery on Santa Cruz Island?

Yes. Near the main ranch complex is *La Capilla de la Santa Cruz del Rosario,* the Santa Cruz Island chapel, built in 1891. Immediately surrounding it is a small cemetery in which several island employees and members of the Stanton family are buried.

1000. Is mass celebrated in the Santa Cruz Island chapel?

Mass has been celebrated in the chapel on Santa Cruz Island on an irregular basis for almost a century, and annually on May 3 since 1968. It is a Roman Catholic chapel. May 3 is the Feast of the Holy Cross. The Santa Cruz Island Foundation restored the chapel in time for its centennial mass celebration in 1991.

1001. What Channel Islands services are available?

CHANNEL ISLAND DIRECTORY

ASPEN HELICOPTERS, INC.
2899 W. 5th Street
Oxnard, CA 93030
Phone: (805) 985-5416   FAX: (805) 985-7327
    For information concerning helicopter and fixed-wing services to various Channel Islands.

DOUG BOMBARD ENTERPRISES
P.O. Box 5044
Two Harbors, CA 907040
Phone: (310) 510-0303   FAX: (310) 510-0244

(SANTA) CATALINA AIRPORT-IN-THE-SKY
P.O. Box 2739
Avalon, CA 90704
Phone: (310) 510-0143   FAX: (310) 510-3509
For airport information.

(SANTA) CATALINA CAMPING
P.O. Box 5044
Two Harbors, CA 90704
Phone: (310) 510-8368   FAX: (310) 510-0244
    For camping reservations at Two Harbors, Parson's Landing, Little Harbor, Blackjack, Conservancy Cove Camps, and Catalina Yurt cabins at Goat Harbor; see also Hermit Gulch.

(SANTA) CATALINA CHANNEL EXPRESS
Berth 95
San Pedro, CA 90731
Phone: (310) 519-1212   Toll Free: (800) 995-4386
    For express boat service from San Pedro and Long Beach to Avalon and Two Harbors.

(SANTA) CATALINA CRUISES
320 Golden Shore
Long Beach, CA 90802
Phone: (800) 228-2546 (800-CATALINA)
    For the largest ships and the lowest fares to Avalon.

(SANTA) CATALINA ISLAND CHAMBER OF COMMERCE & VISITORS
BUREAU
P.O. Box 217
Avalon, CA 90704
Phone: (310) 510-1520   FAX: (310) 510-7606
http://www.catalina.com
    Open seven days a week for information about transportation, hotels,
attractions, activities and events on Santa Catalina Island. Call for a free visitor
guide.

(SANTA) CATALINA ISLAND CONSERVANCY
P.O. Box 2739
Avalon, CA 90704
Phone: (310) 510-1520   FAX: (310) 510-7606

(SANTA) CATALINA ISLAND COMPANY'S DISCOVERY TOURS
P.O. Box 737
Avalon, CA 90704
Phone: (310) 510-TOUR

(SANTA) CATALINA ISLAND MARINE SCIENCE CENTER
P.O. Box 398
Avalon, CA 90704

(SANTA) CATALINA ISLAND MUSEUM
P.O. Box 366
Avalon, CA 90704
Phone: (310) 510-2414
The museum is open daily from 10:30 a.m.-4:30 p.m. Admission is $1.50 for
adults, $1.00 for senior citizens, and 50¢ for children under 12.

(SANTA) CATALINA PASSENGER SERVICE
400 Main Street
Newport Beach, CA 92661
Phone: (714) 673-5245
    For boat transportation from Newport Beach to Santa Catalina Island.

(SANTA) CATALINA TRAVEL CONNECTION
P.O. Box 1511
Avalon, CA 90704
(310) 510-0683

CHANNEL ISLANDS ARCHIVES
Santa Barbara Museum of Natural History
2559 Puesta del Sol
Santa Barbara, CA 93105
Phone: (805) 682-4711
   For information and reference material concerning the California Channel Islands.

CHANNEL ISLANDS AVIATION
305 Durley Avenue
Camarillo, CA 93010
Phone: (805) 987-1301   FAX: (805) 987-8301
   Airplane concessionarie to Channel Islands National Park.

CHANNEL ISLANDS NATIONAL PARK
1901 Spinnaker Drive
Ventura, CA 93003
Phone: (805) 658-5700   FAX: (805) 658-5799
   For camping permits and information about Anacapa, Santa Barbara, Santa Cruz, Santa Rosa and San Miguel islands.

HERMIT GULCH CAMPGROUND
P.O. Box 747
Avalon, CA 90704
Phone: (310) 510-8368   FAX: (310) 510-8369

ISLAND EXPRESS HELICOPTER SERVICE
900 Queens Way Drive
Long Beach, CA 90801
Phone: (310) 510-2525   FAX: (310) 510-9671
   For information regarding helicopter transportation to Santa Catalina Island from Long Beach and San Pedro terminals.

ISLAND PACKERS, INC.
867 Spinnaker Drive
Ventura, CA 93003
Phone: (805) 642-1393   FAX: (805) 642-6573
E-mail: ipco@isle.net
   Concessionaire to Channel Islands National Park. For information about boat schedules, rates and trips offered from Ventura Harbor to the five islands

within Channel Islands National Park, as well as to the western part of Santa Cruz privately owned by The Nature Conservancy.

NATURAL RESOURCES OFFICE
Naval Air Station, North Island.
P.O. Box 357040
San Diego, CA 92135-7040
Phone: (619) 545-2583
    For information regarding San Clemente Island.
NATURAL RESOURCES OFFICE
Naval Air Station
Point Mugu, CA 93042
    For information regarding San Nicolas Island.

PETROLEUM HELICOPTERS, INC.
302 Moffett Place
Goleta, CA 93117
Phone: (805) 964-0684   FAX: (805) 683-6355

SANTA CRUZ ISLAND FOUNDATION
1010 Anacapa Street
Santa Barbara, CA 93101
Phone: (805) 963-4949   FAX: (805) 963-9433
E-Mail: scifmail@west.net

SANTA CRUZ ISLAND RESERVE
Marine Science Institute
University of California
Santa Barbara, CA 93106
Phone: (805) 893-4127   FAX: (805) 893-8062
E-mail: donnam@msi.ucsb.edu
    For information regarding the Santa Cruz Island Reserve located on Santa Cruz Island.

THE NATURE CONSERVANCY
Santa Cruz Island Preserve
213 Stearns Wharf
Santa Barbara, CA 93101
Phone: (805) 962-9111   FAX: (805) 962-2673
Landing Permits: (805) 962-2673
    For information about the western nine-tenths of Santa Cruz Island.

UNIVERSITY OF SOUTHERN CALIFORNIA
WRIGLEY INSTITUTE FOR ENVIRONMENTAL STUDIES AT SANTA
CATALINA ISLAND
P.O. Box 5069
Avalon, CA 90704
Phone: (310) 510-0811   FAX: (310) 510-1364
　　For information regarding the former Catalina Marine Science Center.

VAIL & VICKERS
123 W. Padre St.
Santa Barbara, CA 93101
Phone: (805) 682-7645   FAX: (805) 682-1897

WRIGLEY MEMORIAL & BOTANICAL GARDEN
P.O. Box 2739
Avalon, CA 90704
Phone: (310) 510-2288   FAX: (310) 510-2354
E-mail: wmgarden@catalinas.net
　　Garden is open daily from 8:00 a.m. to 5 p.m. Admission for adults is
$1.00 and children under 12 are free.

INDEX

By Question Number